WITHDRAWN

OXFORD ENGLISH MONOGRAPHS

General Editors

CHRISTOPHER BUTLER   VINCENT GILLESPIE

DOUGLAS GRAY   EMRYS JONES

ROGER LONSDALE   FIONA STAFFORD

MARIANNE MOORE
AND CHINA

Orientalism and
a Writing of America

CYNTHIA STAMY

OXFORD
UNIVERSITY PRESS

PS
3525
.O5616
Z8288
1999

OXFORD
UNIVERSITY PRESS

Great Clarendon Street, Oxford OX2 6DP
Oxford University Press is a department of the University of Oxford.
It furthers the University's objective of excellence in research, scholarship,
and education by publishing worldwide in

Oxford New York

Athens Auckland Bangkok Bogotá Buenos Aires Calcutta
Cape Town Chennai Dar es Salaam Delhi Florence Hong Kong Istanbul
Karachi Kuala Lumpur Madrid Melbourne Mexico City Mumbai
Nairobi Paris São Paulo Singapore Taipei Tokyo Toronto Warsaw

and associated companies in Berlin Ibadan

Oxford is a registered trade mark of Oxford University Press
in the UK and certain other countries

Published in the United States
by Oxford University Press Inc., New York

© Cynthia Stamy 1999

The moral rights of the author have been asserted
Database right Oxford University Press (maker)

First published 1999

All rights reserved. No part of this publication may be reproduced,
stored in a retrieval system, or transmitted, in any form or by any means,
without the prior permission in writing of Oxford University Press,
or as expressly permitted by law, or under terms agreed with the appropriate
reprographics rights organizations. Enquiries concerning reproduction
outside the scope of the above should be sent to the Rights Department,
Oxford University Press, at the address above

You must not circulate this book in any other binding or cover
and you must impose the same condition on any acquirer

British Library Cataloguing in Publication Data

Data available

Library of Congress Cataloging in Publication Data
ISBN 0-19-818460-3

1 3 5 7 9 10 8 6 4 2

Typeset by Graphicraft Limited, Hong Kong
Printed in Great Britain
on acid-free paper by
Biddles Ltd,
Guildford and King's Lynn

237100

For

HAYDEN AND CLAIBORNE

Preface

Marianne Moore's poetry offers an extraordinarily rich site from which to analyse a tradition of American orientalism which focused upon China. *Marianne Moore and China* examines why she chose to participate in that tradition and analyses why her borrowing of Chinese models of all kinds—from poetry to painting and philosophy—was so critical to the formation of her verse. Moore's poetry is part of a long tradition of satirical critique in orientalist writing which finds its roots in English literature. Early America inherited an eighteenth-century European tradition of critical prose writing, in the form of epistolary fictions from so-called 'Chinese' authors, which was used to voice subversive commentaries on the state. In the late eighteenth and early nineteenth centuries, American authors, such as Franklin and Emerson, went on to produce similar critiques directed at American social concerns. In the early twentieth century, this tradition of critique in orientalist prose was adopted by American poets, who borrowed Far Eastern poetic models to permanently transform the ways in which poetry in English was being written by launching a literary assault upon what they saw as outmoded methods of versification. Moore used the Far East to express her own dissatisfaction with contemporary trends in the writing of poetry, and embraced the more ancient culture of China as a means of resisting the American habit of looking to Europe as a singular source of cultural tradition 'at home'.

She employed features of the ancient Chinese *fu* technique in her poems and used images of Chinese supernatural creatures in an effort to establish an alternative to logic and narrative linearity and to facilitate the moral didacticism for which her poetry is known. At the same time that Moore's poems with Chinese imagery represent a deliberate departure from the familiar, the substitution of a Far Eastern literary model for a classical one is a characteristically Modernist break with tradition and resembles, in this respect, the resistance to neo-classicism apparent in eighteenth-century English orientalist writing.

Preface

Similarly, Moore's use of Chinese painting theory and philosophy in the creation of her poems enabled her to explore alternatives to Western perspectival principles and to Western ways
of narrating visual experience. *Marianne Moore and China* also
examines the ways in which Chinese linguistic features provided
Moore with models for her compound nouns and syntactical
ellipses, and gathers evidence to show that her abiding concerns
for precision, brevity, and restraint have both Confucian and
Puritan antecedents. Additionally, this book analyses the degree
to which her collection of quotations, from which she fashions
so many of her poems, and her citation of them in numerous
appended notes, are complicit in the same process of acquisition
and display which characterizes the activity of the museum, the
preoccupations of the curio-collector, and the pursuit of minute
detail in orientalist discourse generally. Moore's consistent ingenuity in employing Chinese forms and methods makes her work a
particularly fruitful source for investigating orientalism and its
contribution to modern poetry.

Marianne Moore and China is intended for readers interested
in Modernist poetry, American literature, and the subject of
orientalism. I have assumed that most readers will not be familiar with Chinese language, poetry, painting, or philosophy
and have provided sufficient background information on these
subjects as they arise. The scope of this book, therefore, while
wide-ranging, should be accessible to anyone drawn to Moore's
poetry, and my hope is that readers will find the analysis of her
orientalism to be a compelling means of arriving at a more
complete understanding of her work as a poet.

For their careful and encouraging supervision of this book
when it was the subject of my D.Phil. thesis at Oxford, I would
like to thank Tom Paulin and Dr T. T. Liu. Christ Church,
Oxford was instrumental in enabling me to complete valuable
research on Moore's manuscripts by awarding me a research
travel grant. I am additionally grateful to the University of
Oxford for awarding me an Oxford University Scholarship,
and to the Committee of Vice-Chancellors and Presidents for
granting me an overseas research student award. I would also
like to thank the Bodleian Library, the British Library, and the
Rosenbach Museum and Library (Philadelphia) for access to their

plentiful resources and rare collections. I am particularly grateful to Ms Leslie Morris, former Curator of the Rosenbach Museum and Library, for her assistance with the Moore manuscript collection.

C.S.S.

Acknowledgements

Publication of material from the Marianne Moore Archive is by kind permission of the Rosenbach Museum and Library.

Publication of material by Marianne Moore is by kind permission of the Literary Executor of the Estate of Marianne Moore.

Reproduction of material from the journals and notebooks of Ralph Waldo Emerson is by permission of the Ralph Waldo Emerson Memorial Association.

Material reproduced from *The Journals and Miscellaneous Notebooks of Ralph Waldo Emerson* is by kind permission of the editors William H. Gilman, Alfred R. Ferguson, George P. Clark, and Merrell R. Davis and the publisher, Harvard University Press.

Publication of an excerpt from a letter by Elizabeth Bishop to Robert Lowell (bMS Am 1905 (183)) is by permission of the Houghton Library, Harvard University.

Excerpt from letter from Elizabeth Bishop to Robert Lowell, dated 25 June 1961 © 1998 by Alice Helen Methfesel. Reprinted by permission of Farrar, Straus & Giroux, Inc., on behalf of the Estate of Elizabeth Bishop.

Unpublished letters by Ezra Pound copyright © 1999 by Mary de Rachewiltz and Omar S. Pound. Used by permission of New Directions Publishing Corporation.

Publication of an excerpt of an invitation from Natalie Clifford Barney to Marianne Moore is granted by kind permission of François Chapon, Literary Executor of the Estate of Natalie Clifford Barney.

Excerpt from *Shih-Ching: The Classic Anthology as Defined by Confucius*, copyright © 1954, 1982 by the President and Fellows of Harvard College. Reprinted by permission of Harvard University Press.

Contents

Note on Transliteration

Chinese words which appear in this book are transliterated in Pin Yin orthography, which is the modern standard version of transliteration. In keeping with scholarly works on Chinese subjects, however, the names of Chinese authors and Chinese texts dated before the twentieth century are transliterated according to the Wade–Giles system, the accepted standard orthographical method employed before the development of Pin Yin.

Major Chinese Dynastic Periods

Hsia	legendary
Shang	c.1523–c.1028 BC
Chou	c.1030–722 BC
Spring and Autumn	722–481 BC
Warring States	480–221 BC
Chin	221–207 BC
Western (Former) Han	206 BC–AD 8
Eastern (Later) Han	AD 25–220
Three Kingdoms	221–65
Western Chin	265–317
Eastern Chin	317–420
Northern and Southern Dynasties	420–581
Sui	581–618
T'ang	618–906
Five Dynasties	907–60
Liao	907–1125
Northern Sung	960–1126
Southern Sung	1127–1279
Chin	1115–1234
Yuan	1260–1368
Ming	1368–1644
Ch'ing	1644–1911

Abbreviations

I

Oriental Precedents: The Novelty of America and its Modernist Reform

Everyone who writes about the Orient must locate himself vis-à-vis the Orient; translated into his text, this location includes the kind of narrative voice he adopts, the type of structure he builds, the kinds of images, themes, motifs that circulate in his text—all of which add up to deliberate ways of addressing the reader, containing the Orient, and finally, representing it or speaking in its behalf. None of this takes place in the abstract, however. Every writer on the Orient (and this is true even of Homer) assumes some Oriental precedent, some previous knowledge of the Orient, to which he refers and on which he relies. Additionally, each work on the Orient *affiliates* itself with other works, with audiences, with institutions, with the Orient itself. The ensemble of relationships between works, audiences, and some particular aspects of the Orient therefore constitutes an analyzable formation—for example, that of philological studies, of anthologies of extracts from Oriental literature, of travel books, of Oriental fantasies—whose presence in time, in discourse, in institutions (schools, libraries, foreign services) gives it strength and authority.

(Edward Said, *Orientalism*, 20)

MOORE AS AMERICAN ORIENTALIST

In one of her earliest journals, Marianne Moore made the following notations on two meetings of the local Ladies' Missionary Society:

The meeting was opened with prayer; after which, the roll was called, each of those present reciting a verse of scripture as her name was called . . . the subject for discussion—'The Chinese' was introduced . . . Mrs. King read an article on the Chinese & their peculiarities . . .

Mrs. Barr & Mrs. Merwood read articles on the easiest ways & means to adopt, to convert the Chinaman . . .[1]

The entries in this notebook are not dated, although they begin as early as 1907, when Moore had already begun to write verse of her own and was a student at Bryn Mawr. Moore's notes on the Ladies' Missionary Society appear to serve as a faithful and detailed transcription of the day's discussions. Given the clerical background of the Moore family and the fact that her mother, Mary Warner Moore (1862–1947), was also in attendance, Marianne's presence at the Missionary Society meeting is not unusual. However, this early encounter is significant in that, as Carl T. Jackson has remarked, 'the missionary movement would steadily gather momentum and become one of the crucial influences in America's encounter with the Orient'.[2] Already, as a young adult, Moore was experiencing the East as strange and peculiar. China's unfettered ability to resist American religious assimilation, the Christian framework which was so important for the Moore family, must have made it seem even more alien, and possibly more exotic, to the young poet. These entries situate Moore's early experience of what constituted the 'foreign', and display the sense that a 'local' interest necessarily entails an awareness of the ways in which that interest might translate geographically. And, of course, access to the society itself readily identifies Moore's American upbringing not only to be Christian, but middle-class as well.

Moore's work features a markedly international and academic focus from the early poetry onward and Chinese subjects, references, and models increasingly become constituent elements in her ranging and decidedly eclectic output. Her affinity for scholarly work on Chinese subjects from poetry to painting, calligraphy, chinoiserie, textile design, and religious history is evident not only in her poetry and appended notes, but also in prose work throughout her writing career. In a 1923 review of *Hymen*[3] by

---

[1] RL VII:01:01. Notebook 1250/1, 1907–15. It was also at this time that Moore was studying Oriental History at Bryn Mawr. See the summary of Moore's college courses published in the *Marianne Moore Newsletter*, 5/1 (Spring, 1981), 14.
[2] Carl T. Jackson, *The Oriental Religions and American Thought: Nineteenth-Century Explorations* (Westport, Conn., and London: Greenwood Press, 1981), 9.
[3] H.D., *Hymen* (London: Egoist Press, 1921).

H. D. in *Broom*, Moore wrote: 'In this instinctive ritual of beauty, at once old and modern, one is reminded of the supernatural yellows of China'.[4] She reviewed books on Chinese poetry and painting as well for *The Dial* in the 1920s and, in addition to consistently revealing her active interest in sinology, quoted Confucius repeatedly in reviews and essays on quite disparate subjects until the end of her writing career. Moore's orientalism, both imaginative and scholarly, was clearly a productive engagement and exploration. It informs the considerable breadth of her writing not only in terms of subject-matter, but also philosophically, creatively, and, as I will demonstrate in later chapters, in terms of poetic technique as well.

Edward Said's analysis of the multitude of personal, scholarly, and (always) ideological investments in the East is essential to a thorough appreciation of Moore's practice of orientalism. He establishes the scope of this endeavour in *Orientalism*:

Anyone who teaches, writes about, or researches the Orient—and this applies whether the person is an anthropologist, sociologist, historian, or philologist—either in its specific or its general aspects, is an Orientalist, and what he or she does is Orientalism . . . Orientalism is a style of thought based upon an ontological and epistemological distinction made between 'the Orient' and (most of the time) 'the Occident'.[5]

Said's study systematically outlines the degree to which orientalist practices, be they scholarly, imaginative, overtly political, sociological, etc., all entail a psychological investment in a constructed notion of 'the Orient', 'the Oriental', and Oriental sensibilities. The Orient, for Said, arises out of a network of interwoven, interdependent, and schematically secure notions or 'knowledges' of the East, sometimes, though by no means always, founded on an informed, logical structure which has to varying degrees some correspondence to the reality of the East. This emergent complex of discourses arises out of 'a sovereign Western consciousness' resulting from Western hegemony over the Orient since the late eighteenth century.[6] Said's analysis is more useful for examining European orientalism until the early twentieth

---

[4] *Broom*, 4 (Jan. 1923), 133–5, as quoted in *CPR* 81.
[5] Edward Said, *Orientalism* (New York: Vintage, 1979), 2.   [6] Ibid. 7–8.

century and does not fully address the very different tradition of orientalism which developed in America from the late eighteenth century onward.[7]

For my purposes here, however, Said makes a serious effort to examine the far-reaching and elaborate network of orientalist relationships and interdependencies, particularly within the scholarly community, which are so pertinent to the attempt to understand Moore's poetry. One of the objectives of this chapter is to give some indication of the extent of American literary orientalism, particularly as it involves China, and to establish the identifiable influences of that tradition on Marianne Moore's work. Her American orientalism stands outside of what Aijaz Ahmad has described as Said's narrow analysis of '*a* Europe, or the West, as a self-identical, fixed being which has always had an essence and a project, an imagination and a will'.[8] Yet what can be retrieved from *Orientalism* is a contextualization of the scholarly system within which Moore manoeuvres so fruitfully. What is fascinating about Moore's orientalism is the ways in which she both employed and contributed to that network, the individual investments she may have had in that participation, and the degree to which her utilization of orientalist texts worked to pre-empt the intrusion of the corresponding reality of China. Moore's particular use of the Far East, namely China, within this constellation of discourses is problematized, firstly, by her being American and therefore not directly inheriting the specifically European idea of the Orient which Said's analysis relies upon. Secondly, her orientalism is augured in the orientalism of the American Transcendentalists, is specifically Emersonian, and is therefore historically belated.

Moore was involved in the imaginative production of the Orient; she posited China as a repository of wisdom, forbearance, peace, and tranquillity. Above all, she found in her studies of

---

[7] The methodology of *Orientalism* has generated a number of thorough and intelligent critiques. Among them, Aijaz Ahmad's essay, 'Orientalism and After: Ambivalence and Metropolitan Location in the Work of Edward Said', in *In Theory: Classes, Nations, Literatures* (London and New York: Verso, 1992), systematically unseats many of Said's premises and strategies. Other works which contest Said's book include, for example, Robert Young, *White Mythologies: Writing History and the West* (New York: Routledge, 1990), and Marilyn Butler, 'Orientalism', in David B. Pirie (ed.), *The Romantic Period* (London: Penguin, 1994), 395–447.
[8] Ahmad, 'Orientalism', 183.

China a series of qualities which are not usually associated with the Near East which Said's study focuses upon. What for orientalists, whose notions of the Orient rose out of literature about the Near East, was a stereotype of Eastern decadence, laziness, backwardness, irrationality, depravity, sensuality, despotism, and degeneracy, for Moore was a specifically Chinese association with precision and detail, fastidiousness, brevity, concentration, wit, and wisdom. Moore's reverence for what she saw as uniquely Chinese attributes arose out of a complex set of associations, not only with the execution of Chinese paintings and artefacts or with the forms of Chinese poetry, but with what she saw as China's ancient and enduring culture. Much of her poetry is in one way or another caught up in an ongoing meditation on what America is, what its enduring qualities are, and how to find in America what has traditionally been sought in Europe.

There is something about the sheer historical accretion of European experience and culture which, for Americans, has always implied a formidable depth and superiority, in comparison with which America is pristine, inchoate, and naïve. While Moore takes issue with European precedence in some of her poems, it is the way in which she locates in China a cultural superiority to Europe itself that is of particular interest. This manoeuvre is justified not only because of China's historical longevity, the enduring sophistication of its arts and its inventiveness, but also because for Moore it served to remove and displace the struggle for American definition to another and, for her, a superior site. Ralph Waldo Emerson made much the same move when he noted in his journal, 'The East is grand,—& makes Europe appear the land of trifles.'[9] Chapter 2 takes up in detail Moore's deliberate efforts to discover and locate 'at home' those 'foreign' qualities she thought worthy of America. What is pertinent to this discussion is the ways in which this procedure is complicit in the range of orientalist tasks to which Said refers, as well as the degree to which the American orientalism to which Moore subscribed is subsumed within a larger, established proto-nationalist project. For America throughout its literary history has been preoccupied with a nationalist imperative to bring itself into existence, to invent itself.

[9] *JRWE* ix. 322.

In *Orientalism*, Said argues for the very recent arrival to America of the practice of orientalism. America's direct political and military involvement in the Orient is largely confined to the period from the Second World War onward, since which time it has dominated the East.[10] But Moore's practice of finding equivalences in the East preceded American hegemony in that part of the world and is, as I have noted above, a distinctly Emersonian endeavour. This is not unexpected since Emerson is considered to be the first, and unsurpassed, orientalist in the tradition of American literature. However, there is evidence of a nascent American orientalism which predates even the interest of the Transcendentalists in the East. In the 1770s, Benjamin Franklin founded the American Philosophical Society whose charter, set out in the preface to the first volume of its *Transactions* (1771), reveals that one of its aims was to examine Chinese philosophy.[11] Franklin himself published extracts from the Confucian *Analects* in the *Pennsylvania Gazette* and, in 1838, the society he founded published the first American monograph on the Chinese language.

Franklin's literary interest in China was also revealed in his 'Letter from China', published in a London magazine in 1788, where this Pennsylvanian polymath experimented with an Oriental tale. It recounts the travels of two sailors in China who had left Captain Cook's expedition in Macao. The piece exposes the superficiality of Franklin's acquaintance with Chinese religious practices. One of Franklin's sailors observes that the Chinese 'have a sort of religion, with priests and churches, but do not keep Sunday, nor go to church, being very heathenish'. However, the 'letter' displays Franklin's wry humour when it reports why the Chinese did not attend church to pray as Europeans did: 'they paid the priests to pray for them, that they might stay at home and mind their business; and that it would be a folly to pay others for praying, and then go and do the praying themselves'.[12]

Besides Franklin, John Adams, the second American president, was the only American thinker of the Enlightenment to exhibit an interest in Asian thought.[13] Emerson expanded upon this

[10] Said, *Orientalism*, 4 and 290.
[11] Richard C. Rudolph, *China and the West: Culture and Commerce* (Los Angeles: UCLA, 1977), 7–8.
[12] Jackson, *Oriental Religions*, 14.   [13] Ibid. 29.

early American interest in the Far East shown by two of its foremost thinkers and writers. Like Franklin and Emerson, Moore's
orientalist practices are bound up with an enduring American
mandate to articulate America, to define and, to a certain extent,
to produce it, philosophically and literarily. Her library holdings
contain a considerable number of Emerson's published works
including copies of *Representative Men: Seven Lectures* (1849),
Essays of 1841 (with notes in her handwriting), and *Nature*
(1836), all three of which are dated and signed 'Marianne Moore,
October 1904'. There is a 1906 edition of Emerson's *Essays and
Addresses* with clippings enclosed, as well as copies of *Society
and Solitude* (1870) and *Complete Essays and Other Writings*
(1883). In an early notebook entry, circa 1909, Moore wrote
that she had read Emerson's talks to young men.[14]

No other writer figured so prominently in Moore's early career
as did Emerson, whose work was informed by Eastern philosophy from his Harvard days onward. In addition to being very
familiar with Indian philosophies (Buddhist, Hindu) and referring to Asia collectively at times, Emerson's journals reveal an
intimate knowledge of Chinese philosophy (Buddhist, Confucian,
Mencius) and contain a range of pointed remarks about an
enormous variety of Chinese subjects ranging from methods
of worship to tea. His journals allude to and quote liberally
from Confucian texts such as the *Analects*, *The Great Learning*,
The Doctrine of the Mean, and the *Shi King*. These quotations
then found their way into the composition of a number of his
lectures such as 'Social Aims', 'Society', 'The Heart', 'Ethics',
'Spiritual Laws', 'Character', and 'Religion'. An early journal entry
from 12 February 1822 reveals that Emerson was well enough
acquainted with Chinese history to compare it with Italian
history.[15] His personal library, in addition to his wide reading
at the Boston Athenaeum, provided him with a vast array of
Chinese texts in which to steep his inquisitive mind.[16] Emerson

---

[14] RL VII:01:01, Notebook 1250/1, 1907–15.   [15] *JRWE* i. 83.
[16] For example, in his reading notebooks Emerson lists his sources as: *The
Chinese Classical Work, Commonly Called The Four Books*, trans. Rev. David Collie
(Malacca, 1828), made up of the 'Memoirs of Confucius' and the 'Memoirs of
Mencius'; *The Works of Confucius*, trans. Joshua Marshman (Serampore, 1809);
The Phenix; A Collection of Old and Rare Fragments (New York, 1835); James Legge,
The Chinese Classics, 5 vols. (Hong Kong and London, 1861–72); and E. R. Huc,
A Journey through the Chinese Empire, 2 vols. (London, 1855).

shared with his American and English contemporaries, such as
Thoreau, Carlyle, and Whitman, an avid interest in East Asia.
Indeed, Thoreau bequeathed to Emerson a large number of his
texts on the law, theatre, mythology, philosophy, and poetry of
Hindu tradition.[17]

Among the Transcendentalists, Emerson, Alcott, Thoreau, and
Whitman were all receptive to the East and in this respect shared
the interests of the Romantic movement. What was unique about
their response, however, as Yu Beongcheon has noted, was the
'total absence of literary exoticism and cultural dilettantism'. 'At
once existential and mythical, they responded to the Orient as
a mandate of history, as a matter of birthright', he continues;
'whatever separate paths they pursued, it was the Orient that
helped clarify their sense of direction.'[18] Cleo McNelly Kearns
goes even further when she insists that Transcendentalist interest
in Eastern philosophy was inextricable from their identity as
American writers. She comments that 'nothing for Emerson or
Whitman could have been more primally American, as they made
it, or more confirming of their prophetic and artistic place in
their own culture than their receptivity to Eastern thought'.[19]
The English Romantics' interest in the Orient, however, was
as a literary backdrop, and their references to the East were
primarily geographical and not religious, mythological, political,
or philosophical. 'Certainly the English held a somewhat more
fantastic conception of the Orient than did either the Germans
or the Americans, and their Orientalism was generally not
serious but rather a matter of exotic settings for poems', Arthur
Versluis has aptly noted; 'for them the "Eastern" images and
references were scarcely more than exotic decoration, employed
for effect and having little substance.'[20]

The exotic Eastern settings of English Romantic poetry were
also quite varied and bore little relation to the cultures from which
they were extracted. For Byron the 'Orient' was the Ottoman

[17] *JRWE* xv. 252–5 (1862).
[18] Yu Beongcheon, *The Great Circle: American Writers and the Orient* (Detroit: Wayne State University Press, 1983), 22.
[19] Cleo McNelly Kearns, *T. S. Eliot and Indic Traditions: A Study in Poetry and Belief* (Cambridge: Cambridge University Press, 1987), 190.
[20] Arthur Versluis, *American Transcendentalism and Asian Religions* (New York and Oxford: Oxford University Press, 1993), 29.

Middle East, for Shelley it was India. For De Quincey, China and the Far East were Oriental. Each attached more significance to architecture, topography, and national garb than to the Eastern traditions of thought out of which these very disparate cultures had arisen. Transcendentalism, on the other hand, was primarily a religious literary enterprise and one which embraced aspects of Oriental philosophies in an effort both to bolster and reaffirm existing Christian doctrine and to challenge and transform the prevailing interpretations of that doctrine. Moore responded to this Transcendentalist imperative to look to the East, and did so in a similar incumbent, reactive manner. Yu Beongcheon validates this assertion when he goes on to note that 'by translating Columbus's passage to the Orient into a symbolic return to the source of light, the source of life, [the Transcendentalists] all set a singularly American pattern of orientalism for ensuing generations to follow'.[21] This spiritual necessity to look East to find America is again observable in the poetry of a later Transcendentalist, Walt Whitman. In 'Facing West from California's Shores' (1860) from *Leaves of Grass*, Whitman finds emotional renewal in his Eastern voyage.

Facing west from California's shores,
Inquiring, tireless, seeking what is yet unfound,
I, a child, very old, over waves, towards the house of maternity,
the land of migrations, look afar,
Look off the shores of my Western sea, the circle almost circled;
For starting westward from Hindustan, from the vales of Kashmere,
From Asia, from the north, from the God, the sage, and the hero,
From the south, from the flowery peninsulas and the spice islands,
Long having wander'd since, round the earth having wander'd,
Now I face home again, very pleas'd and joyous,
(But where is what I started for so long ago?
And why is it yet unfound?)[22]

The search which causes Whitman to look unceasingly to the East yields only questions and yet brings him joy. The 'house of maternity' is perhaps the ancestral shores of Asia, the continent in which so many American writers sought some sense

[21] Beongcheon, *The Great Circle*, 22.
[22] Walt Whitman, from 'Leaves of Grass', in *The Portable Walt Whitman* (New York: Penguin, 1978), 186.

of provenance, the New World from the Old. Later, in an entry written in the summer of 1878 from *Specimen Days*, Whitman wrote more explicitly about the generative possibilities of Asia:

The East.—What a subject for a poem! Indeed, where else a more pregnant, more splendid one? Where one more idealistic-real, more subtle, more sensuous-delicate? The East, answering all lands, all ages, peoples; touching all senses, here, immediate, now—and yet so inde-scribably far off—such retrospect! The East—long-stretching—so losing itself—the orient, the gardens of Asia, the womb of history and song—forth-issuing all those strange, dim cavalcades—

Florid with blood, pensive, rapt with musings, hot with passion,
Sultry with perfume, with ample and flowing garments,
With sunburnt visage, intense soul and glittering eyes.

Always the East—old, how incalculably old! And yet here the same—ours yet, fresh as a rose, to every morning, every life, to-day—and always will be.[23]

Again, the East is posited as ancient and enduring and, like Emerson and later Moore, Whitman cites this cultural histor-icity as something which accompanies America's newness, that America is eternally new just as the East is timelessly old.

There is, however, something very emotive and sensual about Whitman's vision of the East which is distinctly absent in Emerson and Moore. Both Moore and Emerson experience China as text; theirs is an academic, rather detached, encounter. Emerson was, on the whole, taking stock of China and East Asia with the eye of a scholar of comparative religions. He develops in his journals an ongoing critique and valuation of religious texts and gleans from them a means of support for his argu-ment for the supremacy of Christian doctrine. 'I find an analogy also in the Asiatic sentences to this fact of life', he writes in his journal in 1841. 'The Oriental genius has no dramatic or epic turn, but ethical, contemplative, delights in Zorastrian oracles, in Vedas, & Menu & Confucius', he continues, 'these all embracing apophthegms are like these profound moments of the heavenly life.'[24] Confucianism was for somewhat obvious reasons very amenable to Emerson as a doctrine whose central aphoristic tenets were often indistinguishable from the teachings

---

[23] Ibid. 534. Entry for 22 July 1878.   [24] *JRWE* viii. 11 (1841).

of Christ. 'Confucius', Emerson noted in his journal, 'anticipated the speech of Socrates, and the *Do as be done by*, of Jesus.'[25] He exploited those similarities and put them to use in his lectures, but remained uncertain as to the cultural superiority of China as a whole.

This kind of selective affinity is also very typical of Moore, whose wide and varied interest in China, as will be evident in later chapters, always skirted contemporary history and politics. Her orientalism is belated in that it determinedly avoided the current reality of a China which was, in her time, mired in social and political turmoil. Moore's historically belated orientalism, her Emersonian orientalism, facilitated the apparently apolitical nature of her interest in China. It enabled her to endow China with a timeless, ethereal quality suited to the needs and preoccupations of her poetry. China represented a utopic space where turbulent exchanges within culture, class, and even gender were momentarily suspended. Compared with Moore, Emerson was far less sentimental and deliberately disengaged from the realities of contemporary events. He at times grumbles in his journals about 'Chinese narrowness',[26] and China's 'crockery Gods',[27] and is on the whole deeply paternalistic about all non-Christian peoples. However, in his more perspicacious moments he is certainly not unaware of the posturings and concerns of contemporary colonialism:

The earth is shaken by our engineries. We are feeling our youth & nerve & bone. We have the power of land & sea, & know the use of these. We count our census, we read our growing valuations, we survey our map, which becomes speedily old, our railway, telegraph. We interfere in S. America, in Canton, & Japan, & discover Antarctic continents & polar sea. We are the brag of the world, & value ourselves by these feats.[28]

The 'we' he asserts in this passage is clearly Western and European, and the passage implies a collective responsibility for the impetuousness of Western imperialism. Emerson had quite clearly taken note of what Said calls 'the fact of empire'.[29]

---

[25] Ralph Waldo Emerson, *The Journals of Ralph Waldo Emerson*, (ed.) Edward Waldo Emerson and Waldo Emerson Forbes (Boston, Mass., 1909–14), ix. 535.
[26] *JRWE* xiv. 58 (1856).   [27] *JRWE* ii. 378 (1824).
[28] *JRWE* xiv. 263 (1859).   [29] Said, *Orientalism*, 14.

Emerson practised a distinctly American form of orientalism which, as I have pointed out, sought in the Far East a means of defining and shaping America in a process of self-analysis. 'It is useful to know the <productions> state of man in circumstances widely dissimilar', he wrote in his journal of 1824, 'it is a help to an inference concerning our progress.'[30] It is at the same time clear that he employed the same register of binaries common to all orientalist projects. In his journal of 1845, Emerson sets out the following pairings:

Asia	Europe
Unity	Variety
Infinity	Boundary
Fate	Freedom
Caste	Culture[31]

What is significant about these orientalist dichotomies is that America stands outside the binary, before Europe/Asia became West/East. This is what distinguishes American from European orientalist positions until the time of American intervention in the Far East from the Second World War onward. What Moore and Emerson share is this sense of being part of a tertiary term outside the opposition and yet as a scion, so to speak, of Europe, also implicated in the binary. With one coast facing Europe and the other facing the Far East, America's interstitial position necessitates some kind of resolution and synthesis. From another perspective, America in this model need not define itself in opposition to Asia. Neither does the East become a surrogate self, but rather is viewed as an ancestor from whom qualities such as patience and sagacity will no doubt be inherited by the relatively new American nation.

Like Moore, Emerson reached to Asia as to an ancient progenitor whose cultural durability offered America a kind of acquired wisdom, while at the same time he saw America as the energetic offspring destined to rescue the family of mankind:

Asia, Africa, Europe, old, leprous & wicked, have run round the goal of centuries till we are tired and they are ready to drop. But now a

---

[30] *JRWE* ii. 229 (1824). The angle brackets around <productions> indicate alternate choices of terms included in Emerson's manuscripts.

[31] *JRWE* ix. 333 (1845).

strong man has entered the race & is outstripping them all. Strong Man! youth & glory are with thee. As thou wouldst prosper forget not the hope of mankind. Trample not upon the competitors though unworthy. Europe is thy <mo>father—<support her Asia> bear him on thy Atlantean shoulders. Asia, thy grandsire, regenerate him. Africa, their ancient abused <slave> bondman. Give him his freedom.[32]

Within this broken triumvirate, Asia alone is seen as uncontaminated both physically and morally, unlike 'leprous' Africa and 'wicked' Europe. The 'Strong Man' of America can revitalize Asia, indeed rescue the world, but only by virtue of 'his' lineage with both Europe and Asia. In a journal entry some twenty years later, Emerson offered a less mythical and more complex assessment of the divisions within mankind. 'Some men have the perception of difference predominant, and are conversant with surfaces & trifles, with coats & coaches, & faces, & cities; these are the men of talent. Hence Paris & the western European, and New York & New England. And other men abide by the perception of Identity; these are the Orientals, the philosophers, the men of faith & divinity, the men of genius.'[33] No longer is difference delineated along national boundaries. In this new dichotomy, Emerson no doubt is a 'man of faith' and as such shares qualities with 'the Orientals'.

For Emerson and for Moore, looking to other nations was decidedly not to be confused with emulating other nations. For both, the project of finding equivalences and making comparisons was never incorporative but always exploratory. Each was concerned with the building of America, but always reluctant to use other than indigenous materials. 'The less America looks abroad, as now, the grander its promise', Emerson wrote in his journal of 1864.[34] This kind of self-reflection is an abiding feature of American culture. America, preconceived as a New World, is historically defined by its departure from all other cultures. 'Shake off from your shoes the dust of Europe and Asia', Emerson noted in his journal of 1855.[35] The persistent search for authenticity is a crucial component of the process which is America, and this process is generated by a perceived lack of

[32] *JRWE* ii. 218 (1824).   [33] *JRWE* ix. 72 (1844).
[34] *JRWE* xv. 431 (1864).
[35] Emerson, *Journals*, (ed.) Emerson and Forbes, viii. 568.

origin and history. Emerson's and Moore's evident anxiety about defining America is itself constitutive of American identity, an identity seemingly eternally in the throes of the process of individuation. Separated across historical time, both their concerns remain much the same. 'The young men in America take little thought of what men in England are thinking or doing', Emerson wrote in 1864. 'That is the point which decides the welfare of a people,—*which way does it look?*', he asked, 'if to any other people, it is not well with them.'[36] Differentiating itself first from Europe and then from the rest of the world is the project of becoming America. 'A true nation loves its vernacular tongue. A completed nation does not import its religion. Duty grows everywhere, like children, like grass, and we need not go to Asia to learn it.'[37] This statement informs the poetry of Marianne Moore. 'England', written early in her career (first published in *The Dial* in April 1920), reasserts Emerson's imperatives. America is the land in which 'letters are written | not in Spanish, not in Greek, not in Latin, not in shorthand, | but in plain American'. America is linguistically undefined, a 'languageless country' which speaks a version of English in which the letter *a* is mispronounced. The poem is entitled 'England', but the ultimate contest to establish America as distinct, sufficient, and even equal to 'all that noted superiority' is with the East: 'The sublimated wisdom of China, Egyptian discernment, | the cataclysmic torrent of emotion | compressed in the verbs of the Hebrew language, | . . . if not stumbled upon in America, | must one imagine that it is not there? | It has never been confined to one locality.'[38] To look 'far enough' is to be able to stumble upon, to recognize, those qualities which inhere in America. To become 'a true nation', to arrive at 'America', is for both Emerson and Moore a duty, and one which preoccupied their writing throughout their careers.

Emerson was an editor of *The Dial* magazine, in his day subtitled *A Magazine for Literature, Philosophy, and Religion*. Emerson's two years as editor (1842–4) allowed him the opportunity to offer his views on Far Eastern philosophy and related subjects alongside of articles reviewing contemporary

---

[36] *JRWE* xv. 430 (1864).   [37] Ibid. 431.
[38] 'England' will be discussed further in later chapters. All poems by Moore appear in *CP* unless otherwise noted.

American literature.[39] In July 1842, with Emerson's debut as editor, 'Ethnical Scriptures' began a series of extracts from religious literatures as a permanent feature in *The Dial*. Between 1842 and 1844, Emerson and Thoreau offered selections from Marshman's *Works of Confucius* and Collie's *Chinese Classical Work*.[40] Thoreau's interest in the East was initially ignited by Emerson and, though he showed a strong interest in India, his writings, particularly *Walden*, are evidently informed by Confucian, Hindu, and Buddhist readings. Emerson's and Thoreau's use of Far Eastern sources was, however, very different. While Thoreau took from Eastern philosophy ideas that he could translate directly into a new way of living (as he did at Walden Pond), Emerson's interests in the East were to a large extent a literary enterprise. He assimilated Eastern religious texts into his thought and writings with a rhetorical emphasis rather than reiterating, or often even acknowledging, the source of these ideas. Emerson's journals, which also functioned as his reading notebooks, are therefore a vital source with which to trace the progress of his Eastern researches and the evolution of his thought. Arthur Versluis calls attention to the pragmatic and discursive quality of Emerson's use of Asian sources:

In keeping with his tendency to regard 'Eastern doctrines' from a literary perspective, Emerson had little knowledge of the Buddhist denial of transmigration; rather, his point of view generally assimilated Vedantic and Confucian thought, which were much more amenable to literary use . . . Confucianism had a similar attraction, for it too translated into terms easily assimilable to the nineteenth-century American mind, terms of merit and morality.[41]

Of course, these terms were of immense importance to Moore, whose poetry locates the moral and the moral worth of nearly all that it encounters. Emerson's habit of gleaning useful aphorisms, ideas, and texts for his essays, which would promote understanding and translate into wisdom, became Moore's practice as well. In an early, unpublished, manuscript version of 'The

<hr/>

[39] For a detailed discussion of the early evolution of *The Dial*, see Joel Myerson, *The New England Transcendentalists and the Dial: A History of the Magazine and its Contributors* (Rutherford, NJ: Fairleigh Dickenson University Press, 1980).
[40] Jackson, *Oriental Religions*, 59. For citation of texts see n. 16 above.
[41] Versluis, *American Transcendentalism*, 70.

Steeple-Jack', Moore quoted Emerson's remark that 'one is not
fitted to be a scholar without the heroic mind'.[42]

It will become increasingly clear in later chapters that Moore
sought what was helpful for her poetry in a bold and seemingly
unpremeditated manner, and always approached her sources with
scholarly acumen. Her use of Chinese texts and subjects was
always deliberate and studied, whether her aim was a greater
resolution of the subject at hand or a deliberate obfuscation
of its meaning. It is clear that Emerson was pivotal to Moore's
development as a distinctly American poet at a time when the
anti-traditional and international influences upon modern poets
were decidedly strong. Her American orientalism is one identifiable inheritance from Emerson, as was her determination 'to
be a scholar'. It seems that for both of them this determination
was an important component of their interest in China, and
Emerson's example certainly led Moore to look to the Far East to
'imagine'[43] what she needed at home. As Frederic I. Carpenter
observed in one of the earliest works on this subject, *Emerson
and Asia*, 'Emerson's example has encouraged Americans to seek
out for themselves the wisdom of Asia at its sources.'[44]

SUBVERSIVE ORIENTALISM

Orientalist works have traditionally taken the form of a critique
of resident institutions, prominent persons, or the contemporary
state of affairs. This guise has often been loosely worked and
obvious, thus facilitating the appropriate 'reading' of a piece.
Both English and European literature since the sixteenth century
reveal examples of this kind of satirical writing. Within this genre,
there has been a persistent appearance of satirical orientalist
pieces which use China or Chinese characters as their ruse, and
this satirical model eventually found its way into early American
orientalist writing. This tradition of critique in orientalist prose
writing was, in the Modernist period, adopted by several poets
who borrowed Chinese poetic models to permanently transform

---

[42] RL I:04:23.   [43] See the concluding lines of 'England'.
[44] Frederic Ives Carpenter, *Emerson and Asia* (Cambridge, Mass.: Harvard University Press, 1930), 249–50.

the ways in which poetry in English was being written. Not only did these efforts succeed in undermining established poetic techniques—dependence upon metaphor, for example—but they also introduced poetic methodologies which continue to inform contemporary verse. American literary orientalism, then, inherited an eighteenth-century European orientalist tradition of critical prose writing about Europe and went on to produce similar critiques directed at American social concerns in the nineteenth century. In the twentieth century, this tradition was embraced by American poets who imported Far Eastern poetic forms 'directly' in order to launch a literary assault upon what they saw as outmoded methods of versification. What is interesting about this development is not only that it is initially American poets who co-opt Eastern models, but that the eighteenth-century European satirical models are eventually discarded by American poets in favour of a more direct borrowing of Far Eastern forms.

Examples of the use of China as exemplar exist at least as early as the sixteenth century. In the Baroque era, the romance of chivalry was followed by the heroic-gallant romance and the novel. Ludovico Arrivabene's *Il magno Vitei* (The Great Vitei) (1597) was the first prose romance of significant length to marvel at Asian rulers and the nations they governed. As the 'first king of China', Vitei is portrayed as an excellent prince who presides over the most virtuous nation known to mankind. Vitei's military exploits against neighbouring nations, his learning, inventions, and virtue, are all celebrated by Arrivabene. Asia is shown as a land of both real and fabulous wonders. This Italian homily is an early example of what was to become in the eighteenth century a more widespread notion that China was a model society which Europe should emulate. China is depicted by Arrivabene as a highly organized society with exceptional lay morality ruled by exemplary princes with model governance. *Il magno Vitei* was later followed by *Lob des Krieges-Gottes* (Praise of the Gods of War) (1628) by the father of German Baroque poetry Martin Opitz. In this poem Opitz asserts that Mars sent Europeans by sea to China's fertile shores where artillery, printed books, and porcelains were made.[45] No doubt this poem inspired another

---

[45] Donald F. Lach and Theodore Nicholas Foss, 'Images of Asia and Asians in European Fiction, 1500–1800' in Robin W. Winks and James R. Rush (eds.), *Asia in Western Fiction* (Honolulu: University of Hawaii Press, 1990), 18–19.

German writer, Gottfried Wilhelm Leibniz, to study Far Eastern sources. By 1687, Leibniz's journal entries reveal that he had read Confucius, and in 1697 his *Novissima Sinica* was published, advocating exchange between China and European civilizations.[46] In the eighteenth century, Jesuit missionaries were already writing of their experiences in China and compiling sizeable volumes of information about its religious philosophy and culture generally. They depicted China as a land governed by Confucian orthodoxy, 'home of the *sage chinois*', and this characterization prompted writers such as the French free-thinker La Mothe Le Vayer to voice dissatisfaction with European society for its failure to live up to the Chinese ideal.[47]

Epistolary fictions had a long-standing popularity among satirical orientalist prose writers as well. As Lach and Foss point out in their study, Europeans travelling in Asia corresponded with those at home through letters, travelogues, and reports. Undoubtedly, the notion of fictional 'letters' purportedly written by Asian travellers to Europe was a reflection of these authentic epistolary exchanges. They provided a means through which criticisms of European society could be launched by 'foreign' exotics and comparisons made to supposedly superior Far Eastern institutions. The presence of the Japanese embassies of 1585 and 1614, as well as Eastern court envoys, substantiates the possibility that this kind of correspondence did in fact take place. These epistolary fictions were also reinforced by the arrival in the West of visitors from the Far East, which included the young Chinese Christian convert, Michael Shen Futsung, educated by Jesuit missionaries and brought to Oxford in 1687 to help with the Chinese library. Arcadius Hoang, another young Chinese, came to Europe in the 1720s. The fictive letter became a popular literary device in the late seventeenth century, when European authors began to base their works on the correspondence of imaginary Easterners.[48]

---

[46]   Rudolph, *China and the West*, 8–9.

[47]   Lach and Foss, 'Images of Asia', 25.

[48]   Ibid. 25–6. Examples of this genre include: *Marana's Turkish Spy* (1687); *Montesquieu's Two Persians* (1721); the *Lettres chinoises* (1739) of Jean Baptiste de Boyer; and the Marquis d'Argens and Elizabeth Hamilton's *Translations of the Letters of a Hindo Rajah* (1797). Frederick the Great of Prussia's six satirical letters from a fictional Chinese official, *Relation de Phihihu* (1760), mock the pope, referred to as 'the Grand Lama of Rome'.

English examples of this kind of epistolary fiction include ' "Eubulus" On Chinese and English Manners' (1738),[49] written by Samuel Johnson (1709–84), which uses Chinese philosophy to criticize the monarchy. Learning and industry, 'Eubulus' points out, are ranked by the Chinese over laziness and privilege: 'nobility and knowledge are the same'. The fictional author's name, 'Eubulus', meaning 'prudent and well advised', implies a kind of classical wisdom and, while not an Easterner, he is evidently imaginary. 'Eubulus' describes the ideal emperor who ruled with reason, law, and morality, who 'scorn'd to exert [his] power in defence of that which they could not support by argument'. He goes on to portray an English prince as reluctant to behave according to Chinese principles until 'forced' to do so. Johnson was bitter over the recognition of scholarship and industry in China, while in England George II (r. 1727–60) spoke broken English and spent the majority of his time in Hanover. These implied comparisons with Chinese government serve as an overt corrective to the English government without inviting the potential reprisals, literary or otherwise, which might have attended either diatribe or invective.

Another good example is a 'letter' of 12 May 1757, entitled 'A Letter from Xo Ho, a Chinese Philosopher at London, To his Friend Lieu Chi, at Peking',[50] written by Horatio Walpole (1717–91). This piece, which features an exotic 'outsider' who discovers that 'reason in China is not reason in England',[51] was very popular in England and, according to a note by its author, went through five editions in two weeks. Xo Ho summons a series of contemporary political situations and observations to show that China and England have little in common, and indeed that England resembles no other country. 'These people are incomprehensible . . . They are unlike the rest of the western world . . . an Englishman has no fixed ideas . . . his caprices are his own', he writes, 'while all are free to fell their *liberty*, the richest or craftiest may purchase it . . . all they ask [of politicians] is news;

[49] Samuel Johnson, ' "Eubulus" On Chinese and English Manners' in the *Yale Edition of the Works of Samuel Johnson*, (ed.) Donald J. Greene, vol. x: *Political Writings* (New Haven and London: Yale University Press, 1977), 14–18.

[50] Horatio Walpole, 'A Letter from Xo Ho, a Chinese Philosopher at London, To his Friend Lieu Chi, at Peking', in *The Works of Horatio Walpole, Earl of Oxford*, vol. i (London: printed for G. G. and J. Robinson and J. Edwards, 1798), 205–9.

[51] Ibid. 206.

a falsehood is as much news as truth'.[52] Again, the ruse is meant to be understood and even humorous, as Xo Ho goes on to wonder at the English calling their season 'summer' when there is no corresponding sunshine. However, some of his observations are quite critical and discerning. 'They do not oppose their king from a dislike of royal power but to avail themselves of his power', he writes of English politicians; 'they are as little in earnest about liberty.'[53] Walpole's 'letter' epitomizes this kind of orientalist epistolary fiction, exposing the degree to which Chinese institutions were idealized in this period. Thinly veiled criticism of this sort likewise enabled authors to adopt the innocent authorial persona of the foreigner abroad, for as Xo Ho observes, 'every thing here is reversed'.[54]

Similarly, Oliver Goldsmith's *The Citizen of the World* (1762)[55] features a Chinese commentator, Lien Chi Altangi, who satirizes both European social mores and contemporary stereotypes of China. Goldsmith relies heavily not only upon his reading of Voltaire's work on China but also, like his orientalist satire-writing forebears, upon Jesuit missionary accounts. Unlike previous Asian critiques, Goldsmith's *Citizen of the World* lampoons the English enthusiasm for things Chinese and mocks the dilettantish Sinophilia which embraces and co-opts Chinese products in seeming ignorance of their original use and meaning.[56] Goldsmith's work represents one of the only satires which targeted the English obsession with Chinese 'ideas' and chinoiserie.

Orientalist satires and polemics based upon researches into Far Eastern culture frequently appeared in eighteenth-century European literature by authors such as Friedrich Schlegel (1772–1829), Johann Gottfried von Herder (1744–1803), and Voltaire (1694–1778). Voltaire's *Essai sur les mœurs* (1745) corroborates the idea that China and India represented 'the true elders of the family of mankind' and that European philosophy and culture was founded in the East.[57] His satirical, didactic discourses

[52] Horatio Walpole, 205–6.   [53] Ibid. 205.   [54] Ibid. 209.
[55] Oliver Goldsmith, *The Citizen of the World; or, Letters from a Chinese Philosopher Residing in London to his Friends in the East* (London, 1762).
[56] Lach and Foss, 'Images of Asia', 26–7.
[57] Raymond Schwab, *The Oriental Renaissance: Europe's Discovery of India and the East 1680–1880* (New York: Columbia University Press, 1984), 152. *Essai sur les mœurs* first appeared in fragments originally published in the *Mercure de France* from April 1745 to June 1746 and later from 1750 to 1751.

sometimes feature an Asian (usually Chinese) visitor who extolls China, the acme of civilized societies, and disparages Europe as an inferior civilization and society. Herder went so far as to claim in *Ideen zur Philosophie der Geschichte der Menschheit* (1784–91) that the Orient was the 'soil of God, rightly elected for this purpose'.[58] British interests in the Far East, particularly in India, made English writers unusually prone to offer comparisons between England and the East. Marilyn Butler refers to this in her essay, 'Orientalism'. 'As Britain transformed itself into an Eastern empire, most of the orientalizing poets, at least some of the time, imagined such empires as lightly allegorized, defamiliarized versions of the British state', she observes, 'an imagined over-throw "otherwhere", the plot of poem after poem, stands for revolution anywhere, including the British empire, including metropolitan Britain—an entirely different proposition.'[59] While many of these literary polemics concerned the Far East gener-ally or countries other than China, the orientalist satire on the whole served many of the same purposes as a means to caution or upbraid contemporary European institutions and to deflate Eurocentric notions of superiority and originality.

Early accounts by English travellers reveal the awe with which China was regarded.[60] A Cornish adventurer, Peter Mundy, wrote of his impressions when he accompanied the first English expedition there in 1636. 'This Countrie May bee said to excell in these particulers: Antiquity, largenesse, Ritchenesse, healthy-nesse, Plentiffullnesse', he noted, 'for Arts and manner off governmentt I thinck noe Kingdome in the world Comparable to it, Considered alltogether.'[61] By the late eighteenth century, England had become almost Sinomaniacal. Its admiration of China and things Chinese had reached unprecedented pro-portions. The steady rise of interest in China and England's increasing idealization of Chinese institutions can be observed

[58] As cited and translated in Schwab, *The Oriental Renaissance*, 13.
[59] Butler, 'Orientalism', 399.
[60] For a thorough background on European conceptions of China, see Colin MacKerras, *Western Images of China* (Hong Kong, Oxford, and New York: Oxford University Press, 1991).
[61] Peter Mundy, *The Travels of Peter Mundy in Europe and Asia, 1608–1667* (London, 1919), as cited in Raymond Dawson, *The Chinese Chameleon: An Analysis of European Conceptions of Chinese Civilization* (London: Oxford University Press, 1967), 32.

in the writings of Sir William Temple, an avid Sinophile and the first Englishman to write about the Chinese garden. 'An Essay on Popular Discontents',[62] which begins his *Miscellanea* (1701), decries factionalism and the deceitful appearances of men, whose hidden hearts and disguised principles allow them to pretend to loyalty while seething with dissent. The weak heads and hearts of public servants, Temple continues, are to be found in any government, and he describes England as 'our unfortunate Country'.[63] 'All Places and Ages of the World yeild [sic] the same Examples; and if we Travel as far as *China* and *Peru*, to find the best composed Frames of Government that seem to have been in the World', he laments, 'yet we meet with none that has not been subject to the same Concussions, fallen at one time or other under the same Convulsions of State, either by Civil Dissentions, or by Foreign Invasions'.[64] Later, however, Temple voices unconditional praise for Chinese government institutions as unsurpassed in their wisdom and strength:

> For it may perhaps be concluded, with as much Reason as other Theams of the like Nature, That those are generally the best Governments where the best Men govern; and let the Sort or Scheme be what it will, those are ill Governments, where ill Men Govern, and are generally employ'd in the Offices of State: Yet this is an Evil under the Sun, to which all things under the Sun are subject, not only by Accident, but even by natural Dispositions, which can very hardly be alter'd, nor ever were, that we read of, unless in that antient Government of the *Chinese* Empire, established upon the deepest and wisest Foundations of any that appears in Story.[65]

Evidently what was perceived to be the reality of China engendered deep dissatisfaction with England in the late eighteenth century. China, regarded by some writers as a more venerable ancient civilization than Rome or Greece, emerged as a foil to the more popular neo-classical revival of the eighteenth century. China was posited not only as predating classical civilizations, but also as surpassing Greece and Rome in its rational order, morality, and sophisticated taste. It was not until the late eighteenth century that a more informed and balanced notion of China began

---

[62] Sir William Bart Temple, 'An Essay on Popular Discontents', in *Miscellanea* (London: Jonathan Swift; printed for Benjamin Tooke, 1701), 1–95.
[63] Ibid. 44.   [64] Ibid. 18–19.   [65] Ibid. 24–5.

to hold sway. In some respects, a harsh and even critical account of Chinese institutions later became the norm in an apparent reversal of earlier positive enthusiasm about China.[66]

In eighteenth-century America, there is little evidence of this kind of extreme Sinophilia, no doubt because of its weak links with the East. However, it is significant that when American scholarship begins to become actively informed about Chinese texts later in the next century, similar kinds of critique emerge. By the time the European notion of China had sobered in the latter decades of the eighteenth century, Americans were beginning to write their own satirical Oriental tales. Henry Sherburne's *The Oriental Philanthropist* (1800) tells a tale of the heir-apparent to the Chinese throne, Prince Nytan, who narrowly escapes imprisonment by an evil Chinese minister through the intervention of a fairy, and travels to Europe 'preaching the ideals of virtuous living and good government'.[67] A similar conceit is employed in George Fowler's *The Wandering Philanthropist; or, Lettres from a Chinese Written during his Residence in the United States*, published in 1810.[68] Interestingly, Emerson himself is the author of one of these, a short warning on the seductiveness of empty phrases, false virtue, and an ethically bankrupt age.

The Reformer. (after the Chinese)
There is a class whom I call the thieves of virtue. They are those who mock the simple & sincere endeavourers after a better way of life, & say, these are pompous talkers; but when they come to act, they are weak, nor do they regard what they have said. These mockers are continually appealing to the ancients. And they say, Why make ourselves singular? Let those who are born in this age, act as men of this age.— Thus they secretly obtain the flattery of the age.

The inhabitants of the village & of the city all praise them. Wherever they go they are attentive & generous. If you would blame them, there is nothing to lay hold of. They accord with prevailing customs & unite with a polluted age. They appear faithful & sincere, & act as if sober & pure. The multitude all delight in them but they confuse virtue.[69]

[66] Lach and Foss, 'Images of Asia', 27–8.
[67] Jackson, *Oriental Religions*, 5 citing Mukhtar A. Isani, 'The Oriental Tale in America through 1865: A Study in American Fiction' (Ph.D. diss., Princeton University, 1962).
[68] Jackson, *Oriental Religions*, 6.
[69] *JRWE* ix. 32 (1843).

This passage is unique in Emerson's writings. Why he chose to adopt a mock-Chinese tone and phraseology is uncertain. It is clear that he had read and absorbed in detail the entire canon of Chinese classics. Emerson's observations could well be based upon the Confucian *Analects*, though naïve credulity in the face of verbal dexterity is a weakness common to all ages and peoples. 'A virtuous man is certainly capable of making valuable speech', Confucius said, 'but a man of valuable speech is not necessarily a man of virtue.'[70] Emerson's 'ruse', while plain, could well have appealed to a growing public familiarity with Chinese proverbial idioms and, as such, have been accorded serious reflection. The proverbial form also allows for a lack of specificity as to who is being accused and where the 'multitude' resides. Similarly, it supplies some sense of the enduring presence of mockery and posturing in public life as well as its predictable effects upon popular opinion and public sensibilities. These enabling features of Emerson's short venture into orientalist fictionalization are not dissimilar to those of Johnson in the preceding century, though Emerson's slightly more creative use of Chinese idiom is note-worthy. The examples presented thus far expose both the range of orientalist texts from the sixteenth to the nineteenth centuries which could be seen as subversive, and the varying degrees of indirection which they adopt.

In the early Modernist period, a more subtle deployment of 'the exotic' East, in poetry in particular, challenged traditional assumptions of what constituted an appropriate stock of poetic images. This practice expanded both the scope and obscurity of poetic references. Moore consciously chooses images not only from the foreign and exotic Far East, but from twelfth-century Chinese landscape painting, descriptions of Chinese porcelains and jades couched in the art-historical language of the connoisseur as well as poetic models from China's ancient past. These cultural sources are scattered among a vast array of unfamiliar images of exotic and sometimes mythical animals, often of Chinese origin, in a quite radical display of detailed scholarship. What is particularly disarming is that these images, unfamiliar and culturally dispersed

[70] Confucius, *Lunyu zhengyi* (The Analects with Exegesis), in *Zhuzi jicheng* (Collection of Classics), vol. i, (ed.) Liu Baonan, Vii. I. 134, as cited in Zhang Longxi, *The Tao and the Logos: Literary Hermeneutics, East and West* (Durham, NC and London: Duke University Press, 1992), 14.

as they are, are embedded in poems whose language is for the most part demotic. This admixture of the familiar with the remote and even inconceivable creates an internal tension which could be read as a protest against modernity, or a struggle to come to terms with contemporaneity. Likewise, Moore's technical embrace of a prehistoric Chinese poetic form, and one which she does not acknowledge in discussions of her poetic procedures and models, is a deliberate option for the foreign and the historically remote. At the same time that Moore's poems with Chinese imagery represent a deliberate departure from the familiar, the substitution of a Far Eastern literary model for a classical one is a characteristically Modernist break with tradition and resembles, in this respect, the resistance to neo-classicism apparent in eighteenth-century English orientalist writing. For Moore, the establishment of China as a model of morality, precise language, and quiet wisdom is reliant upon a literary tradition which idealized Chinese institutions. Her adoption of the Chinese *fu* style of versification, which will be discussed in a later chapter, likewise presented a seemingly ideal poetic vehicle with which to exhibit her many didactic responses in a form of free verse.

There is also an argument that, in the case of Ezra Pound for example, this tradition of subversive orientalism provided a foundation for the Imagist use of Far Eastern poetic models as a means of purifying language. In Pound's Chinese *Cantos*, a historical meditation on conduct, motives, and morals, the idealization of Confucian mores provides a bulwark and standard against which other cultures and creeds can be measured. This is particularly important in the case of orientalist literary texts in the early twentieth century, when referentiality and the dialectic between the current and classical literary canon establish themselves as critical features of Modernist texts. In *Guide to Kulchur*, Pound makes explicit his devotion to Confucian doctrine over classical philosophy: 'Take the whole ambience of the Analects (of Kung fu Tseu), you have the main character filled with a sense of responsibility . . . Greek philosophic thought is utterly irresponsible. It is at no point impregnated with a feeling for the whole people.'[71] Pound's interest in Confucius appeared quite early in his writing career. *My Thirty Years' War*, Margaret

[71] Ezra Pound, *Guide to Kulchur* (London: Faber & Faber, 1938), 29.

Anderson's autobiography, quotes a letter from Pound from the early 1920s in which he offers Anderson's *The Little Review* an essay on Confucius.[72] Indeed, an argument has been made that Confucianism informed Pound's writing of the *Cantos* from its inception. Hugh Kenner claims that Pound's interest in Confucian philosophy also provided some substantiation for the tenets of the Imagist Manifesto, the emotional examination of *Personae*, and the promotion of precision and brevity in *Lustra*.

There would be no difficulty in showing that the ethos of the *Cantos* is Confucian from the very first, or that, as our juxtaposition of Confucius and the Imagist Manifesto has implied, Pound's conception of aesthetic honesty showed from the first an intrinsic alignment with concepts of personal and governmental honesty, and with inspection of the moral and emotional quality of cultures and civilizations . . . The emotional exploration that underlay *Personae* corresponds to a Confucian injunction. So does the concern for precise observation and verbal exactness that becomes strikingly manifest with the *Lustra* volume.[73]

Similarly, Pound's interest in the ideogrammic method,[74] which drew upon the pictographic composition of Chinese characters, was inaugurated by his search for an alternative verse form free from the traditional conventions of structure and meter. Even Fenollosa's short work, *The Chinese Written Character as a Medium for Poetry*, edited by Pound and originally published in successive issues of *The Little Review* in 1919, highlights the superiority of the Chinese character because it is 'alive', because it carries with it 'a verbal idea of action' and corresponds, in a way that the arbitrary symbolization of an alphabet cannot, to 'the fundamental reality of *time*'.[75] In all of these overtly quite disparate Poundian texts, Chinese philosophy, literature, and language are central to the project of critique and subversion. The presiding impetus and effect of Pound's efforts are ones of revolt, revolution, and reform.

[72] Hugh Kenner, *The Poetry of Ezra Pound* (Lincoln, Nebr., and London: University of Nebraska Press, 1985), 286.

[73] Ibid. 288.

[74] For a fuller discussion of the ideogrammic method, see Laszlo K. Géfin, *Ideogram: History of a Poetic Method* (Austin, Tex.: University of Texas Press, 1982).

[75] Ernest Fenollosa, 'The Chinese Written Character as a Medium for Poetry', (ed.) Ezra Pound *Little Review*, 6/5–8 (Sept.–Dec. 1919); also published San Francisco: City Lights, 1936: see p. 9.

Like Pound, Moore employed features of the Chinese language in her poetry which will be discussed more fully in later chapters. All of the Chinese elements in her poetry, be they verse forms which enable her to incorporate aphoristic preachments into her poems, supernatural beings which establish spatial and temporal freedoms, or a cosmic Chinese painting perspective which alternately reinforces the security of many of her bourgeois notions of sight and insight at the same time as they free her observations from the confines of linear perspective, are means of resistance. At different times, Moore uses Chinese poetry, art, and philosophy to resist the dictates of contemporary verse forms, the influence of European literature and art, the restrictions of a masculine logic, and the imposition of the demands of contemporary politics and mass culture. The subversion she practises is by turns liberating and defensive: it allows her to explore through Far Eastern principles the alternatives to Western traditions of vision and expression at the same time that it permits her to become entrenched in the familiarity of middle-class conservatism. Literary upheaval and renewal, while signalling dissatisfaction and a need for reassessment of poetic technique, often lead to some degree of confirmation of existing poetic practices. Marianne Moore's contribution to a subversive Modernism has not yet been adequately assessed. But what is certain about Moore's orientalist poetic ventures is that without Chinese borrowings she could not have created what Robert Lowell has described as her 'terrible, private, and strange revolutionary poetry'.[76]

---

[76] Elizabeth Bishop quotes Robert Lowell's remark in an unpublished letter to Lowell, dated 25 June 1961. This letter is held in the Lowell Collection (bMS Am 1905 (183)) and is published by permission of the Houghton Library, Harvard University.

2

Useful Travel: Moore's Imaginative Forays Abroad

'Moore's relation to the soil is not a simple one.'
(T. S. Eliot, *The Dial*, December 1923)

Hands that can grasp, eyes
that can dilate, hair that can rise
if it must, these things are important not because a
high-sounding interpretation can be put upon them but
because
they are
useful.
('Poetry' (1919), long version)

DOMESTICATED TEXTS

In 1907, when Marianne Moore's poems were beginning to appear in *Tipyn O'Bob*,[1] the undergraduate magazine at Bryn Mawr, a canon of scholarly works in English on the literature and arts of the Far East was already being established. As her writing career developed, this field burgeoned as private collections[2] of Chinese and Japanese art became available to a public already given to Chinese curio-collecting. By 1930, published work on Chinese art and history as well as commendable, if not definitive, translations of Chinese poetry were widely available in English. In 1922 Arthur Waley published *Zen Buddhism and its Relation to Art* and, in 1923, both an introduction to the study of Chinese painting and a translation of Chinese poems, *The Temple and*

---

[1] Eight poems and eight short stories by Moore appeared in *Tipyn O'Bob*. The title comes from a Welsh expression which means 'a little bit of everyone'.

[2] For example, the Weld–Fenollosa Collection in the Boston Museum (Dr G. C. Weld) was formed from art purchased in Japan before 1884 when the Law of Koko Ho (National Treasures) was established in Japan.

Other Poems. H. A. Giles's *History of Chinese Literature* (1901) was still a standard work, as was Pauthier's 1841 *Les Quatres Livres de philosophie morale et politique de la Chine.* Numerous dictionaries and guides had been published in English and in French (in which Moore was reasonably fluent despite her humble denials). Osvald Siren's several multi-volume histories of Chinese art began appearing in 1925.[3]

In addition to these more substantial sources, a welter of translations of Chinese and Japanese poems steadily appeared in the pages of *The Egoist, The Dial,* and *Poetry* among other literary magazines.[4] In August 1917 T. S. Eliot's 'The Noh and the Image' appeared in *The Egoist.* Eliot, of course, had a long-standing fascination with the Middle and, later, the Far East from his Harvard days onward, and his acquaintance with Eastern philosophies, particularly Buddhist and Hindu traditions, was, as Cleo McNelly Kearns attests, 'profound and extensive'.[5] In 1911 Laurence Binyon published a volume entitled *The Flight of the Dragon,* an art-historical survey of the principles of Far Eastern art giving considerable attention to the Chinese dragon and, in 1925, a collection of his translations of poetry was published as *Little Poems from the Japanese.* Ezra Pound's review of *Flight of the Dragon* in *Blast* ensured that its audience, which would have included Moore, was aware of its publication and of Binyon's many observations about Chinese painting and philosophy, which Pound quoted copiously.[6] Pound refers to *Flight of the Dragon* again in *Gaudier-Brzeska: A Memoir* (1916) as potentially capable of providing the reader with 'some degree of enlightenment'.[7] Indeed, Moore's library contains a copy of *Flight of the Dragon* with no less than nine pages of notes about the text which indicate a close reading.

'Chinese-style' poems were published in Ezra Pound's *Des Imagistes* in March 1914. His *Cathay* appeared in 1915 and *Lustra* (1915) included the contents of *Cathay* as well as four additional

[3] His first multi-volume work included Chinese sculpture from the fifth to the fourteenth centuries (4 vols., London, 1925).

[4] Marianne Moore had herself published poems, reviews and articles in both *The Egoist* and *Poetry* from 1915.

[5] Cleo McNelly Kearns, *T. S. Eliot and Indic Traditions: A Study in Poetry and Belief* (Cambridge: Cambridge University Press, 1987), 29.

[6] Ezra Pound, *Pavannes and Divagations* (London: Peter Owen, 1958), 148–50.

[7] *Gaudier-Brzeska: A Memoir* (New York: New Directions, 1979), 122.

translations of Chinese poems. Pound published several uncollected translations of Chinese poems in magazines such as Margaret Anderson's *Little Review*, of which he was the London editor. In November 1918 his translation of 'Dawn On The Mountains' (Wang Wei) and 'Wine' (Li Po) appeared with other poems. Fenollosa's 'The Chinese Written Character as a Medium for Poetry', with Pound's editing, was also finally published in *Little Review* in four instalments, commencing in September 1919, two of which are contained in Moore's library holdings.

Allen Upward edited *The Sayings of K'ung the Master* (1904), or 'The Sayings of Confucius', for *The Wisdom of the East Series* which was reprinted in *The Egoist* of 1 November 1913. These appeared shortly after the *Poetry* issue of September 1913 in which a sequence of Upward's verses appeared, 'Scented Leaves—from a Chinese Jar', which was neither a translation nor a paraphrase of Chinese poetry but was, as Pound put it, made 'up out of his head, using a certain amount of Chinese reminiscence'.[8] Pound had begun reading the works of Allen Upward in about 1913 and no doubt communicated Upward's enormous influence upon him to Moore.[9] Upward's poems were modern equivalents of, and often humourous homages to, the Confucian epigram, and reveal an intimate acquaintance with the variety of expressions, imagery, myth, and ceremony in Chinese poetry. They capture more than just the aura of the Chinese epigrammatic poem by reflecting that peculiar sadness and mystic sorrow which permeates even somewhat celebratory Chinese verse.

It is within this creative and vibrant milieu of both rigorous scholarly enquiry and selective dalliance with Chinese and, to a lesser extent, Japanese poetry and culture that Marianne Moore began to explore Far Eastern subjects, and in particular Chinese art history. Clearly, numerous resources were available to her, including her acquaintance and correspondence with Ezra Pound with his fund of enthusiasm for Far Eastern culture. Moore's library, now located in the Rosenbach Archive in Philadelphia, contains Chinese art books and pamphlets on Chinese painting, porcelain, and carving, as well as regular clippings and notes of

[8] Letter from Ezra Pound to Harriet Monroe, London, 23 Sept. 1913, in *The Selected Letters 1907–1941 of Ezra Pound*, (ed.) D. D. Paige (New York: Harcourt, Brace, 1950), 22–3.
[9] Bryant Knox, 'Allen Upward and Ezra Pound', *Paideuma*, 3/1 (1974), 71.

the *Illustrated London News* contributor, Arthur Hayden, who specialized in Chinese art subjects.

The 1930s brought a similar outpouring of publications about Chinese language, painting, calligraphy, and literature. In 1931 Richard Wilhelm translated *The Secret of the Golden Flower: A Chinese Book of Life*, an alchemical tract and Taoist text of Chinese yoga, which included a commentary by Carl Jung. Later editions included Wilhelm's translation of the *Hui Ming Ching* (The Book of Consciousness and Life), a Buddhist and Taoist meditational text, written by Liu Hua-yang in 1794. In Chicago in 1935, Lucy Driscoll and Kenji Toda published *Chinese Calligraphy*. That same year a translation of Kuo Hsi's *An Essay on Landscape Painting* and a book on Chinese painting and calligraphy, *The Spirit of the Brush*, both by Shio Sakanishi, appeared in London. Chiang Yee's works, *The Chinese Eye* (London, 1935) and *Chinese Calligraphy* (London, 1938), which today remain seminal texts, in addition to Arthur Waley's *One Hundred and Seventy Chinese Poems* (New York, 1938), form an important contribution to scholarship in English on Chinese subjects. Moore's own library holds Waley's 1938 translation of *The Analects of Confucius* with her notations. Similarly, she had a heavily annotated copy of Witter Bynner's version of *The Way of Life According to Lao Tzu* (1944).

By the time Marianne Moore was writing poems influenced by Chinese '*fu*-style' poetry her own work displayed imagery steeped in the lore and symbology of Chinese art and culture. It will become evident in the following chapters that Moore's footnoted sources do not reveal all of the textual origins of her 'oriental' imagery and vocabulary. Certainly both the use and the increasing sophistication of references in her poems reveal that Moore continued throughout her career to pursue her interests in Chinese art and culture to the point where she could make ample use of scholarly works and original Chinese texts in translation.

Moore used only a single Chinese word in her published poems, in 'Nine Nectarines', referring to the *yu* peach to which the Chinese attribute longevity and life-saving qualities. If she did not understand the fundamentals of pronunciation of the Chinese language, then it is likely that this syllable functioned for her as a proper noun or, as used here, as an adjective. However, if Moore was aware of even the most essential aspects of the Chinese tonal system, the use of this word would have been more elaborate. Transliterations of this kind function as words with an implied musical notation since both Chinese music and Chinese monosyllabic words are distinguished by being distributed on a five-tone scale. This italicized syllable interrupts the quick, staccato pace of the poem while changing the optical surface of the page.[10]

Moore acknowledges the use of a plethora of sources on Chinese art and quotes from these texts in her poems. Surprisingly, she never quotes from Chinese literature in her poems, with the exception of the *I Ching* (Book of Changes, *c*.800 BC) in 'Tom Fool At Jamaica' (1953), but could not have remained unaware of the myriad available translations and scholarly texts. Her later readings, in fact, reflect a movement towards the use of original sources in translation and scholarly materials rather than general reading matter. For example, the *I Ching* translation by Wilhelm and Baynes which she used was a Bollingen Series publication of 1950. In reviewing the sources for Chinese images and references listed in her footnotes, it is both tempting and feasible to consider these and similar available texts as providing inspiration for a range of ideas in her work which go beyond mere allusion to exotic animals and fruits from the East. Many of the sources and references which inform her work are never acknowledged within her poems or their appended notes. As she herself admits in the epigraph to *The Complete Poems of Marianne Moore*, 'Omissions are not accidents'.

Moore, like Emerson before her, sought to synthesize disparate sources in her work, to practise an eclecticism which reached to the foreign for material with which to craft her poetry, and thereby made contemporary in America some of the world's oldest traditions. This naturalization of imported history, ideas, and objects is an essential feature of Moore's poetry. It relies upon a conviction, which she shared with Ezra Pound and William Carlos Williams, that this kind of textual reaching was made possible by a rootedness in the American soil, a surety and conviction that America could sponsor, and locate the familiar in, the foreign. In an essay published in *The Dial* of March 1927,

---

[10] CP 29.

entitled 'A Poet of the Quattrocento', Moore writes of Williams's endorsement of imaginative journeys which are made from 'home', whose impulse to seek out foreign sources is generated by necessity and utility.

In his modestly emphatic respect for America he corroborates Henry James' conviction that young people should 'stick fast and sink up to their necks in everything their own countries and climates can give,' and his feeling for the place lends poetic authority to an illusion of ours, that sustenance may be found here, which is adapted to artists. Imagination can profit by a journey, acquainting itself with everything pertaining to its wish that it can gather from European sources . . . The staying at home principle could not, he is sure, be a false one where there is vigorous living force with buoyancy of imagination . . . He has visited places and studied various writings and a traveler can as Bacon says, 'prick in some flowers of that he hath learned abroad.' In the man, however, Doctor Williams' topics are American . . .[11]

Moore's reference to Bacon's remark reiterates her insistence that what is derived from foreign sources may be fostered in American soil, flowers replanted at home. Williams's topics, according to Moore, remain American despite their source. This is an idea which occupies Moore's poetry as well, as she corroborates the essential Americanness of what is garnered abroad. The 'staying at home principle' to which Williams adheres is yet a reformulation of Moore's own poetic practice of textual 'travel' as a surrogate for real journeys, a means of assimilating a stock of 'knowledge' to elucidate and illustrate her own claims for America. Moore did not travel extensively and her creative procedure can be regarded as a kind of armchair journey. Her search for novelty outside America and her subsequent location of it at home make her originality dependent upon this process of retrieval and assembly. Continually finding that one needn't leave home ('my own back yard') to discover what 'home' is, is somehow reliant upon that 'looking abroad' and reaffirms the very necessity of 'the foreign' to the process of discovering and valuing America. Her poems re-enact that process by demanding that the mind should travel great distances between the geographical sources of her numerous, contiguous images.

[11] Marianne Moore, 'A Poet of the Quattrocento', *The Dial*, 82 (Mar. 1927), 213–15, and *CPR* 144.

Moore takes up a very American pastime with her journeys of the mind. In a journal entry of 1835, Emerson too writes of his imaginative travel as he sits in his chimney corner:

Advantage of the Spiritual man in the fact of the identity of human nature. Draw your robe ever so chastely round you, the surgeon sees every muscle, every hair, every bone, every gland. He reads you by your counterpart. So I read the history of all men in myself. Give me one single man & uncover for me his pleasures & pains, let me minutely & in the timbers & ground plan study his architecture & you may travel all round the world & visit the Chinese, the Malay, the Esquimaux, & the Arab. I travel faster than you. In my chimney corner I see more, & anticipate all your wonders.[12]

Emerson is deeply critical of the American need to make amends through travel for a perceived lack of national culture. In 'Self-Reliance' (1839–40) he wrote that 'it is for want of self-culture that the superstition of Traveling . . . retains its fascination for all educated Americans'.[13] In the same essay, he reiterated his belief that America must find originality and creative sustenance at home and encouraged his countrymen towards self-improvement. 'As our Religion, our Education, our Art look abroad, so does our spirit of society', he wrote, 'all men plume themselves on the improvement of society, and no man improves.'[14] Emerson's cautions are rooted in a mistrust of the 'foreign' as excluding the present and the useful. He urges the American artist to create what is suited to American needs, to establish 'a house' which fits with the American landscape and climate, to refrain from imitation.

Our minds travel when our bodies are forced to stay at home. We imitate; and what is imitation but the traveling of the mind? Our houses are built with foreign taste; our shelves are garnished with foreign ornaments; our opinions, our tastes, our faculties, lean, and follow the Past and the Distant . . . Beauty, convenience, grandeur of thought and quaint expression are as near to us as to any, and if the American artist will study with hope and love the precise thing to be done by him, considering the climate, the soil, the length of the day, the wants of the people, the habit and form of the government, he will create a house

¹² *JRWE* v. 107 (1835).
¹³ Ralph Waldo Emerson, 'Self-Reliance', in *Selections from Ralph Waldo Emerson*, (ed.) Stephen E. Whicher (Boston, Mass.: Houghton Mifflin, 1957), 163.
¹⁴ Ibid. 165.

in which all these will find themselves fitted, and taste and sentiment will be satisfied also.[15]

For Emerson, travel can conceal a desire to avoid the burden of originality, can result in imitation, a belated fondness for the remote. Such diversions 'follow the Past' and fail to acknowledge, appreciate, and celebrate the genuine beauty and uniqueness of the close-at-hand. Like Emerson, Moore bemoans the American 'tendency to remove as one man to Europe',[16] and one is reminded again of those memorable concluding lines of 'England' (1920): 'the flower and fruit of all that noted superiority— | if not stumbled upon in America, | must one imagine that it is not there? | It has never been confined to one locality'. She is equally concerned about the ability of foreign models to bear American meanings. The importation of artistic commodities necessarily demands that new interpretations of them should reflect their original source and not imitate European 'versions'. This is particularly true of European interpretations of Chinese sources, and Moore's poetic musings on that very early Far Eastern import, china, is a good example of her effort both to caution America to maintain its authenticity and to praise its fidelity to the Chinese original.

In *The Geographical History of America*, a book which Moore chose as part of her 'ideal library'[17] and reviewed for *The Nation* in 1936,[18] Gertrude Stein calls attention to the inevitable process of reinscription of dislocated foreign sources when she writes about China and china:

> In china china is not china it is an earthen ware. In China there is no need of China because in China china is china.
> All who liked china like china and have china.
> China in America is not an earthen ware.
> All who like china in America like china in America and all who like china in America do not like to have china in china be an earthen ware. Therefore it is not.[19]

[15] Ibid. 164.

[16] Marianne Moore, editorial comment in *The Dial*, 81 (Nov. 1926), 447, and *CPR* 175.

[17] 'Booklists', in Raymond Queneau (ed.), *Pour une bibliothèque idéale* (Paris: Gallimard, 1956), 228–32, and *CPR* 669.

[18] Marianne Moore, 'Perspicuous Opacity', *The Nation*, 143 (24 Oct. 1936), 484–5, and *CPR* 339–41.

[19] Gertrude Stein, *The Geographical History of America or The Relation of Human Nature to the Human Mind* (New York: Vintage, 1973), 72.

Moore herself refers to this resistance of objects to translation across nations when she writes about china in an early
manuscript version of 'Nine Nectarines' (1934)[20] entitled 'Nine
Nectarines and Other Porcelain'.[21] China is described as 'the
land | of the best china-making first' and Moore later questions
whether the hunting and domestic scenes, the bird and floral
designs, on English and French china could match the Chinese
original.

> A Chinese 'understands
> the spirit of the wilderness'
> and the nectarine-loving kylin
> of pony appearance—the long
> tailed or the tailless
> small cinnamon-brown, common
> camel-haired unicorn
> with antelope feet and no horn,
> here enamelled on porcelain.
> It was a Chinese [ ] who
> imagined this masterpiece.[22]

The poem exposes the different interpretations of 'china' ware, what
kinds of emblems adorn each country's version, and the degree
to which the 'original' has been reinvented and domesticated.
Moore finds in the Chinese 'masterpiece' a 'race that "understands
| the spirit of the wilderness"' which is America's most pro-
minent topographical feature and, indeed, embodies America's
national heritage. Moreover, the unarguably American 'spirit
of the wilderness' further links it with Chinese sensibilities in
this poem, the successive revisions of what 'china' is marking
France and then England as moving further away from the 'best
china-making'.

In much the same way, Moore is evidently careful to use her
Chinese textual sources, not as attempts to adorn the originals
with American 'designs' as she claims Europeans did with China,
but to refashion and adapt Chinese ideas to reflect their consonances in American thought and to highlight what China and

---

[20] 'Nine Nectarines' was first published in *Poetry*, 45 (Nov. 1934), 64–7.
[21] 'Nine Nectarines and Other Porcelain' appears in Moore's manuscripts with
eight stanzas (RL I:03:15), the first four stanzas of which later appeared in 'Nine
Nectarines'.
[22] This appears as the final stanza in 'Nine Nectarines', *CP* 30.

America share. The textual 'travel' to China which Moore continually embarked upon from the very earliest stages of her writing career is testimony to her success at locating in Chinese sources a rich fund of material with which to corroborate American principles and ideas. These texts also provide a means to nurture and reinforce what Moore felt to be America's potential to manifest the 'sublimated wisdom of China',[23] and her persistent efforts to reconcile American and Chinese traits attest to the importance of this project for her poetry.

DOCTRINES OF UTILITY

In 'Answers to an Enquiry',[24] Marianne Moore gave the following response to a question about the purpose of her work:

Q. Do you intend your poetry to be useful to yourself or others?
A. Myself.[25]

In as much as the query is general, Moore's response is beautifully direct and ironically evasive at the same time. Her answer reinforces the sense of her committment to the well-known American doctrine of utility, which endorses the importance of selecting among potential experiences only those which will improve, instruct, and better one personally. The notion of being 'self-made' is fundamental to the assumption of America as a classless society, a 'land of opportunity' and endless possibility where individual efforts can translate into tangible results. It also contributes to the idea that an individual's self-improvement necessarily fosters the more general increase of America's well-being as a nation, that each citizen becomes a distillation or microcosm of America itself. In this light, Moore's poems can be seen as exercises in the pursuit of these goals and as adhering to the Puritan emphasis upon purposefulness and the primacy of the didactic nature of action and experience.

Indeed, poetry as devotional writing was historically a primary form of Puritan literary discourse along with sermons, diaries, spiritual autobiographies, and psalm books. Sermons were

---

[23] From 'England' (1920).
[24] 'Answers to an Enquiry', *New Verse*, 1 (Oct. 1934), 16.　　[25] CPR 674.

mnemonically organized to assist the congregation in following a simple exegesis and later ruminating upon its main points. The doctrine was extracted from the sermon in a numbered series of reasoned statements to which a subsidiary series of numbered 'Uses' or practical applications were attached. The sermon there-fore functioned as a hierarchical verbal outline of the utility of Christian doctrine. Treatises on the structure and import of the Puritan sermon appeared in the early seventeenth century, of which Richard Bernard's *Faithfull Shepheard*[26] and William Perkins's *The Arte of Prophecying*[27] were the most prominent. Both texts exhort the preacher to emphasize the 'application' of the sermon's lesson. In *Faithfull Shepheard*, Bernard stresses the four 'uses' of the text—confutation, instruction, reprehension, and consola-tion.[28] It was as necessary to exhibit the utility of biblical texts as it was to relate the text itself. As John Morgan has observed, the Puritans generally employed the 'Reformed Style' of preach-ing, 'which emphasized the parallel importance of "doctrine" and "use", so necessary to instruction in the existential living of the faith at the core of the puritan thrust'.[29]

These four forms—verse, sermon, psalm book, and private writings—together comprised a system of tutelage focused upon the individual and designed to enable each worshipper to consult memory and text to translate Christian principles into models for everyday thought and behaviour. Within this system, poetry operated as a kind of 'workbook', or personal disquisition on the progress of this method of Christian reflection and the pro-cess of its continual revision. Clearly, Moore's poetry participates in this tradition of practical Puritan morality. She even quotes from Richard Baxter, the seventeenth-century American Puritan author of *The Saints' Everlasting Rest*, in three early poems, 'Pedantic Literalist' (1916), 'Marriage' (1923), and 'An Octopus' (1924). Many of her poems depend upon a kind of personal and didactic pedagogical method. She derives a 'lesson' from natural

---

[26] Richard Bernard, *Faithfull Shepheard . . . Wherein is . . . set forth the excellencie and necessitie of the Ministerie . . .* (London, 1607).

[27] William Perkins, *The Arte of Prophecying. Or a Treatise Concerning The Sacred And Onely True Manner And Methods Of Preaching* (Cambridge, 1609).

[28] Bernard, *Faithfull Shepheard* (expanded version, 1621), 274 ff.

[29] John Morgan, *Godly Learning: Puritan Attitudes towards Reason, Learning, and Education, 1560–1640* (Cambridge: Cambridge University Press, 1986), 121.

observation and the intimate, detailed analysis of objects, and remains committed to locating a pragmatic wisdom in specificity and fact. Moore often concludes her poems with apophthegms, pithy questions or compact summations of the import of the observations she has made within a poem. They often sound as if they were derived from Puritan epigrams, and indeed they share a certain stunted, cautionary phrasing. The final lines of an early poem, 'In This Age of Hard Trying, Nonchalance Is Good and' (1916)[30]—'The staff, the bag, the feigned inconsequence | of manner, best bespeak that weapon, self-protectiveness'—or the ending to 'Those Various Scalpels' (1917)[31]—'But why dissect destiny with instruments | more highly specialized than components of destiny itself?'—are curiously reminiscent of Puritan maxims such as 'Knowledge without wisdom may be soon discerned; it is usually curious and censorious',[32] or 'Pleasures come like oxen, slow and heavily, and go away like post-horses, upon the spur'.[33] Both strive to be short and memorable, to take on the condensation of Scripture.

Indeed, the abiding feature of Puritan plain-style writing is its similarity to biblical verse. As Alan Heimert and Andrew Delbanco point out in *The Puritans in America*, the Puritan's first literary principle was 'reverence for the language of scripture'.[34] Advocation of biblical 'style' represented a proximity to biblical teachings. Sacvan Bercovitch makes this clear in *The Puritan Origins of the American Self* when he notes that, for the Christian, the mere reading of Scripture was insufficient; the Bible was considered to be the comprehensive 'sole norm'. The Puritans formulated their theory of the plain style on this basis. 'To speak plainly was not primarily to speak simply, and not at all to speak artlessly', Bercovitch observes, 'it meant speaking the Word—making language itself, as self-expression, an *imitatio Christi* because it conformed to scripture . . . The plain

---

[30] First appeared in *Chimaera*, 1 (July 1916), 52, 55, and later in *CP* 34.
[31] First appeared in *Lantern* (Bryn Mawr), 25 (Spring 1917), 50–1, and later in *CP* 51.
[32] Quotation of Thomas Manton in *The Golden Treasury of Puritan Quotations*, compiled by I. D. E. Thomas (Edinburgh: Banner of Truth Trust, 1977), 163.
[33] Quotation of Joseph Hall, ibid. 313.
[34] Alan Heimert and Andrew Delbanco (eds.), *The Puritans in America* (Cambridge, Mass. and London: Harvard University Press, 1985), 11.

stylist condemned eloquence for its own sake.'[35] Compare this
description of the Puritan plain style to William Carlos Williams's
description of Moore's writing:

There is almost no overlaying at all. The effect is of every object
sufficiently uncovered to be easily recognizable. This simplicity, with
the light coming through from between the perfectly plain masses, is
however extremely bewildering to one who has been accustomed to look
upon the usual 'poem' . . . The 'useful result' is an accuracy to which
this simplicity of design greatly adds. The effect is for the effect to remain
'true'; nothing loses its identity because of the composition, but the
parts in their assembly remain quite as 'natural' as before they were
gathered. There is no 'sentiment'; the softening effect of word upon word
is nil; everything is in the style.[36]

Moore's style resembles that of the Puritan text more than it does
the Bible. Puritan literary 'methods' dispensed with the symbology
of Christian verse and emphasized explication and clarity over
exhortation and liturgy.

The kind of useful didacticism which characterizes Puritan
teaching is likewise a salient feature of Confucian doctrine. The
early American plain style could easily be viewed as an example
of Confucian pragmatical language. As Zhang Longxi has pointed
out, Confucius thought that language could express utility in terms
of moral behaviour:

While reluctantly granting words the value of usefulness, he nevertheless
remained suspicious of the value of language per se and of any extra-
vagant use of it . . . His attitude toward language at times came close
to a completely utilitarian one, as he insisted, 'So far as words can get
to the point, that is enough' . . . Confucius is certainly not endorsing
the use of language from a purely rhetorical or literary point of view,
since all his teachings invariably point in a single direction—namely,
the perfection of morality in society as well as in individual life. It is
therefore simply impossible to consider the nature and function of language as separated from moral and political issues in the framework
of Confucian ideology.[37]

[35] Sacvan Bercovitch, *The Puritan Origins of the American Self* (New Haven and
London: Yale University Press, 1975), 29–30.
[36] William Carlos Williams, 'Marianne Moore' (1925), in *Imaginations*, (ed.)
Webster Schott (New York: New Directions, 1970), 318.
[37] Zhang Longxi, *The Tao and the Logos: Literary Hermeneutics, East and West*
(Durham, NC and London: Duke University Press, 1992), 14–15, and quoting his
own translation of Confucius from *The Analects*.

Moore's familiarity with the works of Confucius is particularly evident in her prose writing. The utility of Confucian
prose is highlighted by Moore in her essay, 'Impact, Moral and
Technical; Independence Versus Exhibitionism; and Concerning
Contagion': 'A master axiom for all writing, I feel, is that of
Confucius: "When you have done justice to the meaning, stop."
That implies restraint, that discipline is essential.'[38] Similarly, a
revised manuscript version of her poem 'Silence' (1924) includes
an added final line in which she invokes Cotton Mather's pre-
cept to 'Be Short',[39] and this makes plain the essential congruity
of Confucian and Puritan literary advice. Moreover, these proscriptions were part of Moore's personal educational experience
as well, and were still memorable in 1956 when she wrote
'Values In Use'.[40] The poem refers to discussions of writing at
school: 'Be abstract | and you'll wish you'd been specific; it's a
fact. | . . . Certainly the means must not defeat the end.'

The value and usefulness of brevity and plain speech are
reconfirmed as she locates again in Puritan and Confucian teachings the same cautions for writing. Moore was certainly well versed
in Confucian philosophy: her library holdings include not only
a translation of *The Analects of Confucius*[41] with her annotations,
but her correspondence with Ezra Pound about Confucius is
plentiful and her copy of Pound's *Confucius: The Great Digest
and Unwobbling Pivot* (1951) is also personally annotated.
Confucian and Puritan doctrines of utility, then, not only share
common tenets, they also both found a modernist advocate
in Marianne Moore. 'Much wisdom', she wrote in 1965, 'is
epitomized by Confucius.'[42]

In an essay entitled 'Discipline', Emerson espouses a version
of both the Puritan and Confucian doctrines of utility:

In God, every end is converted into a new means. Thus the use of commodity, regarded by itself, is mean and squalid. But it is to the mind
an education in the doctrine of Use, namely, that a thing is good only so

---

[38] Marianne Moore, in the *Harvard Summer School Conference on the Defense
of Poetry* (Cambridge, Mass.: Harvard University, 1951), 71–6, and *CPR* 435.
[39] RL I:04:17.
[40] First published in *Partisan Review*, 23 (Fall 1956), 506. See *CP* 181.
[41] Arthur Waley (trans.), *The Analects of Confucius* (New York: Random;
London: Allen & Unwin, 1938).
[42] Moore, *Women's Wear Daily* (17 Feb. 1965), 5, and *CPR* 600.

far as it serves; that a conspiring of parts and efforts to the production of an end is essential to any being. The first and gross manifestation of this truth is our inevitable and hated training in values and wants, in corn and meat.[43]

Christian and American pragmatics, concerned primarily with progress and renewal, are plaited together in Emerson's thought. While Moore does not attribute her concern with utility to Christian sources, her arguably Emersonian and Confucian philosophy of the use of language finds parallels in early American Puritan theories of writing.

Moore struggled with the meaning of what it is to be an American artist throughout her writing career. This concern suffused not only her poetic production but also her prolific output as an essayist and reviewer. Moore's continuous analysis of the 'Americanness' of America and American art makes available a unique example of not only the tradition of questioning where the artist lies within the new and somewhat inchoate 'tradition' of American art, but also the ongoing adaptation that is necessary to establish the artist as distinctly American when that 'America' is undergoing cataclysmic and unparalleled change and transformation. So we have, in Moore, a particularly rich site in which to observe and draw conclusions about the strategies she employed and the anxieties which generated this abiding interest in establishing a dialogue with a tradition in process.

To be an artist in America for Moore is, in some ways, to be proficient in everything, to be a jack of all trades, to call upon references from a multitude of sources, to *use*. Moore shares this quality with the Native American or 'nature-born' artist. And Moore's method of using natural sources in particular betrays a certain respect for nature, very different from the more widely accepted Modernist idea that nature is unfeeling and therefore a neutralization of it is without consequences. However, the utilitarianism which characterizes Moore's use of natural images and data is subsumed within an interest in the practicality or expediency of nature's processes. Her procedure is dedicated to the conversion of visually acquired information into practical knowledge. Therefore her poems can be seen as compilations of

---

[43] Ralph Waldo Emerson, 'Discipline', from *Nature* (1833–6), in *Selections from Ralph Waldo Emerson*, (ed.) Whicher, 39.

practical information with a kind of homespun wisdom that is reminiscent of the familiar American almanac. They impart information in a way that implies that their practical concerns also fulfil recognized needs, provide a contribution to everyday life. To some extent, her preference for the practical exposes her sense of what is needed from American poetry, and this again appears to be rooted in the perception of America as a nation in its formative stages. As John Quincey Adams wrote in a letter of 1780, 'the Usefull, the mechanic Arts, are those which we have occasion for in a young Country'.[44] Moore's poems are not narrowly metaphysical and in that respect her concerns are decidedly American, define a distinctive American expression, and are attuned to what would be useful for a 'young Country'. For her, natural facts and perceptions are both practical and personal, and her poems are replete with them. Like early New England writing, Moore does more than carefully observe natural phenomena. She applies features of the plain style in privileging accuracy in her representations and observations of nature and of life and adheres to a classic eighteenth-century prescription for utilitarian prose—to be edifying, effective, and maintain the standards of good sense. The natural phenomena she refers to are autonomous, detailed, and retain their localized identity.

What intrigues Moore is not so much nature as science. It is, for instance, the locomotive features of the plumet basilisk which she values in her 1933 poem of that name. These portions of the poem epitomize Moore's attention to the beauty of the physical design of the creature:

> In Costa Rica the true Chinese lizard face
> is found, of the amphibious falling dragon, the living fire-work.
> He leaps and meets his
>   likeness in the stream and, king with king,
> helped by his three-part plume along the back, runs on two legs,
>   tail dragging; faints upon the air; then with a spring
> dives to the stream-bed, hiding as the chieftain with gold body hid in
>   Guatavita Lake

. . . .

---

[44] John Adams, *Familiar Letters of John Adams and his wife Abigail Adams, During the Revolution*, (ed.) Charles Francis Adams (Cambridge, Mass.: Riverside Press, 1876), 318.

If
beset, he lets go, smites the water, and runs on it—a thing
    difficult for fingered feet. But when captured—stiff
and somewhat heavy, like fresh putty on the hand—he is no longer
the slight lizard that
    can stand in a receding flattened
S—small, long and vertically serpentine or, sagging,
span the bushes in a fox's bridge.[45]

'The Fish' (1918) and 'To A Snail' (1924) ('the curious phenomenon of your occipital horn'), and 'Elephants' (1943) are additional examples of this kind of reverence for the biological and
the anatomical. As Jeredith Merrin has noted, Moore 'conjoins
scientific inquiry with a kooky delight in the strange'.[46]

  Even Moore's personal valuation of her writing technique is
conceived of in the language of science. 'I never "plan" a stanza.
Words cluster like chromosomes, determining the procedure.'[47]
Her adherence to scientific processes in the creation of her
verse was an allegiance shared by several of her fellow poets.
Pound advised poets to 'consider the way of the scientists' and
not attempt to 'retell in mediocre verse what has already been
done in good prose'.[48] T. S. Eliot, too, advocated poetry that
approached 'the condition of science'.[49] For these poets, artistic
processes conform to natural, ordered, scientific procedures
and adhere to design. For Moore, it was as if science allowed
access to the value of nature. 'Science's method of attaining to
originality by way of veracity is pleasing', she wrote in 1931.[50]
And this sentiment is echoed in a verse of her poem, 'Four Quartz
Crystal Clocks':

                                The sea-
          side burden should not embarrass
          the bell-boy with the buoy-ball
          endeavoring to pass

[45] CP 20–4.
[46] Jeredith Merrin, *An Enabling Humility: Marianne Moore, Elizabeth Bishop,
and the Uses of Tradition* (New Brunswick, NJ and London: Rutgers University Press,
1990), 16.
[47] Moore, interview with Donald Hall, in *A Marianne Moore Reader* (New York:
Viking, 1961), 263.
[48] Ezra Pound, *Literary Essays*, (ed.) T. S. Eliot (London: Faber & Faber, 1954),
12, 6, 5.
[49] T. S. Eliot, *Selected Essays* (New York, 1950), 7.
[50] Moore, 'Experienced Simplicity', *Poetry*, 38 (Aug. 1931), 281.

> hotel patronesses; nor could a
> practiced ear confuse the glass
> eyes for taxidermists
>
> with eye-glasses from the optometrist.[51]

Even fraudulent nature cannot approximate science; clear glass cannot aspire to the complexity of lenses and the laws of optics.

The science of Moore's poetry consists not only in its overtly meticulous composition, but also in its emulation of scientific usefulness, of technology. 'The exact way in which anything was done, or made, or functioned', Elizabeth Bishop once remarked, 'was poetry to her.'[52] Moore seemed to be acutely aware of the splitting of art and culture, and recognized the need to repair that separation by submitting her art to practical concerns. For some artists, culture became the enemy of art, especially that part of culture which had become highly capitalized and industrialized. Ignoring the notion that there was no longer a place for any genuine, authentic or pathic kind of art, Moore instead embraced art as commodity, as practical and industrial. 'Always sensitive to the articulation of parts, to the bones and struts of living and non-living entities', Daniel L. Guillory has observed, 'Marianne Moore makes no fundamental distinction between the older technology of bodies and the newer, imitative structures that followed.'[53] She addresses some of her poems, such as 'To a Steam Roller' (1915), 'Four Quartz Crystal Clocks' (1940), and 'Granite and Steel' (1966), directly to the American technological climate. 'To A Steam Roller' celebrates the impersonal quality of technology and implies that nature and industry resist comparison. In 'Granite and Steel' Moore offers a hyperbolic paean to the triumphant building materials of the Brooklyn Bridge, describing them as 'Enfranchising cable', 'Caged Circe of steel and stone', ' "O path amid the stars I crossed by the seagull's wing!" I "O radiance that doth inherit me!" I —affirming inter-acting harmony!', and the bridge itself as 'a double rainbow'.[54]

[51] Moore, 'Four Quartz Crystal Clocks', *Kenyon Review*, 2 (Summer 1940), 284–5, and *CP* 115–16.

[52] Elizabeth Bishop, 'Efforts of Affection: A Memoir of Marianne Moore', in *The Collected Prose*, (ed.) Robert Giroux (London: Chatto & Windus, 1984), 149; written between 1969 and 1979, and first published in *Vanity Fair* in May 1983.

[53] Daniel L. Guillory, 'Marianne Moore and Technology', in Patricia C. Willis (ed.), *Marianne Moore: Woman and Poet* (Orono, Maine: University of Maine Press, the National Poetry Foundation, 1990), 83.

[54] *CP* 205.

For Moore, the aesthetic of technology is continually grounded in the practical facts of technological progress.[55] Much of the energy which generated these poems could also be described as patriotic. Lisa M. Steinman has examined Moore's recognition of the creative American imagination that made industry both its subject and inspiration:

Moore's usual praise of science, technology, and business involves redefinition, and it serves the larger purpose of defending America as a country that might value creativity and imagination. Consistently, her attention to verbal detail reclaims or redefines the technological and scientific virtues of effectiveness, accuracy, and precision. These redefined virtues underlie Moore's invocations of American technology and science . . . Scientific accuracy is then not the accuracy of machines but of observers; moreover, precision and effectiveness include giving value to the world thus viewed; they become forms of imaginative possession and also activities. Moore wrote that 'precision is a thing of the imagination' and 'precision . . . creates movement'.[56]

In defence of American industry, Moore redefined American traits and incorporated commercial ingenuity into America's long-standing reputation for practical concerns. Steinman continues to appraise Moore's efforts to identify accomplishments in science and industry with the strength of the American imagination and creativity on the one hand, and poetry with practicality and fact on the other:

If Moore's defense of poetry is in terms of science and fact, I have argued that this is in part because criticisms of American society had raised the problem of how to launch a defense of American poetry without ignoring the commercial and industrial values for which America was famous . . . [This was] the dilemma American culture presented to its poets in the early twentieth century, as witnessed by Moore's self-consciousness about how to reconcile American practicality with creativity, or accuracy with imagination.[57]

Moore's attitude more closely resembles Gertrude Stein's, in that both artists sought to celebrate the American respect for

---

[55] This is additionally supported by the presence of Alan Trachtenberg's *Brooklyn Bridge: Fact and Symbol* (New York: Oxford University Press, 1965) in Moore's library.

[56] Lisa M. Steinman, *Made in America: Science, Technology, and American Modernist Poets* (New Haven and London: Yale University Press, 1987), 117, and quoting from Moore's *Predilections* (New York: Viking, 1955), 4, 141.

[57] Steinman, *Made in America*, 128–9, 131.

both industry and the industrial. They are equally aware that products don't appear out of nowhere, and that beautiful objects also have to be made. A passage from Stein's 'The Difference Between the Inhabitants of France and the Inhabitants of the United States of America' calls attention to this: 'Another case is the case of that American the American of whom it is said can he say so. This American of whom it is said can he say so says practically that he practically says that he unites windows and windows when windows and windows are in their place and he wishes to stop that is to remain where he is.'[58] Stein calls attention to the American as self-consciously aware of his essential usefulness, that he is part of a larger effort of building America. This sense that the American surround is adequate to, and even an augur of, creativity, originality, and artistic fecundity is very different from earlier European notions that American soil could not nourish its inhabitants and, in fact, might siphon creative energy away and thereby impoverish the artist. Like Hawthorne, Moore believed that America could produce the greatest works of art in the world, without imitation and true to a sense of national individuality. She wrote in 'A Poet of the Quattrocento': 'it is not folly to hope that the very purest works of the imagination may also be found among us.'[59]

However, the situation of the American artist is not dependent upon locale, but rather relies upon a capacity for self-nurture for its inspiration. In other words, the American artist is uniquely capable of extracting from the environment whatever sustenance is necessary. As Moore said of James, 'Henry James belongs to "the race which has the credit of knowing best, at home and abroad, how to make itself comfortable." '[60] Moore's sense of the American artistic tradition is inextricable from her concern with usage. In an interview in 1938, she allies growing up in America with becoming American, implying that there is a useful aspect to this internal citizenship: 'As for American tradition . . . childhood associations dye the imagination and a thing that is one's own can double the use of it, as Henry James said of

---

[58] In Gertrude Stein, *Useful Knowledge* (New York: Payson & Clarke, 1928), 45.

[59] Marianne Moore, 'A Poet of the Quattrocento', *The Dial*, 82 (Mar. 1927), 213, and *CPR* 144.

[60] Marianne Moore, 'Henry James as a Characteristic American', *Hound and Horn*, 7 (Apr.–May 1934), 363–72, and *CPR* 320.

Hawthorne.'[61] The description is so like that of the 'Wolf's wool' which 'cannot be sheared' in her poem, 'The Student' (1932), that it seems clear that Moore's sense of imaginative value and practical use are germane to her idea of what it is to be an American artist. It is part of the indivisibility of the American from America, a permanent tie to the geography and landscape of a vast continent.

TAXONOMIES AND THE CAPACITY FOR FACT

Achieving dominion over the natural world has historically been defined by the ability to inventory and categorize its enormous diversity. In the Bible, Genesis delegates to man the power to name the creatures of the earth as a sign of man's control and hegemony. The book of Job, too, presents a veritable bestiary of creatures. Moore's poetry attends to the process of naming, and she is concerned with naming animals largely from distant lands, exotic beings often of Chinese origin. These animals (and plants) are foreign in a sense and yet, at the same time, domesticated by her seemingly vast and detailed acquaintance with their physical and locomotive attributes, what makes them uniquely suited to their environments. She situates that 'suitedness' as exemplary and somehow worthy of imitation. Moore's concern with this kind of nomenclature, of distinguishing types and kinds and what makes each unique, is indicative of an American posture. It exposes a deliberate anchoring *in* America, a looking 'abroad' as it were, to find *there* figures and attributes which are worthy and, more importantly, which are qualities we can locate here at home, in our very midst. So that Moore's is a colonial gesture of a kind, but a colonization of qualities which inhere, which are shared and which are discoverable, replicable, and proximate. In very much the same way that America is constituted in the act of naming, Moore's activity of nomenclature is a continual re-enactment of 'discovery'. What makes her project different is that she is concerned to discover similarities, to locate things 'at home', to make a concordance between home and 'abroad', and this is made particularly evident in the final stanza of her

---

[61] Marianne Moore, 'Enquiry', *Twentieth Century Verse*, 12/13 (Oct. 1938), 114.

early poem, 'England' where she observes that the 'wisdom of China', 'Egyptian discernment', and the compressed emotion of Hebrew verbs ('all that noted superiority') can be 'stumbled upon in America'. While still a kind of colonizing gesture, it is not an effort to 'bring home' what is not one's own but rather to locate equivalences and to *name* them. In effect, Moore's exercise is a liberatory one. It relieves America from an indebtedness to Europe and, at the same time, vitiates the claims that 'abroad' makes on American originality. This process is one which at once values what is 'foreign' while rendering it not so. Moore cuts the ties that bind America to its past and to the world without setting it adrift.

In many ways, the task that Moore sets herself is a distinctly American one. It addresses American anxieties about its own national 'authorship', its self-naming, and in doing so validates practicality. She summons America to itself and asks it to see what it has to hand. Moore directs America's gaze homeward in the end. Her work fulfils a need. In her poems, essays, and reviews, she consistently endorses the American valorization of useful-ness and subscribes to the notion that poetry should be didactic and fulfil the requirements of usage by responding to a demand for art. Implicit in this overt commentary is the adoption of a strategy of metadiscourse, simultaneous critique, or narration of method almost as an ongoing reminder and justification of her poetic project, of the *telos* embedded in her work. Moore's poems are a modern example of what Alexis de Tocqueville (1805–59) described in *Democracy in America* as the American taste for the useful, or the 'pragmatic'.[62] By subscribing to strict methods of composition such as metrical grids and espousing spareness as a poetic watchword, Moore is self-consciously aware of her poetry and prose as craft. The philosophy of pragmatism had become the concern of nineteenth-century American thinkers with whose works Moore was well acquainted. 'There can *be* no difference anywhere that doesn't *make* a difference elsewhere', wrote William James, 'no difference in abstract truth that doesn't express itself in a difference in concrete fact and in conduct consequent upon that fact, imposed on somebody, somehow, somewhere and somewhen.' 'Pragmatism is uncomfortable away

---

[62] Alexis de Tocqueville, *Democracy in America* (London: Patrick Campbell, 1994).

from facts', he continued, enlarging upon Charles Sanders Peirce, who first gave currency to the term in a series of published papers in the 1870s. 'The attitude of looking away from first things, principles, "categories", supposed necessities; and of looking towards last things, fruits, consequences, facts', was James's explanation of the orientation of pragmatism.[63] Moore refers to and quotes William James on several occasions in her prose writings,[64] concerned as she was with the application and consequences of her writing and its contribution to the 'production' of America.

Moore's method of finding Europe and Asia 'at home' is intimately linked to the echoic structure of her poetic texts. Just as she 'travels' to other lands for her stock of poetic images, Moore retraces that journey for her reader through her annotations. She participates in a poetic economy, catering to an American taste for the useful. Implicit in this cartographic process is the notion that the reader can reduplicate the procedure, take the journey, and find out the same 'things'. This is a scientific enquiry; the 'account' of the journey must be a verifiable and repeatable 'experiment'. There is a kind of levelling process at work here, something very different from the efforts of other Modernist writers to always remain at least at one remove. What Moore removes, she puts within reach in her annotations, or so her gesture might be read. Unlike Eliot and Pound (despite his own belief that his work was accessible), Moore seems to expose her poetic process. The poetic inventories of observation and fact she offers to her reader resemble traveller's inventories, as they share little by little the discovery of a place of origin. The privilege Moore grants to vision, a subject which will be taken up in depth in a later chapter, makes her acts of description simultaneously a visual appropriation of space, a process of reducing the distance between America and abroad. Her strong insistence on the visual over the tactile in her very descriptive poetry asserts travelling and seeing as means of traversing space. This visual appropriation and eclecticism was an established method for 'making' America. 'Already manifest in Franklin and Jefferson was this sense of America as a historic experiment', Yu Beongcheon

---

[63] William James, 'What Pragmatism Means' (1906), in *Pragmatism: A New Name for Some Old Ways of Thinking* (1907; Cambridge, Mass.: Harvard University Press, 1978), 30, 38, 32.

[64] William James's daughter, Peggy, was a friend of Moore's at Bryn Mawr.

has noted, 'a sense of determination to search far and wide, to appropriate anything and everything useful, even from the Orient, in order to make a success of their common undertaking, the creation of a new nation, a new civilization which would inherit the world.'[65] Unlike the European orientalism which had such different methods and aims, Beongcheon continues, 'this pioneering spirit characterized the American response to the Orient'.[66]

Moore's poetic practice adheres to these American imperatives for usefulness and self-definition. This may in large measure be the source of what some have described as Moore's, and indeed many American artists', detachment from their work, a sense that usage prevails over the personal response to inward, internal pressures which characterizes ideal art. A symptom of this detachment may be observed in Moore's preference for the emblematic over the metaphoric, and for the visual over the tactile. Tony Tanner makes this distinction for Emerson when he writes that 'perhaps the difference between an emblem and a metaphor is that an emblem is a sign existing at a definite remove from what it signifies and composed of different material; while a metaphor merges the sign and the thing signified'.[67] In this respect, Moore again exhibits an American trait, and Tanner's further observations on the American Romantics are, I think, equally applicable to Moore's writing.

A purely or predominantly visual relationship with nature in fact can indicate a state of alienation or detachment from it . . . To be linked to a thing only by sight is at the same time to be severed from it, if only because the act of purely visual appropriation implies a definite space between the eye and the object. And American writers have been predominantly watchers.[68]

Geoffrey Crayon's passive and observant 'spectatorship' in Washington Irving's *The Sketch Book of Geoffrey Crayon, Gent.* (1819–20) is certainly a good example of this, as is Chillingworth's in Hawthorne's *The Scarlet Letter* (1850). Tanner goes on to

---

[65] Yu Beongcheon, *The Great Circle: American Writers and The Orient* (Detroit: Wayne State University Press, 1983), 22.

[66] Ibid.

[67] Tony Tanner, *Scenes of Nature, Signs of Men* (Cambridge: Cambridge University Press, 1987), 32.

[68] Ibid. 30.

trace this characteristic common among American writers from Thoreau and Emerson to James and Hemingway.

This disengaged quality in Moore's work has been read psychoanalytically as well, particularly by Stanley Lourdeaux. Lourdeaux interprets the subject-matter of her poetry as symptomatic of this quality of detachment and sees it as 'a dominant fantasy of modernist poetry—the desire to resolve one's relation to an absent yet significant Other'.[69] He continues:

Moore's poetry remained limited mostly to naturalistic scenes and animals because her speaker's ego remained *subsidiary* to external appearances. To avoid symbolization is, finally, to isolate oneself from characterization and audience. Moore's speaker strikes her readers as the absent as well as significant Other . . . As a way to free the significant Other or animal subject in her poems from manipulative symbolic projection, Moore developed a particular stylistic strategy for the modernist dissociated image—introjected splitting. With this new strategy, she taught her readers freedom from anxious introjection. That is, she offered precise surface accounts of exotic creatures, leaving their identities independent of her poetic voice. The creatures seemed absent once described.[70]

The detachment that Moore exhibits may result from her quasi-scientific approach to her writing. Both 'the poet and the scientist', she said, 'must strive for precision'.[71] Her search for accuracy relies upon a hoarded stock of knowledge and 'facts' which are cultivated and ordered. Factual detail is at least as predominant and consistent a feature of her poetry as syllabic counting, moral epigrams, and her praise of American technology. In a stanza from her poem, 'Invitation to Miss Marianne Moore' (1955), Elizabeth Bishop offers these components as part of an ideal 'landscape' particularly suited to summon Moore:

> Bearing a musical inaudible abacus,
> a slight censorious frown, and blue ribbons,
>   please come flying.
> Facts and skyscrapers glint in the tide; Manhattan
> is all awash with morals this fine morning,
>   so please come flying.[72]

---

[69] Stanley Lourdeaux, 'Marianne Moore and a Psychoanalytic Paradigm for the Dissociated Image', *Twentieth Century Literature*, 30/2–3 (Summer–Fall 1984), 370.
[70] Ibid.   [71] Moore, interview with Donald Hall, 44.
[72] Bishop, 'Invitation to Miss Marianne Moore', in *Complete Poems* (London: Chatto & Windus, 1991), 82.

Moore makes self-evident Wallace Stevens's claim that 'poetry seeks out the relation of men to facts.'[73] Moore's linkage of the ability to record observation with the process of systematic thought is a tenet she shared with Stevens. In 'Adagia', Stevens writes that 'accuracy of observation is the equivalent of accuracy of thinking'.[74] Moore's reading notebook for 1916–21 records an uncited quotation about poetry which ignores facts as eventually having a 'weakening effect on the mind'.[75] There is a rarefied, intellectual tone to Moore's poems which is devoid of sentiment or any moving emotion; hers are analytical, worked lines, with a distilled, mannered quality to them. Her 'surface accounts' of creatures are never more than generic; they move among phylae but stop short of the individual. Because she epitomizes with common, factual traits rather than risking the specificity of exempla, her accounts retain their accuracy and her creatures, as Lourdeaux observes, remain 'absent'.

Moore's method is a visually accretive one. As Lisa M. Steinman put it: 'Scientific accuracy is then not the accuracy of machines but of observers; moreover, precision and effectiveness include giving value to the world thus viewed; they become forms of imaginative possession, and also activities.'[76] Moore's immersion in visual detail verges on the voyeuristic. 'The power of the visible | is the invisible', she writes in 'He "Digesteth Harde Yron"' (1941). The primacy of natural vision upon which epistemology is based becomes consciousness itself. Through Moore's dispersal of gaze among the multitude of disparate images in her poems, desire is produced primarily through visualization, and the atemporal quality of her poetry augments and makes urgent a need for a visual grounding of her referents. In her clipping collection in the Rosenbach Archive, Moore marked a copy of *The Listener* of 2 January 1967 in which an article by John Holloway, 'The Dickensian Environment', appeared. The underlined portion was Holloway's recommendation to

[73] Wallace Stevens, 'From Miscellaneous Notebooks', in *Opus Posthumous*, (ed.) Milton J. Bates (London: Faber & Faber, 1989), 204.
[74] Wallace Stevens, 'Adagia', ibid. 185.
[75] RL VII:01:01. Notebook, 1916–21.
[76] Steinman, *Made in America*, 117.

disregard associations, evocations, poetry, quasi-human life and activity in things; ignore sensuous evocativeness in its rich quiddity. Instead, note measurement and quantity, draw on the visual sense; but leave aside touch, and scent, and anything else that brings the object too close or involves it too livingly with the observer. Aim, in other words, at the absolutely maximum degree of 'depatinization'.[77]

Moore achieves an even greater distance, or 'depatinization', by never privileging visual or technical description over legend and lore, exhibiting a pre-Linnaean notion of what constitutes descriptive accounts of natural forms. Her reading notebooks and clipping files reveal that she spent considerable time sifting through both scientific treatises and a range of histories on animal and plant subjects, clipping items from geographical magazines and travel accounts. Articles such as 'Bob Davis Reveals'[78] and Rau's 'Built on a Fabled Past'[79] stand out. Her library holds works such as *Animal Sagacity* (1824), Nash's *101 Legends of Flowers* (1927), Ditmars's *Strange Animals I have Known* (1931), De Beer's *Alps and Elephants* (1955), Urzidel's *Das Elefantenblatt* (1964), Fox's *The Personality of Animals* (1952), Vaughan-Jackson's *Animals and Men in Armor* (1958), Bates's *Animal Worlds* (1963), Point's *Wilderness Kingdom* (1967), Gray's *Animal Locomotion* (1968), Burkhardt's *Signals in the Animal World* (1967), and Fitter's *Vanishing Wild Animals of the World* (1968), many of which are annotated by Moore.

Her poetry shows that fact and fable are equally adequate for her taxonomic purposes. Biological detail is often a substitute for an organic quality in her work; mythology and legend, like scientific minutiae, prevent the subject coming 'too close' or being 'too livingly with the observer'. In an early manuscript version of 'The Plumet Basilisk' (1933), Moore included four additional stanzas at the end of the section entitled 'In Costa Rica'. These lines show that Asia, and particularly China, provide a source of that myth and story so critical to establishing this remove:

---

[77] RL Vertical File: Literary History/Criticism.
[78] Bob Davis, 'Bob Davis Reveals: Facts about the Ear, Eye and Nose of Wild Animals', *New York Times* (Moore writes 'November or December 21, 1931').
[79] Santha Rama Rau, 'Built on a Fabled Past', *New York Times Book Review* (6 Oct. 1957), 5.

                                        This is the
feather basilisk
   of travellers' tales, of which a pair stood
bodyguard beside Confucius' crib: aquatic thing
      lizard-fairy detested by such dragonhood
as Michael fought

  .   .   .   .

                                   When two plumet
territories touch,
   the masters of them are dramatic
without shedding blood, exerting charm as Chinese dragon—
   whiskers in a crystal handle charm; or as thick-
flowering orchids gather dragons, in the East, by forming
   clouds for them.[80]

Moore's research ensures that her poetic accounts of natural life
are authentically drawn. However, regardless of whether she is
describing nature or china, her poetry is always circumscribed
by the visual; tactility and sensuality are strangely absent. The
unnatural distance which this creates, and the clinical and analytical withdrawal from her subjects which results, firmly place her
among what Tony Tanner refers to as the American 'watchers'.
Another theorist has enlarged upon this capacity to 'watch' and
promotes the idea that it is a consistent feature of the modern
era as a whole. In his essay, 'Scopic Regimes of Modernity', Martin
Jay writes that 'the modern era . . . has been dominated by the
sense of sight in a way that set it apart from its premodern pre-
decessors and possibly its postmodern successor . . . Beginning
with the Renaissance and the scientific revolution, modernity has
been normally considered resolutely ocularcentric', he continues,
'the invention of printing . . . reinforced the privileging of the visual
abetted by such inventions as the telescope and the microscope.'[81]
The fact that Moore's observations are resolutely focused upon
the detail reaffirms this proposition, and her undergraduate
training in biology makes the microscopic the foundation of her
poetic 'evidence'.

   With the advent of natural histories, which Michel Foucault
posits began with the publication of Jonston's *Historia naturalis*

---

[80] RL I:o3:35.
[81] Martin Jay, 'Scopic Regimes of Modernity', in Hal Foster (ed.), *Vision and Visuality* (Seattle: Bay Press, 1988), 3.

de quadripedidus in Amsterdam in 1657, 'the whole of animal
semantics has disappeared',[82] and the mechanism of sight and the
data of vision became invested with an unprecedented power:

> Observation, from the seventeenth century onward, is a perceptible
> knowledge furnished with a series of systematically negative conditions.
> Hearsay is excluded, that goes without saying; but so are taste and smell,
> because their lack of certainty and their variability render impossible
> any analysis into distinct elements that could be universally acceptable.
> The sense of touch is very narrowly limited to the designation of a few
> fairly evident distinctions (such as that between smooth and rough);
> which leaves sight with an almost exclusive privilege, being the sense by
> which we perceive extent and establish proof, and, in consequence, the
> means to an analysis *partes extra partes* acceptable to everyone . . .[83]

Visual observations also subscribe to the scientific requirement
of repeatability; they can be confirmed. Even the mythological
and the fabulous are in Moore's poems footnoted as sources, as
history, and as such refer to a textual authority outside her poems.
She invites, and has pre-empted, any questioning of the veracity
of her poetic reportage by means of what Joanne Feit Diehl has
termed her 'visual overspecificity'.[84] Visual detail and the support-
ing documentation of notes are part of an effort to authenticate
the status of her poetry as literature of fact. So that none of her
observations and recountings are left open to doubt and scrutiny,
she is always left holding 'that weapon, self-protectiveness'.[85]
Perhaps Moore's commitment to the visible is another means of
democratizing her poetic writing. The 'proof' that Foucault refers
to can be seen as a demand of scientific enquiry that observable
phenomena can be translated into demotic speech 'acceptable
to everyone' or, as Moore describes it in 'England', 'in plain
American which cats and dogs can read!'

---

[82] Foucault, *The Order of Things: An Archaeology of the Human Sciences*
(London and New York: Routledge, 1970), 129.

[83] Ibid. 132–3.

[84] Joanne Feit Diehl, *Women Poets and the American Sublime* (Bloomington and
Indianapolis: Indiana University Press, 1990), 61.

[85] From final line of 'In This Age of Hard Trying, Nonchalance Is Good and' (1916).

3
A Chinoiserie of Manners and Marvellous Creatures

'Myths are primal—do not die.'
(Marianne Moore, 'The Classics and
the Man of Letters')
'I should say again that the East loved infinity, & the West
delighted in boundaries.'
(Ralph Waldo Emerson, journal entry of 1845)

A COSMIC PERSPECTIVE

'One notes the surprising usefulness of animals as aids to self-expression',[1] Marianne Moore wrote in 'Art and Interpretation', her review of the Museum of Modern Art's 'Exhibition of the Marvelous' in 1937. Her observations are appropriately linked to her opinions of the marvellous, for Moore was inspired by the dragons (*long*), kylin or Chinese unicorns (*qilin*), basilisks,[2] tortoises (mythological figures in Chinese lore), and other strange, if not magical, beings which populate her poems. These and other imaginary beasts were of enormous interest to Moore, and her library and file collection attest to the range and depth of her study of them. References to dragons appear in published poems such as 'The Plumet Basilisk' and in its notes, 'Half Deity' (1935),[3] and 'O To Be A Dragon'. Additionally, Moore kept a file labelled 'Dragons, Mythological Beasts' in her library and kept a picture

---

[1] RL II:01:30, p. 3 of four-page unpublished manuscript, dated 1 Mar. 1937.
[2] The basilisk is a fabulous reptile (also known as a cockatrice) hatched by a serpent from a cock's egg, blasting by its breath or look; it is also the name of a small American lizard with a hollow crest inflated at will.
[3] 'Half Deity' was first published in *Direction* (Peoria, Ill.), 1 (Jan.–Mar. 1935), 74–5, later appearing in *What Are Years* (1941). It was not included in *Complete Poems* (1968).

of a dragon in her sitting-room.[4] Two undated, unpublished, and possibly unfinished, poems refer to dragons as well. ' "Am I a Brother to Dragons and a Companion to Owls?" '[5] reinforces the raw and dangerous qualities of the dragon, whose insensitivity the author believes reminds her of her own. It also displays Moore's relatively early acquaintance with dragon lore, though in this poem it is not clear that it is Far Eastern. The copious notes which are enclosed in her copy of Laurence Binyon's *The Flight of the Dragon* (1911), which devotes an entire chapter to the dragon, reveal a close and detailed reading. The unpublished 'In "Designing a Cloak to Cloak his Designs," You Wrested from Oblivion a Coat of Immortality for your own Use'[6] intimates a familiarity with Chinese dragons, as the poem implies that the two masters the dragon serves are good and evil.

Moore's fascination with dragons of the Far East can be seen as symptomatic of her apparent need to invest China and things Chinese with an originary potency, to place moral statements against a ground of the ancient and even prehistoric. Ernest Ingersoll situates the Chinese dragon within the context of myth and legend when he notes that 'everywhere the dragon, when first heard of, is associated with the genesis of the arts of civilization in China'.[7] Dragon myths predate the Honan sage Fu Hsi, whose appearance marks the legendary, as distinguished from the mythical, period which preceded him.[8] The initial appearance of dragons in China is therefore mythologically contemporaneous with the beginning of art itself and with transmitted oral history. Moore's choice of this particular mythical being, along with several other similarly imaginary creatures, indicates the value she places upon the historically remote as lending credence to the enduring nature of her moral observations. In her foreword to *A Marianne Moore Reader*, Moore states that 'the Tao led me to the dragon in the classification of primary symbols'.[9]

---

[4] The contents of Moore's sitting-room have been rehoused in the Rosenbach Museum in Philadelphia.

[5] RL I:01:03. This poem notes Moore's address at the top of the manuscript as 343 North Hanover St., Carlisle, which dates it between 1909 and 1916.

[6] RL I:02:29.

[7] Ernest Ingersoll, *Dragons and Dragon Lore* (New York: Payson & Clarke, 1928), 52.

[8] Ibid.

[9] *A Marianne Moore Reader* (New York: Viking, 1961), p. xiv, and *CPR* 551.

The dragon inhabits a space where moral outcomes are fixed, and this preordination produces the kind of freedom she craves in a poem like 'O To Be A Dragon' (1957). The Chinese dragon's ability to both exceed boundaries or disappear altogether is indicative of the enormous span of its potential moral behavior. When it ascends to heaven it becomes invisible, but when on earth it can swell to fill up all the space between heaven and earth.[10] The dragon's lack of restriction is what this poem celebrates, and the power it represents can be exercised at will and without consequences. The dragon has the ability to continually transmogrify and never assume a final shape. To inhabit the extremes of a moral continuum is Manichaean long before the arrival and acceptance of that doctrine in China during the eighth century.[11] However, Ernest Ingersoll observes that the polarities of every moral framework are already embodied in the figure of the Chinese dragon:

The dragon was born in the youth of the East, a creature engendered between inward fear and outward peril, was nurtured among prehistoric wanderers, and has survived in the hinterlands of ignorance and superstition because it embodied the underlying principle of all morality—the eternal contrast and contest between Good and Evil, typified by the incessant struggle of man with the forces of nature and with his twofold self. In the East the dragon, like primitive gods, was by turns deity and demon . . .[12]

These kinds of observations throw an interesting light upon 'O To Be A Dragon', which becomes a longing for a moral freedom that is absent in other poems. The fantasy in the poem articulates an idealistic desire for unity and absolute, unrestricted liberty and independence, an anomalous yearning amidst the calls

[10] Wolfram Eberhard, *Chinese Symbols: A Dictionary of Hidden Symbols in Chinese Life and Thought*, trans. G. L. Campbell (London and New York: Routledge & Kegan Paul, 1986), 84.

[11] The Chinese conquest of eastern Turkistan reopened caravan routes to West Asia which allowed Manichaean missionaries to enter China in the late seventh century. In 731, the Chinese emperor ordered a Manichaean bishop to compose a catechism which informed him of Manichaean doctrines, scripture, and discipline. In order to gain acceptance, true Manichaeism was mixed in this compendium with Taoism and Buddhism leading, in 732, to an imperial edict granting freedom to worship in the Manichaean religion and its subsequent widespread acceptance. See Victor H. Mair, *Painting and Performance: Chinese Picture Recitation and its Indian Genesis* (Honolulu: University of Hawaii Press, 1988), 50–1.

[12] Ingersoll, *Dragons*, 13.

for discipline and orderliness in much of Moore's poetry and prose. 'The dragon, symbol of nature's elemental forces', writes Wen Fong, 'is known in Chinese mythology for its capacity for infinite and unpredictable transformations.'[13]

Like the dragon, Moore disappears and reappears, is minute or 'immense', just as the lines of 'O To Be A Dragon', and many of her poems, can become abbreviated or quite lengthy, often without regard for any fixed and unalterable pattern. Edward H. Schafer observes that 'any creature endowed with exceptional spiritual powers could appear to the world as a dragon'.[14] It is a desire for spiritual as well as physical power which Moore is fascinated by in this poem. 'A reverence for mystery is not a vague, invertebrate thing', Moore wrote in 1922, 'the realm of the spirit is the only realm in which experience is able to corroborate the fact that the real can be also the actual.'[15] In the *I Ching*, from which Moore quoted in 'Tom Fool At Jamaica', the dragon signifies the power of wisdom and is a symbol of change and willed transformation. As Mai-Mai Sze remarks, 'the awe and reverence with which the dragon was regarded were part of the general attitude toward nature'.[16] Moore's ode, in this light, becomes a paean to her natural retinue. Notwithstanding that the dragon for the Chinese is a manifestation of *yang*, the male essence, the power of the dragon is not gendered and may embody a formidable female, and often matriarchal, power. In fact it was possible, according to the Chinese, for real human women to become visibly dragon-like and reptilian. 'These manifestations need not be transient, latent or figurative apparitions, such as serpents or rainbows, but as dragons proper', Sze notes; 'the records of such epiphanies are very old.'[17] The dark, watery, fertile aspects of the dragon are shared with the female principle, *yin*. Interestingly enough, as Schafer points out, 'in the more elevated story world of true dragon women, "dragon" is an honorable epithet

---

[13] Wen Fong, *Images of the Mind* (Princeton, NJ: The Art Museum, 1984), 169.

[14] Edward H. Schafer, *The Divine Woman: Dragon Ladies and Rain Maidens in T'ang Literature* (Berkeley and Los Angeles: University of California Press, 1973), 17.

[15] Moore, 'Is The Real The Actual?', *The Dial*, 73/6 (Dec. 1922), 622, and *CPR* 74 (here mistitled as 'Is The Real Actual?').

[16] Mai-Mai Sze, *The Tao of Painting* (Princeton, NJ: Princeton University Press, 1963), 98.

[17] Ibid. 27.

attached to a desirable feminine being'.[18] Perhaps this, too, is what Moore alludes to as her 'felicitous phenomenon'.[19]

So many of Moore's poems employ animal imagery as a kind of moral template upon which to assess human behaviour, possibly because animals are such models of conformity: they never fall short of what is expected of them. 'Because so much of our own world is evil', Randall Jarrell notes about Moore, 'she has transformed the Animal Kingdom, that amoral realm, into a realm of good; her consolatory, fabulous bestiary is more accurate than, but is almost as arranged as, any medieval one.'[20] Real animals come to embody the sturdy virtues to which, Moore repeatedly asserts, man should aspire. This is often thought to be an exaggerated belief in the Far East, where Buddhism has exerted so much influence. Moore certainly believed it to be true when, in 1933, she noted Emily Dickinson's 'Japanesely fantastic reverence for tree, insect, and toadstool'.[21] Part of the 'reverence' for nature that Moore and Dickinson share is attributable to the kinds of animals and plants that both poets chose to write about —ones that are incapable of challenging or violating the simplified moralities which polarize and place their conventional attitudes. Randall Jarrell offers an explanation of the methodology which permits this kind of natural confirmation in Moore's poetry:

How often Miss Moore has written about Things (hers are aesthetic–moral, not commercial–utilitarian—they persist and reassure); or Plants (how can anything bad happen to a plant?); or Animals with holes, a heavy defensive armament, or a massive and herbivorous placidity superior to either the dangers or temptations of aggression . . . Nature, in Miss Moore's poll of it, is overwhelmingly in favour of morality; but the results were implicit in the sampling—like the *Literary Digest*, she sent postcards to only the nicer animals . . .[22]

Imaginary animals, like the Chinese kylin, unicorn, and dragon, assert the only alternatives to unalloyed goodness, their status as fabulous beings already situating their representation in the realm of the impossible.

---

[18] Schafer, *The Divine Woman*, 117.
[19] See final line of 'O To Be A Dragon', *CP* 177.
[20] Randall Jarrell, 'Her Shield', in *Poetry and The Age* (London: Faber & Faber, 1955), 178.
[21] Moore, 'Emily Dickinson', *Poetry*, 41 (Jan. 1933), and *CPR* 292.
[22] Jarrell, 'Her Shield', 178.

Moore exhibits a consistent need to locate an all-encompassing vantage-point from which to view both tangible and fantastical representations of experience. In 'Sea Unicorns and Land Unicorns' (1924), non-Chinese unicorns are described in sixteenth-century cartographical terms and the language of heraldry. Evidence for their existence lies in 'pictures' and they are 'etched like an equine monster of an old celestial map'. We are, as in many of Moore's poems, grounded in the devices of portrayal in this poem, made to consult documents and artwork to corroborate even imaginative reality: 'Upon the printed page, | also by word of mouth, | we have a record of it all'. Moore's poetry displays her ability to combine spiritual imagination with a refusal to be confined to any single perspective among these temporally indeterminate, fabulous creatures. Imaginary or magical objects, as Sartre points out, 'do not appear, as they do in perception, from a particular angle; they do not occur *from a point of view* . . . they are "presentable" under an all-inclusive aspect'.[23] In the Chinese context, as James J. Y. Liu notes about the T'ang dynasty poetry of Tu Fu (AD 712–70), 'nature is seen as it presumably always is, not from any personal angle'.[24] Kuo Hsi (c.1020–90), a famous Northern Sung dynasty painter, included a similar observation in his essay on landscape painting, 'A Father's Instructions' (*Lin-ch'uan Kao-chih*, 1080): 'Those who study flower painting take a single stalk and put it into a deep hole, and then examine it from above, thus seeing it from all points of view.'[25] A constantly moving perspective perpetually realigns and redraws the boundaries of a perceived object, allowing time and a shifting sight to mark out in minute detail the particularities of the subject. Moore's roving perspective, and nearly microscopic examination of subjects, augments the fantastic qualities of her exotic, and often imaginary, creatures.

She points out in an essay entitled 'Is the Real the Actual?' (1922) that spiritual imagination is 'especially potent in interpreting subjects which are spiritual, seeming to derive feeling from the

---

[23] Jean-Paul Sartre, *The Psychology of Imagination* (London: Methuen, 1978), 141.
[24] James J. Y. Liu, 'Time, Space, and Self in Chinese Poetry', *Chinese Literature: Essays, Articles, Reviews*, 1/2 (July 1979), 149.
[25] Quoted in Laurence Binyon, *The Flight of the Dragon* (London: John Murray, 1911), 63. Moore also quotes Kuo Hsi in her foreword to Clay Lancaster, *Prospect Park Handbook* (New York: Walton H. Rawls, 1967), 7.

subject rather than to have to bring feeling to it as in the theme which is palpable and easily comprehensible'.[26] Possibly Moore conceived of this kind of supernatural subject as 'spiritual', which would account for the emotionally expressive qualities of 'O To Be A Dragon', a poem which in this respect is almost unique among Moore's work. Supernatural tales have formed a repository of visually expressive images and provided an enduring artistic inheritance for the Chinese poet for centuries. The magical beings which the Chinese have endowed with such immense significance have continually succeeded in capturing the imaginative energies of the poet. It is difficult to ascertain whether supernatural and mythical beings embody a spiritual or noumenal significance which draws poets to them, or whether it is their fantastical aspect that allows the poet to lend a personally contrived importance to these somewhat indeterminate figures.

David Hawkes, in his article on the supernatural in Chinese poetry, describes an aspect of this interchange between the Chinese poet and the symbology the poet employs. 'However true it may be that poets are capable of using for their imagery and inspiration a mythology in which they have long ceased to believe, symbols have, as it were, lives of their own', he writes, 'and it is arguable that some of the characteristic mental attitudes that poets adopt may be in part formed by the symbols, rather than the reverse.'[27] In her 'Comment' in *The Dial* in August 1927, Moore stresses that it remains possible for our literary conscious-ness to respond with wonder and a somewhat primitive sense of mystery to primeval beings: 'Needless to say, we dissent from the serpent as deity; and enlightenment is preferable to super-stition when plagues are to be combated', she notes; 'a certain ritual of awe—animistic and animalistic—need not, however, be effaced from our literary consciousness.'[28] Supernatural imagery, as I have pointed out, released her from the exigencies of a single visual, and often temporal, perspective. Likewise, these images lacked fully elaborated and circumscribed definitional boundaries and thereby permitted Moore to ascribe a personal significance to them which was compatible with their accumulated legendary

[26] Marianne Moore, 'Is The Real The Actual?', 620, and *CPR* 73.
[27] David Hawkes, 'The Supernatural in Chinese Poetry', *University of Toronto Quarterly*, 30 (1960–1), 322–3.
[28] Marianne Moore, 'Comment', *The Dial*, 83/2 (Aug. 1927), 178.

and literary contents. The 'ritual of awe' she tries to promote through her poetry arises from that very interplay between her notion of 'spiritual imagination' and the symbological potency of Chinese myth.

Moore calls attention to the ways these symbols are separated from us, as indistinct yet potentially powerful beings who abide in a realm apart, when she speaks of the death of two dragons[29] brought from the Island of Komodo as 'a victory, making emphatic to us our irrelevance to such creatures as these, and compulsorily our mere right to snakes in stone and story'.[30] Their power as fabulous creatures continues to inhabit their earthly forms as the palpable creatures which for millennia inspired myth and magic. For even ordinary dragons were 'mortal creatures with an innate gift for concealing themselves'.[31] Very few human beings populate Moore's poetic world, her celestial and terrestrial bestiary usurping the usually predominant place of man. Yet Moore's presentation of the 'real' and 'unreal' versions of mysterious beings, particularly in a poem like 'The Plumet Basilisk', works to dispute man-made categories, ultimately commenting upon human nature by moving back and forth between objective, mimetic representation and the description of apparent impossibility. The poem's initial grounding in the 'real' facilitates the resultant unease and disorientation by foregrounding the relation between the real and unreal as the poem's central concern.

It would seem that these extraordinary dragon creatures take on their legendary, mythological guises in some of Moore's poems and become something between what Tzvetan Todorov terms the 'hyperbolic marvellous' and the 'exotic marvellous'.[32] This distinction is particularly useful for examining the ways in which Marianne Moore uses these fabulous creatures in her

[29] René Grousset, in *Chinese Art and Culture*, trans. Haakon Chevalier (London: Andre Deutsch, 1959), 21, cites the work of archaeologist Jung Keng who has concluded, after conducting extensive research, that at least fifteen 'types' of dragon exist. See Jung Keng, *The Bronzes of the Shang and Chou*, 2 vols., *Yenching Journal of Chinese Studies*, Monograph Series, no. 17 (Beijing: Harvard–Yenching Institute, 1941).
[30] Moore, 'Comment', *The Dial* 83/2 (Aug. 1927), 179.
[31] Schafer, *The Divine Woman*, 19.
[32] Tzvetan Todorov, *The Fantastic: A Structural Approach to a Literary Genre*, trans. Richard Howard (Ithaca, NY: Cornell University Press, 1975), 54–5.

poems,[33] by creating phyla for the exotic and examining their reported traits and characteristics. The value attached to codifying poetic features and procedures lies in its ability to allow us to observe the means by which a rapport may be established between the poet and the reader. This is particularly true in Moore's case, where we find several methods of presentation which rapidly replace one another within and among her poems. Sometimes she assimilates and subsumes these mysteries into conventional or scientific categories, as in 'The Plumet Basilisk', and at other times, as in 'O To Be A Dragon', emphasizes their supernatural capabilities of enlargement, disappearance, and escape. These operations work to combine elements that are strange to one another, and constitute a protest against both the constraints of invoking the invisible and against the rigidity of distinctions between the real and the imaginary. In another review, entitled 'Concerning the Marvellous', covering the same Museum of Modern Art exhibition in 1937, Moore wrote of the artists' 'primitive tendency to depict side by side, the real and the imaginary'.[34] Moore practises a kind of poetic primitivism in her poems that include Chinese supernatural creatures which allies her work with that of Modernist painters who engaged in a similar practice of juxtaposition to question the meaning of modern culture, the criteria of 'civilization', and the democracy of what ordinarily passes for appropriate subject-matter for art. Moore situates the supernatural with the ordinary in a refusal to affirm unities of time and space, dispensing with chronology, three-dimensionality and the rigid and artificial generic categories which separate animate and inanimate objects, thereby disturbing the 'rules' of artistic representation.

The genre of the marvellous is characterized not by an attitude towards the described events, but by the nature of those events. Among several distinctions within the marvellous there is, in Todorov's terms, the 'hyperbolic marvellous' which is supernatural

---

[33] While Todorov states that 'the fantastic can subsist only within fiction: poetry cannot be fantastic' (ibid. 60), scholars have argued that Todorov's definition does not in fact exclude the accommodation of poetry within its bounds: see e.g. Lance K. Donaldson-Evans, 'Demons, Portents, and Visions: Fantastic and Supernatural Elements in Ronsard's Poetry', in Maryanne Cline Horowitz *et al.* (eds.), *Renaissance Rereadings: Intertext & Context* (Urbana and Chicago: University of Illinois Press, 1988), 225–35.

[34] RL II:01:30, p. 3 of four-page manuscript.

only by virtue of its dimensions, and surpasses that which is familiar to us.[35] As he points out, 'this form of the supernatural does not do excessive violence to reason'.[36] The 'exotic marvelous', on the other hand, embodies what is supernatural but is not presented as such, the natural and the supernatural melded together into a single, so-called 'narrative'. Todorov states that the implicit reader is supposed to be 'ignorant of the regions where the events take place' and, consequently, has no reason for calling them into question'.[37] These distinctions operate as boundaries and categories which circumscribe and later assimilate the fantastic once the period of hesitation or uncertainty on the part of the reader/listener has ended.[38] The 'fantastic' derives from the Latin, *phantasticus*, and originates in Greek, meaning 'that which is made visible, visionary, unreal'. The term conflates the otherwise incommensurate ideas of visibility and unreality.

Hesitation, according to Todorov, results from indecision 'as to whether apparently inexplicable events can be explained according to the laws of nature, or whether in fact they are the result of supernatural intervention'. 'Once this hesitation passes', he writes, 'the *fantastique* will be incorporated either into the category of *l'étrange* (the supernatural explained) or *le merveilleux* (the supernatural accepted).'[39] This choice between acceptance and explanation of the fantastic is, in Moore's poetry, often approached but never made. Ambivalence never ceases in a poem like 'The Plumet Basilisk', where the 'true Chinese lizard face | is found, of the amphibious falling dragon, the living firework', in Costa Rica.

> He runs, he flies, he swims, to get to
> his basilica—'the ruler of Rivers, Lakes, and Seas,
> invisible or visible,' with clouds to do
> as bid—and can be 'long or short, and also coarse or fine
> at pleasure.

These are the very qualities which Moore longs for in 'O To Be A Dragon', but in this poem she is also interested in ecosystems and details of animal classification, and adopts a detached, clinical manner.

---

[35] Todorov, *The Fantastic*, 54.   [36] Ibid. 55.   [37] Ibid.
[38] Donaldson-Evans, 'Demons, Portents, and Visions', 226.   [39] Ibid.

This is the serpent dove peculiar
to the East; that lives as the butterfly or bat'
can, in a brood, conferring wings on what it grasps, as the air
plant does.

We can see how Moore adopts successively different attitudes
throughout 'The Plumet Basilisk', imposing at one time *le
merveilleux* and at another *l'étrange*, wonder following taxonomic
analysis in an endless relay of speculation and scientific reportage.
It is as if she tries to embody two potential, antithetical outcomes
of the fantastic at once, neither dismissing nor corroborating
either viewpoint. The reader is suspended in a state of hesitation
which characterizes the fantastic by Moore's insistent, pervasive
perspective. Both myth and magic are made credible as Moore
attempts to maintain, or to constantly re-enact, those moments
of hesitation to which Todorov refers.

In 'O To Be A Dragon', Moore chose from among several
species of a dragon the *long* dragon (dragon being a generic
term), a bringer of rain and a whimsical spirit of changeable
aspect. Other dragon types exist, among which the *jiao* stands
out as a close approximation to the ill-omened basilisk, or
cockatrice,[40] which Moore describes in 'The Plumet Basilisk'. In
the opening line of an unpublished (and undated) poem entitled
'Eloquence', she humorously alludes to the sinister quality of
fluid speech with yet another reference to the basilisk, or *jiao*.
The dragon basilisk is a species with qualities of its own whose
origin, as with all dragons, is irretrievably lost in time. In
'Eloquence', it becomes evident that Moore is familiar with the
basilisk's attributes and uncertain provenance. Moreover, her
poem 'The Plumet Basilisk' is remarkably similar to a Chinese
collectanea,[41] or reference book, which makes distinctions between
the *jiao* and other divine serpents. The following lines by Guo
Bu from the Han dynasty (206 BC–AD 220) offer an example of
the kind of descriptive discrimination which these collectanea
include:

[40] Schafer, *The Vermilion Bird: T'ang Images of the South* (Berkeley and Los
Angeles: University of California Press, 1967), 218. Schafer employs the Wade–Giles
system, in which *jiao* would appear as *kau*.
[41] 'Collectanea' is the Latin neuter plural of *collectaneus*, meaning 'passages, remarks,
etc., collected from various sources; a collection of passages, a miscellany'.

Neither snake nor dragon,
Scaly, many-colored, shining, refulgent,
It prances and jumps on wave and billow.[42]

These watery creatures likewise appear in the poetry of the famous T'ang dynasty poet, Tu Fu.[43] While creatures such as the dragon, unicorn, and tortoise have supernatural status in both Chinese literature and in Marianne Moore's poems, other 'real' animals, by virtue of their exotic origins, take on supernatural qualities in her poetry as well. For example, the pangolin is an animal found in Africa as well as in Asia[44] and is, in Moore's poem 'The Pangolin' (1936), a creature who becomes steadily more supernatural as the poem progresses.

This hesitation or uncertainty about the ultimate status of her animal subjects is one which invites comparison with similar uncertainties about nature in Romantic poetry. 'If Shelley had been a Chinese poet', Laurence Binyon said in 1933, 'his ode [to the West Wind] would inevitably have been addressed to the Dragon.'[45] Binyon's remark highlights the simultaneous natural and supernatural qualities in nature to which poets of so many periods have been drawn. While similarities between mythical creatures found in Romantic poetry and those which appear in Moore's poems could no doubt also be established by further analysis, it has been argued by many scholars that the rise of the fantastic, and the use of supernatural subjects in literature which established that genre, resists precise dating and may have originated in the Renaissance period or earlier.[46] It is important to emphasize here that the supernaturally endowed dragons which appear in Anglo-Saxon literature such as *Beowulf* are fundamentally different from the Chinese creatures which appear in Moore's poems, whose aspect and representation are quite distinct.

[42] Kuo P'u, *Ch'uan Shang Ku San Tai Ch'iu Han San Kuo Liu Ch'ao Wen*, cited in Schafer, *The Vermilion Bird*, 310 n. 133.

[43] Ibid. 219.

[44] Ibid. 230. The pangolin is a mammal of the genus *Manis*, the greater part of whose body is covered with horny scales; a scaly ant-eater.

[45] Laurence Binyon, *The Spirit of Man in Asian Art*, a Charles Eliot Norton Lecture delivered at Harvard University, 1933–4 (Cambridge, Mass.: Harvard University Press, 1935), 70. Quotation is from the third lecture, entitled 'The Conception of Landscape Art in China: Taoism and Zen'.

[46] Donaldson-Evans, 'Demons, Portents and Visions', 225.

Moore's ability to defer, or dispense with, temporal reference in many of her poems is also linked to Chinese poetry. In Chinese poetry, the indistinction between past, present, and future, brought about by the absence of any indication of tense morphology, lends a timeless, ethereal quality to descriptive poems. Among its many attributes, 'the simultaneous separation and fusion of past and present is one of the marvels of Chinese poetry', as Hans Frankel has observed; 'a Chinese poet is always free to keep time indefinite'.[47] Moore's poems ordinarily occupy an eternal present tense where all time is made simultaneous; it suspends chronology and maintains the sense of a current dialogue with the reader amidst the profusion of apparently disordered observation. This mode of address, as will be evident in later chapters, simultaneously helps to retain the reader's attention and Moore's control, and therefore works to further her didactic purposes. It conveys a magical mode of thinking that initially distracts the reader from the ultimate moral import of her poems, and gives the impression that her single, often reductive 'truths' are arrived at through a kind of descriptive debate. Bonnie Costello highlights a context within which this strategy can be understood. 'Moore's poems enter into a long and varied tradition of emblematic literature', she notes, 'in which images are juxtaposed to ideas or morals with which they have little natural but primarily an abstract connection.'[48] However, the poetic sincerity of such a tactic, that suddenly strands the reader on an aphorism or epigram which does not proceed out of what has gone before, nor progress towards synthesis, can be called into question.

Her sudden, radical shifts from description to a kind of prayer or paraphrastic utterance disarm the reader, who might return to previous stanzas in an ultimately futile attempt to gain a purchase on the sometimes artificial sequence of the 'narrative' of her sentences. These 'ethical crystallizations', Richard Howard observes, 'occur like geodes in her poems'.[49] The ultimate decision as to whether or not her procedure bolsters or dismantles

---

[47] Hans Frankel, *The Flowering Plum and the Palace Lady: Interpretations of Chinese Poetry* (New Haven and London: Yale University Press, 1976), 128.

[48] Bonnie Costello, *Marianne Moore: Imaginary Possessions* (Cambridge, Mass.: Harvard University Press, 1981), 40–1.

[49] Richard Howard, 'Marianne Moore and the Monkey Business of Modernism', in Joseph Parisi (ed.), *Marianne Moore: The Art of a Modernist* (Ann Arbor, Mich. and London: UMI Research Press, 1990), 6.

her efforts rests with the reader's openness to this kind of 'play' between the opposing energies of the imaginative tour and the indisputable verity. Indeed, as Bonnie Costello has remarked, Moore was often led to write poems that 'defy the lessons they purport'.[50] Certainly this is true of longer poems whose sheer volume of description and observation overpowers the short maxims which accompany them. 'Words were a kind of finery which she loved to put on', James Fenton has observed, 'facts were adored for their glamour rather than their factuality.'[51] Elizabeth Bishop, in a more familiar setting, similarly observes that 'as in the notes to her poems, Marianne never gave away the whole show . . . The volubility, the wit, the self-deprecating laugh, never really clarified those quick decisions of hers—or decisive intuitions, rather—as to good and bad, right and wrong . . . her meticulous system of ethics could be baffling.'[52] We can only speculate about other reasons for Moore's wishing to maintain a cosmic perspective within some of her poems. Certainly it seems to serve no other purposive, teleological scheme within her verse. James J. Y. Liu's observation about this aspect of Chinese poetry, however, provides a plausible explanation for the compensatory effect of Moore's methods: 'Against this cosmic perspective, one's own misfortunes appear insignificant.'[53]

EMBLEMS OF RESTRAINT

The Chinese dragon's association with the aristocratic and the genteel produces another set of questions about Moore's obvious devotion to dragon imagery in several of her poems. Most of the texts she read about dragons were scholarly and based upon art-historical studies of these creatures as they appeared upon Chinese imperial silk robes and in seventeenth-century scroll paintings. Among Moore's library holdings is Annette B. Cottrell's *Dragons*, published by the Museum of Fine Arts, Boston, and

---

[50] Costello, *Marianne Moore*, 197.

[51] James Fenton, 'Becoming Marianne Moore', *New York Review of Books* (24 Apr. 1997), 43.

[52] Elizabeth Bishop, 'Efforts of Affection: A Memoir of Marianne Moore', in *Elizabeth Bishop: The Collected Prose*, (ed.) Robert Giroux (London: Chatto & Windus, 1984), 154–5.

[53] Liu, 'Time, Space and Self', 152.

illustrated with museum pieces. The rarefied nature of these depictions and legends of Chinese dragons is evident in the carefully wrought, gilded carvings and detailed scroll paintings in which they appear. Chinese dragon lore reveals little evident similarity to European dragon lore.[54] Cottrell calls attention to the enormous disparity between the two types of dragon, the Chinese or 'Oriental' dragon being described as 'an elegant aristocrat'[55] and 'believed to be a close relative to the Emperor'.[56] Other texts support these descriptions and underscore the ethereal and imperial nature of this powerful, divine, supernatural animal. In a study of 'Imaginary Beings', Jorge Luis Borges, in a chapter on the 'Eastern Dragon', notes that 'history traces the earliest emperors back to Dragons';[57] in another chapter, on the 'Chinese Dragon', he observes that in the *I Ching* or *Book of Changes*, the dragon 'signifies wisdom'. In addition to being the imperial emblem, the emperor's throne was called 'the Dragon Throne', his face 'the Dragon Face'. 'On announcing an emperor's death', Borges notes, 'it was said that he had ascended to heaven on the back of a Dragon.'[58]

Moore kept a large file on dragons, and handwritten annotations in her books on the subject reveal that she discerned and marked the differences between Far Eastern dragon lore and that of, for example, Islam and India.[59] In her notes to 'The Plumet Basilisk', Moore cites Frank Davis's article 'The Chinese Dragon' to offer this observation: 'The dragon "is either born a dragon (and true dragons have nine sons) or becomes one by transformation." There is a "legend of the carp that try to climb a certain cataract in the western hills. Those that succeed become dragons." '[60] There are evident parallels to the barriers of social class in this kind of mythological story. 'The Plumet Basilisk' was first published twenty-four years before the appearance of 'O To

[54] For a wide-ranging discussion of world dragon lores, see Ingersoll, *Dragons and Dragon Lore*.

[55] Annette B. Cottrell, *Dragons* (Boston, Mass.: Museum of Fine Arts, 1962), introduction (pages unnumbered).

[56] Ibid., unnumbered page detailing eighth-century Chinese bronze dragon.

[57] Jorge Luis Borges, *The Book of Imaginary Beings* (New York: Dutton, 1969), 82.

[58] Ibid. 65.

[59] For example, her own annotations in her copy of the December 1955 *Metropolitan Museum of Art Bulletin* referring to the Persian dragon on p. 88.

[60] Frank Davis, 'The Chinese Dragon', *Illustrated London News* (23 Aug. 1930).

Be A Dragon' (1957). As two poems about dragons, written so many years apart, 'The Plumet Basilisk' exhibits the same kind of longing expressed in 'O To Be A Dragon', but not so much for power in and of itself, as for the distance it creates. This impression is further reinforced by Moore's 'Comment' in *The Dial* in 1927, in which she cites *The Historie of Foure-Footed Beastes* (1607) by Edward Topsell (1572–1625) when she writes that 'among all the kinds of serpents there is none comparable to the Dragon'.[61] For Moore, it seems, the dragon inhabits a realm above and beyond all others.

Other Chinese mythological elements come to stand for the social qualities Moore expects both of herself and others. The Chinese kylin appears in Moore's 'Nine Nectarines': 'A Chinese "understands | the spirit of the wilderness" | and the nectarine-loving kylin | of pony appearance—the long- | tailed or the tailless | small cinnamon-brown, common | camel-haired unicorn | with antelope feet and no horn, | here enameled on porcelain.' Ezra Pound's translation of the Confucian Odes (*Shijing*) similarly emphasized the quiet, natural restraint of the kylin, or Chinese unicorn, a personal emblem of Confucius.[62] The kylin's forbearance, these lines imply, arises at least in part out of its ancient, noble lineage: 'Wan's line | and clan.' This is a direct reference to the royal line of the Chou dynasty (*c.*1030–722 BC) which continued to reign during the lifetime of Confucius.[63]

> Kylin's foot bruiseth no root,
> Ohé, Kylin.
> In Kylin's path, no wrath,
> Ohé, Kylin.
> Kylin's tooth no harm doth,
> Ohé, Kylin:
> Wan's line
> and clan.[64]

[61] Moore, 'Comment', *The Dial*, 83 (Aug. 1927), 178, and *CPR* 187.

[62] The plumet basilisk was also associated with Confucius for Moore. In a manuscript version of 'The Plumet Basilisk' (1933), she writes: 'This is the | feather basilisk | of travellers' tales, of which a pair stood | bodyguard beside Confucius' crib' (RL I:03:35).

[63] David Hsin-fu Wand, 'The Dragon and the Kylin: The Use of Chinese Symbols and Myths in Marianne Moore's Poetry', *Literature East and West*, 15/3 (1971), 481.

[64] *The Classic Anthology Defined by Confucius*, trans. Ezra Pound (Cambridge, Mass.: Harvard University Press, 1954), 6.

Moore's prose constantly calls for restraint in writing and this
concern is mirrored in her private demands for a polite social
restraint in others. On the envelope of a letter from Ezra Pound
dated 7 September 1954 is a pencilled verse by Moore as a
response to Pound, which refers to Pound's translation of *The
Classic Anthology Defined by Confucius* in which his lines
about the kylin appear:

> 4 misdemeanors
>   in one letter
> profanities & blasphemy
> But I confess, Confucius,
> [is a] Well as my
> French sage has said,
> 'Sweet speech does no *harm*
> none at all.' I refer to
> the anthology[65]

No doubt Moore is referring to Pound's explicit language and
mild habit of swearing (sometimes in a comic way, as in
'demme' for 'damn me') in his letters. Behaving well and maintaining propriety at all times is part of the genteel social presence
which Moore required in private, just as, as Robert Pinsky
points out, 'gentility and idiosyncrasy are unquestionably part
of the true social presence in the poems'.[66] Randall Jarrell confirms his view when he writes:

One is often conscious while reading the poetry, the earlier poetry especially, of a contained removed tone; of the cool precise untouchedness,
untouchableness, of fastidious rectitude; of innate merits and their
obligations, the obligations of ability and intelligence and aristocracy
—for if aristocracy has always worn armour, it has also always lived
dangerously: the association of aristocracy and danger and obligation
is as congenial to Miss Moore as is the rest of the 'flower and fruit
of all that noted superiority'. Some of her poems have the manners or
manner of ladies who learned a little before birth not to mention money,
who neither point nor touch, and who scrupulously abstain from the
mixed, live vulgarity of life.[67]

---

[65] RL V:51:02.
[66] Robert Pinsky, 'Marianne Moore: Idiom and Idiosyncrasy', in *Poetry and the
World* (New York: Ecco, 1988), 47.
[67] Jarrell, 'Her Shield', 182.

Equally, Chinese supernatural beings are complicit in establishing that genteel and idiosyncratic 'social presence' in Moore's poetry. It is not surprising that the kylin and dragon find their way into her stock of images among the other trappings of genteel life which ordinarily appear in her verse. ' "Be gentle and you can be bold" is an ancient Chinese saying', she wrote in her essay ' "We Will Walk Like The Tapir" ' (1943), ' "be frugal and you can be liberal; if you are a leader, you have learned self-restraint" '.[68] David Hsin-Fu Wand has noted that the kylin is a 'good-natured beast, which possesses all the ideal traits of a *junzi* or Confucian gentleman, "bruiseth no root" with its "foot" and feeds only on nectarines and peaches, much as the Greek gods do on nectar and ambrosia'.[69]

Not only is the kylin a suitably polite animal, but it is 'nectarine-loving' in 'Nine Nectarines'. Moore has substituted nine peaches for nine nectarines in her poem, where the 'peach *Yu*' ('oily peach' or *yu t'ao*) imparts longevity to those who eat it.[70] Wand relates an interesting background to the powers of the peach in Chinese art and literature as a symbol of longevity. According to one legend, Lao Tzu (from whose philosophy Taoism arose) visits the Queen of Heaven, Hsi Wang Mu, and they dine together on the food of the immortals, peaches and pears.[71] An earlier version of 'Nine Nectarines', entitled 'Nine Nectarines and Other Porcelain' (1934), indicates that Moore knew of these legends. This version mentions the imperial happiness and the immortality that the 'peach *Yu*' gives. The kylin and the Chinese peach share a polite history and genteel connotations. Like the dragon, they have an enormous and effortless power. The peach holds the power of immortality, and the kylin, as one of the four Chinese supernatural beings, exerts cosmic power.[72] Again, Moore finds these emblems compelling because they embody the power of restraint and abide by Moore's desire for 'sweet speech' which, like the kylin, 'no harm doth'.

---

[68] Moore, ' "We Will Walk Like The Tapir" ', *The Nation* 156 (19 June 1943), 867, and *CPR* 377.

[69] Wand, 'The Dragon and the Kylin', 481.   [70] Ibid.

[71] Ibid. Wand cites as his source for these remarks Cyril Birch (ed.), *Anthology of Chinese Literature* (Harmondsworth: Penguin, 1967) 167–8.

[72] Sze, *The Tao of Painting*, 11.

Much like her fascination with all kinds of strange and exotic beings, Moore is drawn to the even more impersonal and unknown qualities of the Chinese dragon, whose isolated invocation in 'O To Be A Dragon' could hardly be more indifferent to worldly reference. Her use of the basilisk, kylin, and dragon, all mythological creatures, effectively establishes a distance between Moore's subjects and her reader, a distance which in other poems is brought about by the use of extinct or unusual forms of life. The reader is never allowed to become habitualized to these oddities, as Moore discloses an ever-increasing number of facts and facets of their behaviour, appearance, and habitats. This prevents the reader from confronting most of her poems with a desire to corroborate personal, lived experience, and it also makes it impossible to verify her versions or interrogate their truth. This is not to say that Moore repels her reader on any level. Each of her poems is benevolently organized, with reference material in the notes and an assurance in her descriptive tone which conveys authority. However, she does not encourage rapport. The poems offer a mediated relation to nature, authentic or imaginary, partly because their sources are books and artefacts and partly because she wants to orchestrate the reader's 'visit'. 'One could never master the real world', Bonnie Costello writes of Moore, 'but one could draw emblems and descriptions of the world into a private setting where the world might be brought under imaginary control.'[73]

Sometimes, however, Moore's 'private settings' have codes of conduct, they require manners and a degree of formality, and, like all social intercourse, an implicit understanding of protocol and procedure. Robert Pinsky locates the source of Moore's unnatural reticence in her efforts at self-protection, 'constructing, exposing and disassembling an elaborate fortress'.[74] Another critic, Celeste Goodridge, believes that 'Moore's economy of self-expenditure is contingent upon self-preservation'.[75] The methods she uses to erect that fortress and their consequences for her poetry can be examined through her references to Chinese objects and, in particular, to Chinese supernatural creatures. Not only

---

[73] Costello, *Mariainne Moore*, 6.   [74] Pinsky, 'Marianne Moore', 58.
[75] Celeste Goodridge, *Hints and Disguises: Marianne Moore and her Contemporaries* (Iowa City: University of Iowa Press, 1989), 11.

is the dragon an imperial symbol, but her use of it highlights the fact that Moore never mentions contemporary China in any of her poems, apart from mentioning the last emperor, Pu Yi, as the source of a quotation in her notes to 'Half Deity'. Again, this reference to imperial China, albeit a last remnant of imperial power, reinforces the impression that Moore gravitates towards subjects which exclude the political and which are completely removed from ordinary experience or common knowledge. Her Chinese 'artefacts' are: 'Certain Ming | products' ('Critics and Connoisseurs', 1916); a ' "Chinese cherry" ' ('Picking and Choosing', 1920); 'the East with its snails, its emotional | shorthand and jade cockroaches' ('England', 1920); 'Chinese carved glass', 'landscape gardening twisted into permanence' and 'the Chinese vermilion of | the poincianas' (all from 'People's Surroundings', 1922); the 'survival of ancient punctilio | in the manner of Chinese lacquer-carving' ('Bowls', 1923); 'a Chinese brush' ('The Plumet Basilisk', 1933); 'Chinese flower piece' ('Smooth Gnarled Crape Myrtle', 1935); 'the Chinese lawn' ('He "Digesteth Harde Yron" ', 1941); and 'China's precious wentletrap' ('Logic and "The Magic Flute" ', 1956). Even in her prose writing she privileges what is Chinese: 'The military cape is the most graceful wrap we have—with Chinese straight-up collar', she wrote in 'Dress And Kindred Subjects' (1965).[76] This list is indicative of Moore's practice of gathering Chinese items from the past, or which are out of reach, to suggest meanings which only she can lend to them. Similarly, the rarefied nature of these Far Eastern references invokes an imperial air of manicured gardens, exquisite *objets d'art*, and commissioned paintings. The poetic 'setting' which each of these calls to mind is remote and inhospitable; they tend to command a certain refinement and demand an obligation, even if only to appreciate their fineness. The poems in which they appear span Moore's writing career and work to convey the sense that Moore wishes, in Robert Pinsky's words, 'to consign social experience to a kind of eternal previousness, addressed from behind the walls of idiosyncrasy'.[77] His examination of Moore through the

---

[76] Moore, 'Dress And Kindred Subjects', *Women's Wear Daily* (17 Feb. 1965), 4, and CPR 596.
[77] Pinsky, 'Marianne Moore', 58–9.

'relation of language and poetry to social life and even to social class'[78] is relevant in the light of the very clear manner in which Chinese ingredients are implicated in that relation.

Moore's deployment of things Chinese in her poems is augmented by her respect for Chinese ingenuity and tradition. She writes of the 'sublimated wisdom of China' ('England'), 'the Chinese style' of painting, the 'secluded wall-grown nectarine, | as wild spontaneous fruit was | found in China first', (both from 'Nine Nectarines'), 'Chinese | "passion for the particular," ' ('Tell Me, Tell Me', 1960), and 'an ancient Chinese | melody' and the Chinese acrobat, Li Siau Than, who is 'gibbon-like but limberer' and 'China's very most ingenious man' (both from 'Blue Bug', 1962). The final stanza of 'Nine Nectarines', separated from the rest of the poem, epitomizes these kinds of reference. Moore's catalogue of Chinese capacities and strengths locates what she deems superior, not only in the past and within a distant culture, but within the social portion of China which evidently constitutes the social class capable of endowing China with its most treasured attributes. As David Hsin-Fu Wand points out, 'Miss Moore has miraculously transported the essence of Cathay, or classical China, to the soil of American poetry'.[79]

In this respect, her Sinophilism is reminiscent of thirteenth-century accounts of the wonders of this alien land. Marco Polo's detailed account of China, cited by Todorov as an example of the 'exotic marvelous',[80] also emphasized an aesthetic appreciation of the products of Chinese craftsmanship. In the sixteenth century, Chinese artisans were still being lauded in the travel writings of Lorenzo Corsalis who, in 1515, wrote that the Chinese produce 'silk and wrought stuff of all kinds, such as damasks, satins, and brocades of extraordinary richness'. 'For they are people of great skill', he continued, 'and of our quality.'[81] Another sixteenth-century record by Mendoza expresses similar awe at the architecture of provincial Chinese governors' houses, 'all of which are superbious and admirable and wrought by marvellous art'.[82] Raymond Dawson suggests that this kind of enthusiastic dismay

---

[78] Ibid. 47.   [79] Wand, 'The Dragon and the Kylin', 482.
[80] Todorov, *The Fantastic*, 55.
[81] Raymond Dawson, *The Chinese Chameleon: An Analysis of European Conceptions of Chinese Civilization* (London: Oxford University Press, 1967), 107.
[82] Ibid.

was due in part 'to the aura of exoticism which was associated with all oriental objects and partly to the fact that they carried with them an association with a great empire beyond the seas'.[83]

Likewise, the cult of chinoiserie, which grew steadily from the time of these early voyages until the eighteenth century, as Dawson opines, 'arose in response to Europe's own needs rather than from any desire to become accurately acquainted with Chinese civilization'.[84] And Dawson notes in his book that he finds no differentiation between European and American responses to China. So that Moore's selectivity in choosing China's art, but not her history, China's imperial past, but not her peasantry, is itself a dated orientalist response which reflects an impression of China suited to her own needs. Perceptions of Chinese taste, manners, natural reserve and fastidiousness must have proven an attractive antidote, both for Moore and orientalists of earlier centuries, to Western vulgarity, excess, and increasing uniformity. As Dawson puts it, 'the simple reverence for nature and response to beauty thought to be typical of the Chinese is another aspect of their civilization which has seemed refreshing by contrast with modern Western ugliness'.[85] This romantic vision of Cathay is a form of nostalgia for 'the past' focused upon an idealized subject. The previous chapter called attention to Moore's enthusiasm for a quasi-Confucian moral order, which shared so many attributes of Puritan ethics. Her nostalgia for moral systems is very much like her fondness for an outmoded and naïve fascination with a glamorized China more typical of the seventeenth and eighteenth centuries, and earlier. China's political weakness and imperial pretensions were becoming evident to Europeans even from the late eighteenth century onwards. To indulge in such an outmoded fantasy in the twentieth century embalms this dated and inaccurate vision of an ideal China.

Hugh Honour relates the childhood impressions he had of China from the designs he saw on imported Chinese porcelain. China, for young Honour, was 'a topsy-turvy land of brilliant flowers, weird monsters, and fragile buildings where most European values were reversed'.[86] This description is reminiscent

---

[83] Raymond Dawson, 109.   [84] Ibid. 108.   [85] Ibid. 129.
[86] Hugh Honour, *Chinoiserie: The Vision of Cathay* (London: John Murray, 1961), 2.

of Bryher's[87] memoir, which described Moore as seeming 'to lie perched on a rock above a warm and shallow lake, surveying an earlier globe'.[88] Elizabeth Bishop corroborates Bryher's memory of Moore's immersion in the imagined social graces of another time and place: 'The atmosphere of 260 Cumberland Street was of course "old-fashioned", but even more, otherworldly—as if one were living in a diving bell from a different world, let down through the crass atmosphere of the twentieth century . . . the unaccustomed deference, the exquisitely prolonged etiquette . . . admonitions, reserves, principles, simple stoicism.'[89] And Ted Hughes, in 'The Literary Life' makes similar observations: 'We climbed Marianne Moore's narrow stair | To her bower-bird bric-à-brac nest, in Brooklyn. | Daintiest curio relic of Americana | . . . Her face, tiny American treen bobbin | On a spindle, | Her voice the flickering hum of the old wheel.'[90]

However, Moore read and reviewed books about contemporary China[91] and was alerted to new works on China by Ezra Pound. In a letter to Moore dated 9 March 1957, Pound noted an 'immensely important' book by J. Beldan, *China Shakes the World*.[92] And yet the realities of contemporary China never seemed to penetrate her poetry. Her studied apoliticality in the case of China would not necessarily be remarkable if it did not extend to all of her work. Apart from her quiet pleas for general social tolerance,[93] Moore's most vociferous civic stands were in support of a threatened Brooklyn tree in 'The Camperdown Elm' (1967) and against the wearing of animal fur in 'The Arctic Ox (Or Goat)' (1958). It is an important component of her interest in China generally that it proceeds out of, or even produces, a

---

[87] Bryher's real name was Winifred Ellerman. She and H.D. (Hilda Doolittle) were instrumental in publishing Moore's first volume of poems, entitled *Poems*, in 1921.
[88] Quoted in Charles Molesworth, *Marianne Moore: A Literary Life* (New York: Athenaeum, 1990), 153.
[89] Bishop, ' Efforts of Affection', 137.
[90] Ted Hughes, 'The Literary Life', in *Birthday Letters* (London: Faber & Faber, 1998), 75.
[91] See e.g. her review of Harry A. Franck's *Roving through China* in *The Dial*, 81 (July 1926), 84–5, and *CPR* 245.
[92] RL V:51:01.
[93] For example, these lines from 'The Labors of Hercules' (1921): 'to convince snake-charming controversialists | that one keeps on knowing | "that the Negro is not brutal, | that the Jew is not greedy, | that the Oriental is not immoral, | that the German is not a Hun." '

particular social frame within which she wishes to place herself. In many ways, her connoisseur-like interest in Sèvres china and Chippendale furniture betray a similar self-positioning in relation to an upper-class Europe. Moore's explanatory footnotes, her effort at democratizing her poetry, work instead to increase the volume and burden of her immense number of references. Her allusions to high culture in both her poems and notes are perhaps somewhat intentionally superficial, and she bridges, or gives the impression that she means to bridge, the exclusionary character of privilege and professionalism of her verse. But there are grounds to suspect that these extra 'learning aids' make her gestures towards availability and access appear additionally fraudulent, particularly when they are considered in light of the caveat to her *Complete Poems*, 'Omissions are not accidents'. It is as if Moore warns her readers that the odd attributions and source materials that she has left out were part of yet another project to which we are not party. And yet it also brings back Robert Pinsky's statement about the fortress Moore erects around herself, and the way that these poem notes serve to separate Moore from her own verse and from her prospective audience.

Perhaps it is more meaningful to say that Moore gathers her images from art and nature all over the world, but is never worldly in her poetry. Worldliness implies acquaintance with a gamut of experience, both dramatic and dull, splendid and squalid. Her poetry makes it clear that these were the extremeties of life in which she refused to take part, as in 'We are sick of the earth, | sick of the pig-sty, wild geese and wild men', from 'The Labors of Hercules' (1921). In the first stanza of a late poem, 'Enough: 1969', she expresses similar sentiments when reflecting upon where 'I' would prefer to be: 'Sitting under Plato's olive tree | . . . away from controversy | or anyone choleric.'

This is the kind of statement which has prompted critics such as Sandra Gilbert to highlight Moore's 'overt misandry'.[94] Privately, too, she must have given this impression, given the following lines from Elizabeth Bishop's 'Invitation to Miss Marianne Moore':

---

[94] Sandra Gilbert, 'Marianne Moore as Female Female Impersonator' in Parisi (ed.), *Marianne Moore: The Art of a Modernist*, 35.

> Mounting the sky with natural heroism,
> above the accidents, above the malignant movies,
> the taxicabs and injustices at large,
> while horns are resounding in your beautiful ears
> that simultaneously listen to
> a soft uninvented music, fit for the musk deer,
>   please come flying.[95]

Bishop's lines have both an affectionate and reverential quality about them, no doubt saturated with the complexity of her relationship with Moore. But Bishop has tellingly located that asocial, even anti-social, instinct that is so strongly felt in Moore's poetry and prose. In a way, Bishop is implying here that Moore is attuned to quiet and unobtrusive natural subjects and not to human, social, or mundane events. These lines also imply that Moore's attention is distracted by what is only 'fit' for a smallish, uncommon, and quiescent animal like the musk deer. She cannot merely be a deer, but must be a 'musk deer'; there can't be anything general about Moore. Her unearthly, ascendant qualities are also alluded to in the final line of the stanza—'please come flying'—which ends each of the stanzas in the poem. These lines also accentuate Moore's habit of demoting and dismissing what isn't part of her creed, what she is above, which in these lines is the ordinary daily concourse of life in New York where she lives, her surrounds. Like the dragon and the kylin, she is flying, having preened the unnecessary. Like those genteel creatures, too, Moore is someone to whom 'one' must send an invitation. 'In this world of the poems there are many thoughts, things, animals, sentiments, moral insights', Randall Jarrell explains, 'but money and passion and power, the brute fact that *works*, whether or not correctly, whether or not precisely—the whole Medusa-face of the world: these are gone'.[96] 'One would rather disguise than travesty emotion; give away a nice thing than sell it; dismember a garment of rich aesthetic construction than degrade it to the utilitarian offices of the boneyard', she wrote as early as 1935.[97]

---

[95] Elizabeth Bishop, 'Invitation to Miss Marianne Moore', in *Complete Poems* (London: Chatto & Windus, 1991), 83. First collected in *A Cold Spring* (1955).

[96] Jarrell, 'Her Shield', 183.

[97] Moore, 'Archaically New', in *Trial Balances*, (ed.) Ann Winslow (New York: Macmillan, 1935), 82–3, and CPR 328.

Moore takes from the exotic past, she sifts and separates, littering her poetry with social markers that complement the socially mannered quality of her speech, which Patricia Willis has described as 'enjambed' and 'latinate'.[98] This description identifies both the lengthiness of her agglomerated sentences and the often convoluted quality in the order of words in her poems. It is interesting that Willis and others have used this word 'latinate' to describe Moore's writing, because it also indicates the archaic origins of many of the extraordinary verbalisms to which Moore resorts. This 'latinate' language is also a by-product of modest understatement and a belaboured effort to cover over or camouflage any emotion or excitement in her poems. Joanne Feit Diehl's psychological study of Moore offers this explanation of the delicate balance which generates this aloofness:

Moore thus strives in her poems to maintain a poise between her own conception of aesthetic effectiveness and her impetus to disguise, trans- pose, or deflect the direct experience of human feeling . . . The reticence that marks her imagination can, therefore, be understood as creating a style that maintains a complicated dynamic between competing needs— the goal of evoking powerful emotion and the necessity of protecting, through verbal and metrical controls, the author's subjectivity. Such tension between reticence and a spontaneous expressiveness is associ- ated with Moore's conception of decorum and its relation to intimacy; of manners and morals, of how to conduct one's life, or more broadly, the ethical imperatives that inform style.[99]

In an observation about Henry James, with whom she felt she had so much in common, Moore wrote that he 'was probably so susceptible to emotion as to be obliged to seem unemotional'. But she goes on to note Pound's accuracy in declaring that 'emotions to Henry James were more or less things that other people had, that one didn't go into'.[100] This comment perhaps goes a long way towards explaining what some critics refer to as her natural reticence, and others as her ironic distance from both personal feeling and a personal subjectivity that in America became

[98] Patricia C. Willis, *Marianne Moore: Vision into Verse* (Philadelphia, Pa.: Rosenbach Museum and Library, 1987), 21.

[99] Joanne Feit Diehl, *Elizabeth Bishop and Marianne Moore: The Psychodynamics of Creativity* (Princeton, NJ: Princeton University Press, 1993), 74.

[100] Moore, 'Feeling and Precision', *Sewanee Review*, 52 (Autumn 1944), 406, and *CPR* 401.

increasingly associated with the feminine and the sentimental. The public nature of poetry, perhaps, forces any emotion expressed in it to necessarily entail a social component.

Randall Jarrell discusses Moore's use of understatement in terms of her preference for precision as underscoring truth when he writes that 'she wished to trust, as absolutely as she could, in flat laconic matter-of-factness, in the minimal statement, understatement: these earlier poems of hers approach as a limit a kind of ideal minimal statement, a truth thought of as underlying, prior to, all exaggeration and error; the poet has tried to strip or boil everything down to this point of hard, objective, absolute precision'.[101] Laurence Binyon has called attention to the reasons why Chinese poets and painters have invested nature with so much significance, much as Moore does, to curtail the immediacy of expressed emotion and, possibly, to relay disguised or covert meanings. 'Penetrated with this innate love of suggestion and understatement', wrote Laurence Binyon of Chinese artists, 'we need not wonder that painters and poets preferred to tell of their emotions and experiences, not directly but allusively, under the guise of flower or bird.'[102] But, of course, China has a long history of political persecution of poets and painters, many of the most famous of whom were from the imperial families of deposed dynasties, and for that reason adopted new names, fled into the mountains in retreat, and, from there, wrote encoded poems in which butterflies, persimmons, or plum trees became symbolic references to dynastic reigns, exile, and lament. In the Chinese case, natural elements conveyed both particular emotions and referred to specific imperial families or events. Nature operated as a kind of alternative language which could be used to exchange feeling with impunity.

Moore may have had reason to feel pursued or fear betrayal, but her natural emblems are so often accompanied by studied and exact references to the Chinese art of the connoisseur, or expensive European furniture, that it would be difficult to assign covert meanings to such distinct and numerous *objets d'art* apart from a quiet demand for reserve and gentility. Even Elizabeth Bishop noted in her memoir that 'the Moore *chinoiserie* of manners made giving presents complicated'.[103] In her foreword to *A Marianne*

---

[101] Jarrell, 'Her Shield', 180.   [102] Binyon, *The Spirit of Man*, 31.
[103] Bishop, 'Efforts of Affection', 134.

Moore Reader, Moore asks herself to explain her 'inordinate interest in animals' and replies: 'They are subjects for art and exemplars of it, are they not? minding their own business . . . [they] do not pry or prey—or prolong the conversation; do not make us selfconscious.'[104] This is the implied social understanding between her and her reader. Ironically enough, it is difficult to respond to Moore's poetry without responding to *her*. For a poet who has expended so much effort to occlude herself from her verse, never using 'I' but 'one' in that formal way, she succeeds in making her poems not personal, but peculiar to her, despite her apparent intention to withdraw. Possibly this is due to the very evident activity of the construction of her verse, each stanza so wrought and constrained, full of the kind of disparate detail that implies avid reading and a bibliographic temperament. Moore's is not passive poetry. Her 'attention to detail', according to Richard Howard, 'seemed, often, pathological'. 'Her strategies were so evasive, so deliberately oblique', he notes, 'for all the immediacy of her concern with the animal kingdom.'[105]

Moore's attention to detail, and the orientalist implications of that attention, will be discussed further in a later chapter. At this point, however, it is important to offer another kind of explanation for Moore's seemingly impersonal poetry, one which accounts for her studied avoidance of any autobiographical impulse. Andrew J. Kappel has identified a source of her expressive self-limitation when he observes that 'she would have considered such ambitions sinful'.[106] This may account for the way in which the reader recognizes a personal activity in her poetry, while the poetry constantly disappoints any desire to venture beyond the veneer of compulsive and contingent detail. Perhaps the conspicuous effort of Moore's poetry is generated by that very curtailment of self-expression to which Kappel refers. Or, as David Kalstone has put it, 'the morality is in the method, a way of seeing and celebrating the world of things'.[107] Jeredith

[104] *CPR* 552.
[105] Richard Howard, 'Marianne Moore and the Monkey Business of Modernism', 2.
[106] Andrew J. Kappel, 'Notes on the Presbyterian Poetry of Marianne Moore', in Patricia C. Willis (ed.), *Marianne Moore: Woman and Poet* (Orono, Maine: University of Maine Press, the National Poetry Foundation, 1990), 43.
[107] David Kalstone, *Becoming a Poet: Elizabeth Bishop with Marianne Moore and Robert Lowell* (London: Hogarth, 1989), 52.

Merrin offers a biographical basis for Moore's attraction to this
'way of seeing' when she opines that she 'conceived of her own
poetry as complementary to her brother's vocation'. 'The study
of nature for Moore is a religious act, akin to biblical exegesis',
she writes; 'her employment of natural history for devotional purposes is in accordance with the notion of God's "two books" ',[108]
i.e. the Bible and nature. There remains a suspicion, however, that
this practised humility is not habitual and may itself harbour some
tactical value. As Elizabeth Bishop relates, 'I believe she was
the only person I have ever known who "bridled" at praise,
while turning pink with pleasure.'[109] Granted, Moore's private
responses and her 'public' poetry are two different arenas, which
may corroborate and complement one another or offer divergent
impressions. Even Jeredith Merrin believes that the moral (and
the moral significance) of certain poems 'is almost a rebuke
to her own (and to her engrossed reader's) rapt absorption
in multiplicity and detail'.[110] The animals which did not make
Moore 'selfconscious' are, in Richard Howard's view, not merely
a benign foil for her art. 'She used this extraordinary manner of
apparently exact description to render, in what we might call
a zoophrasty or a zoophrasis, a world of suffused statement
about herself.'[111] On some level, too, she felt herself part of this
animal world. In her own self-description in *Predilections*, she
likens herself to 'an old hop toad', 'a lizard', 'a frog', and 'a
banana-nosed monkey'.[112] No doubt her affinity for the gentle,
tame creatures of the animal world prompted Jeredith Merrin
to describe Moore as 'a sort of declawed and adorable poetic
mascot',[113] and Alicia Ostriker to state that people think of her
as 'a sort of household pet'.[114]

---

[108] Jeredith Merrin, *An Enabling Humility: Marianne Moore, Elizabeth Bishop, and the Uses of Tradition* (New Brunswick, NJ and London: Rutgers University Press, 1990), 23.
[109] Bishop, 'Efforts of Affection', 134.
[110] Merrin, *An Enabling Humility*, 20.
[111] Howard, 'Marianne Moore and the Monkey Business of Modernism', 2–3.
[112] Moore, *Predilections* (New York: Viking, 1955), p. vii.
[113] Jeredith Merrin, 'Marianne Moore and Elizabeth Bishop', in Jay Parini (ed.) *The Columbia History of American Poetry* (New York: Columbia University Press, 1993), 348.
[114] Alicia Ostriker, 'Marianne Moore, the Maternal Hero, and American Women's Poetry', in Parisi (ed.), *Marianne Moore: The Art of a Modernist*, 55.

Whether by the use of Chinese supernatural creatures or ordinary animals, Moore worked very hard to assemble an elaborate camouflage to cloak and disguise emotion in her poetry and in her private life. Her use of animals, real or imaginary, as thinly veiled versions of herself is much like that in the fables she translated. She dwelt in the ladylike, genteel setting of another, and perhaps non-existent, world, where exotic lands were the stuff of fantasy and wonder. The components of that self-fashioned world clearly both confirmed and reinforced one another. This deliberate shelter, ironically, worked only to enlarge interest in what it was meant to protect. Natalie C. Barney, who met Moore only briefly, made plain in a letter of invitation the kind of increased interest that Moore's efforts of self-protective gentility generated:

> Miss Barney sera chez elle
> le Vendredi premier Janvier à 5h
>   et tous les Vendredis suivants . . .
>   should you ever come to Paris—
>
>   .   .   .   .
>
> Thrice protected, by aloofness, a mother, and a mind
> How can our human kind
> Reach you so far behind the blond light of your lashes
> and the coilings of your hair?[115]

[115] RL V:03:28. File: Correspondence.

4

America's Reading of Nature and the Panoramic Gaze of the *Fu*

The first step of a renaissance, or awakening, is the importa-
tion of models for painting, sculpture and writing. The last
century discovered the Middle Ages. It is possible that this
century may find a new Greece in China.

(Ezra Pound, from 'The Renaissance')

RETRIEVING THE ARCHAIC LITERARY MODEL OF THE *FU*

From about 1913, the year of the Armory Show in New York,
American poetry was subject to an increasingly international
influence. Marianne Moore had, before that time, already begun
her vast reading on Chinese subjects. Her poet contemporaries
were similarly delving into scholarly texts on the Far East. From
1901 to 1905, Ezra Pound, William Carlos Williams, and H. D.
were all at the University of Pennsylvania and reading widely in
Eastern literatures. *Poetry: A Magazine of Verse* was founded
in 1912 and published by Harriet Monroe in Chicago, and
Pound, as London editor, was promoting Imagism in its pages.
Of the several imperatives of this new poetic practice, which was
characterized by clarity, precision, and brevity, one feature was
decidedly not in keeping with American poetic traditions. In a
letter to William Carlos Williams of 21 October 1908, Pound articulated an early version of what became the Imagist Manifesto.
He wrote that one of its central tenets was a declared 'freedom
from didacticism'[1] and Wallace Stevens characterized it in much
the same way when he noted that 'Imagism was a mild rebellion

---

[1] *The Selected Letters of Ezra Pound 1907–1941*, (ed.) D. D. Paige (New York: Harcourt, Brace, 1950), 6.

against didacticism.'[2] American poets have continually been given to instructive, even preacherly, verse, a predictable outgrowth of America's Puritan past. Moore embraced many of the Imagist imperatives, and they remained consistent features of her poetry and prose throughout her writing career. However, 'freedom from didacticism' is the one Imagist demand to which she did not subscribe, and her adoption of another Far Eastern literary model, very different from the Imagist's Japanese haiku, is testament to her refusal to espouse all of the strictures of this poetic movement. The didactic quality of her poetry, coupled with her repeated call for precision and restraint in poetic writing, indicates her effort to adapt Imagist methods to the conditions of being an American poet committed to what she saw as a central component of American verse.

Moore can be seen as pursuing some of the literary ideals which she shared with other major literary figures of her time but in a distinctly different and unusual manner. Her original use of the Chinese *fu* style of poetry is one successful instance of her consistent ingenuity in finding and employing 'new' forms in her poetry. The *fu* accommodated some of the articulated principles of Imagism among other established Modernist creeds. As Liu Xie (*c.*465–522) remarked in his *Wen-xin tiao-long*:[3]

The reason for making 'ascension to the height' the peculiar quality of *fu* is that it is the sight of concrete objects which excites the emotions. Since the emotions have been excited by concrete objects, the ideas associated with the objects always remain clear; and since the objects are viewed with feeling, the language used to describe them is always beautiful. Beautiful language and clear ideas complement each other as the symbol and the symbolized. They are like red and purple silk in weaving, and black and yellow pigments in painting. The patterns, though mixed, possess substance, and the colors, though variegated, are fundamentally based. This is the main principle of the *fu* writing.[4]

---

[2] *Letters of Wallace Stevens*, (ed.) Holly Stevens (London: Faber & Faber, 1967), 302: letter to R. L. Latimer of 19 Dec. 1935.

[3] Liu Xie (or Yen-ho) wrote the *Wen-xin tiao-long* (The Literary Mind and the Carving of Dragons) to study the thought and patterns in Chinese literature. He sought to retrieve and reinstate orthodoxy in literary works and adherence to classical form.

[4] Liu Xie, 'Elucidation of *Fu*', in *The Literary Mind and the Carving of Dragons*, trans. Vincent Yu-chung Shih (Hong Kong: Chinese University Press, 1983), 95.

Chinese nature poetry as a whole often displays some urgency in its need to 'place' emotion, to parse a cluster of feelings and ally them with material objects, particular scenes or figures, and natural phenomena. While Moore was not the first modern poet to prefer a Far Eastern form for expressing feelings and truths found in observations of nature,[5] she used the model of the Chinese *fu* in distinctive ways. The self-conscious antiquarianism of her repeated borrowing of *fu* techniques exposes Moore's sense of the problematic nature of modernity, as she employed this ancient formal tributary model to pose questions about the moral and cultural significance of the present.

That Moore was aware of the form's origins and was keeping current with Chinese literary scholarship is revealed in her poem 'In Lieu of the Lyre' (1965) where we find the line: 'rime-prose revived also by word-wizard Achilles— | Dr. Fang'. Achilles Fang wrote his Harvard doctoral thesis (unpublished, 1958) on 'Materials for the Study of Pound's *Cantos*', which explored the relevant Chinese sources and elaborated upon their use in great detail. Fang was selected to write the introduction to Pound's *The Classic Anthology Defined by Confucius*, and an introduction to Pound's translation and commentary entitled *Confucius: The Great Digest and Unwobbling Pivot*. Moreover, Moore cites in her notes to 'Tom Fool at Jamaica' Achilles Fang's annotations to Lu Ji's (261–303) *Wen Fu* (Exposition on Literature), an incisive and enduring work of literary criticism dating from the latter part of the third century,[6] translated by Fang as 'Rhymeprose on Literature' in the *Harvard Journal of Asiatic Studies* in 1951. A copy of this article, as well as a revised version of it published in the Autumn 1952 issue of the *New Mexico Quarterly*, are among Moore's library holdings at the Rosenbach Library. Moore's revised copy is heavily annotated by her and signals the very detailed attention she gave to the subject. Her library also contains a presentation copy of *Studies in Chinese Literature* (1965) given to her by Achilles Fang some thirteen years later, revealing both her abiding interest in Chinese models and her continued

[5] I include in this observation translations of *fu*-style poems and English renditions or equivalences of Chinese poetry of various kinds.

[6] David Hsin-fu Wand, 'The Dragon and the Kylin: The Use of Chinese Symbols and Myths in Marianne Moore's Poetry', *Literature East and West*, 15/3 (1971), 473.

correspondence with Dr Fang. It is clear from her familiarity with his work and from her seeing it as important enough to include in her poems, that Moore took an enormous interest in Chinese literary scholarship and was aware of the resurrection of critical interest in the *fu* 'rime-prose' form in the twentieth century. The presence of *The Art of Letters; Lu Chi's 'Wen Fu', A.D. 302* (1951), a translation and comparative study by E. R. Hughes, among Moore's books makes it additionally inconceivable that the model for many of Moore's poems was not the *fu*.

Chinese literary critics have for centuries commented upon the relationship between man and nature in Chinese poetry, calling attention to the landscape or scenery (*jing*) created or depicted in the poem and its correspondence to human emotions (*qing*). From the earliest anthology of Chinese poems, the *Shi-qing* (Book of Poetry, *c*.1100–600 BC), nature, used as an analogy for human life and as a participant in and conveyor of human emotions, has been almost a commonplace. More than two millennia later, Hsieh Chen (1495–1575) wrote: 'Scenery is the go-between of poetry, emotion is the embryo of poetry. By combining them a poem is made.'[7] The word *fu* means 'display' or 'unfold' and, as a literary subgenre rather than a true verse form, the *fu* has no consistent formal characteristics.[8] In fact, Pauline Yu describes the *fu* as one of several 'rhetorical trope[s]' and cites a T'ang dynasty commentary to support her opinion that the *fu* 'should be viewed more correctly as a technique rather than a form'.[9] An ancient etymology provided by David Hawkes shows that the *fu* comes closest to the English word 'enumerate'[10] and, indeed, Han dynasty *fu* come 'perilously close to being little more than a catalogue of the names of plants, animals, birds, or what not', according to Burton Watson.[11] 'It

[7] Hsieh Chen, *Ssu-ming Shih-hua* 3.2b, cited in Hans Frankel, *The Flowering Plum and the Palace Lady: Interpretations of Chinese Poetry* (New Haven and London: Yale University Press, 1976), 1.

[8] James J. Y. Liu, *The Art of Chinese Poetry* (London: Routledge & Kegan Paul, 1962), 34.

[9] Pauline Yu, *The Reading of Imagery in the Chinese Poetic Tradition* (Princeton, NJ: Princeton University Press, 1987), 105 and 57.

[10] David Hawkes, 'The Quest of the Goddess', in Cyril Birch (ed.), *Studies in Chinese Literary Genres* (Berkeley, Los Angeles, and London: University of California Press, 1974), 64.

[11] Burton Watson, *Early Chinese Literature* (New York and London: Columbia University Press, 1962), 262.

was the function of the *fu* to give exhaustive lists of the trees, plants, fish, etc. that made up the scene being described', he wrote in *Chinese Lyricism*.[12] This urge towards facts, objects, and animals, as well as the need to cite their provenance or map their location, is also a distinctly American concern. Catalogues and lists of American scenes and objects are as typical of early Americans writing about a 'new' country as they are of the poetry of Whitman and, later, Moore.

'*Fu*-style' poems typically explore the reciprocity between man and the natural world and deduce from observations of this inter-action an abstract notion or eternal verity. Often the final four lines are set off metrically and stylistically from the remainder of the poem, forming a *luan* or coda, which approximates to a song or short lyric poem.[13] The purpose of this final utterance is to reprimand or instruct, as many well-known Han writers of the *fu* (for example, Ssu-Ma Hsiang-ju, 179–118 BC, and Yang Xiong, 53 BC–AD 18) and historians of the time (for example, Sima Qian, Ban Gu) have attested.[14] The sacerdotal gravity of much of Marianne Moore's *fu*-inspired poems resembles this aspect of some of the early *fu*, moral precepts being easily recognized as her signature form. However, it is clear from surviving specimens that, despite its frequent compliance with the 'rules' of this par-ticular format, the *fu* did vary somewhat in its intentions and its success in adhering to this didactic model. Some degree of emphasis is often placed upon one or more of its features. Pauline Yu observes much the same mixture of the traditional attributes of the *fu*: 'Certainly Qu Yuan's "Encountering Sorrow" (or *Li Sao*) traditionally acknowledged as the ancestor of the *fu*, can hardly be said to be bent on a literal depiction of the natural world', she writes, 'and the breathtaking catalogues of objects in later expositions seem more intent on incantation, persuasion, or demonstrations of power than mere description.'[15]

The *fu* form, while distinctively Chinese and characterized by a rather rigid, complex metre and several rhyming devices, shares certain features with Romantic poetry. Romantic poetry

---

[12] Watson, *Chinese Lyricism: Shih Poetry from the Second to the Twelfth Century, with Translations* (New York: Columbia University Press, 1971), 133.

[13] Hans Frankel, *The Flowering Plum*, 3.

[14] Watson, *Early Chinese Literature*, 263.

[15] Yu, *Reading of Imagery*, 120.

likewise often shows the relationship between man's creative imagination and the natural world, connecting intimately, through
a heightened vision of external nature, with life's deepest issues.
Wordsworth's vision of the leech-gatherer in 'Resolution and
Independence', who 'Like a sea-beast crawled forth . . . not all
alive nor dead, | Nor all asleep', provides such an example of
that poetic imagination lending meaning to the external world and
natural events. Romantic poems often imbue ordinary objects or
scenes with a sense of mystery and wonder. The initial vision of
the leech-gatherer places him within Wordsworth's imagination
as a core around which the leech-gatherer's woeful tale gathers
meaning, encysting a commonplace encounter within layers
of accretive significance. English Romanticism has exerted an
abiding influence upon American poets to locate in the American
landscape a sense of historical origins and national coherence.
Richard Gray has remarked upon this connection:

Romanticism also encouraged Americans to find consolation in nature
for their alleged lack of culture; or, to be more accurate, it prompted
them to celebrate nature as the true embodiment of their culture—its
openness, its air of possibility, and its innocence. As one historian has
commented, nineteenth-century Americans 'if challenged to produce some
present sign of American greatness . . . could always expatiate on nature
. . . Nature meant many things—the sheer bigness of the country, the
novelty of its fauna and flora, the abundance of life, the sense of room
to spare'.[16]

The *fu* is ideally suited to observing the proliferation of natural
detail from which Moore's poetic commentaries on what constitutes America and Americanness emerge.

Moore peruses rather than inhabits her subjects, examining their
exterior to speculate about their interiors, a method of scrutiny
resembling less a Keatsian interiority than the self-conscious
Imagination of Wordsworth or Coleridge.[17] This is analogous to
a distinction made by John Bayley when he wrote that 'whereas
Keats's participation is instinctive and unrehearsed, expressing
itself in poetry as naturally as the bird does in its movements,

---

[16] Richard Gray, *American Poetry of the Twentieth Century* (London and New
York: Longman, 1990), 12, and quoting from Marcus Cunliffe, *The Nation Takes
Shape 1789–1837* (Chicago, 1959), 135.
[17] John Bayley, *The Romantic Survival* (London: Constable, 1957), 10.

Coleridge's curiosity is analytic—what fascinates him is the nature of his own mental and creative process'.[18] Clearly, Moore is to be located on the Coleridgean side of this distinction. Her poems exhibit a premeditation which prohibits a Keatsian spontaneity. Perhaps this is why her calculated imagery sometimes seems alien to, incongruous, or even at odds with any discernible message which resonates from her poems. Moore's poems are, as Liu Xie's ancient treatise on Chinese literary theory points out about the *fu*, 'works whose themes are plants, animals, and other miscellaneous things, they express feelings which arise in response to external situations, feelings which are reactions to chance experiences with various scenes'.[19] While the Romantic relationship to landscape is fundamentally aesthetic, the *fu* uses landscape as a backdrop, as scenery. Like the '*fu*-style' poems, the axiomatic distillation which Moore arrives at is not personal and special to the poet as it is in much Romantic poetry. Its dictates apply generally, are recognizable as containing kernels of wisdom which the reader is invited to recognize and accept as truth. What is initially perceived as a conventional description of nature, progressing towards a traditional Romantic disclosure of universal truth inhering in natural scenes, becomes more of an eclectic itinerary through a sampler of the strange.

Moore's *fu*-inspired poems exhibit the kind of authority and didacticism which often characterize an ancient poetry. The *fu* was first formulated as a literary form in the writing of the Ancient Poets and enlarged upon in the *Chuci* (the ancient Chinese *Elegies of Ch'u*).[20] Tracing the evolution of the form is hindered by the fact that the putative survivals of the *fu*, which are claimed by some to be the earliest extant examples of the form, cannot be dated with any reasonable accuracy. The anonymity of the first practitioners of the *fu*, and the impossibility of dating its first appearance as a literary technique, augment the sense of its historical longevity. The return to ancient models or revivalism, embodied by the Chinese term *fu-gu*, became a strategem relied upon for effecting radical stylistic redirection. This idea would

---

[18] Ibid. 10.   [19] Liu Xie, 'Elucidation of *Fu*', 93.

[20] The *Elegies of Ch'u* were compiled in the second century AD, but are dated from the Kingdom of Ch'u which flourished from the seventh to the third centuries BC. The *Elegies* have shamanistic origins as songs of tribute and placation to various gods.

have been familiar to Moore through her intimate scholarly acquaintance with works on Chinese poetry and painting, as it continually informs the history and evolution of both media from ancient times. *Fu-gu*, or 'return to ancient verities', is a method of achieving transformation and change and is applied generally to stylistic changes in the Chinese arts, particularly painting. Change for its own sake seeks the new; *fu-gu* enacts change for the sake of returning to precedents in order to revive and revitalize. *Fu-gu* is a revolutionary creed though, at the same time, takes on puritanical overtones. Radical technical innovation coupled with the resurrection of ancient models permits a return to the past in order that the new may emerge. *Fu-gu* is a theory of simultaneous reclamation and renewal.[21] Through the process of *fu-gu*, the immensities of time spanned in Chinese literary periodization are incorporated into the historical reference of the revived *fu*. In this way, Moore's messages are corroborated and lent an authenticity both by her retrieval of an archaic poetic form and by her repeated disclosure of the many links which ally her poetry to an ancient culture. One could describe her poems as translations, or versions of Chinese literary forms and cultural elements, rendered into a distinctly personal utterance.

The *fu* assumed various forms at first, but was from its beginnings differentiated from poetry. The *fu*, while originating in music and dance, was very early distinguished from other poetic forms by being recited or chanted rather than sung.[22] 'Moreover', as Arthur Waley has noted, 'rhyme was something used as an ornament to prose . . . but without that definite pattern of rhythm which distinguishes verse from prose.'[23] Like the Imagists and the practitioners of the *fu*, Moore in her poetry exhibits a sustained use of a form of free verse within a very exacting structure. Her syllabic verse does not create its own rhythm and, therefore, the reader's attention is called to prose rhythms within the poem. As Moore makes clear in her essay, 'Feeling and Precision' (1944), 'you don't devise a rhythm, the rhythm is the person, and the sentences but a radiograph of personality'. 'The following

---

[21] For a discussion of this see Wen Fong, *Images of the Mind* (Princeton, NJ: The Art Museum, 1984), particularly ch. 1, section 4.

[22] Arthur Waley, *The Temple and Other Poems* (London: George Allen & Unwin, 1923), 15.

[23] Ibid. 11.

principles, however, are aids to composition by which I try, myself, to be guided', she wrote: 'if a long sentence with dependent clauses seems obscure, one can break it into shorter units by imagining into what phrases it would fall as conversation.'[24] Her conversational rhythms combine with an internal, subdued rhyme, resulting in a combination which, like the *fu*, could be characterized by the term 'poetic essay'. Indeed Moore's marginalia in her own copy of Achilles Fang's article on rhymeprose in the *New Mexico Quarterly* highlights her interest in the *fu* as 'indirectly substantiating the possibility that verse can be so natural the listener or reader is not aware that it is not prose'.[25] Some sinologists regard the *fu* as 'rhymeprose' or 'poetic essay', primarily because it had been used by the purported originator of the form, the renowned poet and statesman, Qu Yuan (*c*.332–295 BC). Most *fu*, however, were written by professional scholars or officials at the imperial court, or by feudal princes.[26]

As with Marianne Moore's poems, the lines of a *fu* are consistently of unequal length. This, for Chinese poetry, is far more of a departure than for English verse, in that Chinese verse usually subscribes to strict rules and regularized forms. However, this is not to suggest that there is no fixed rhythm in the *fu*. The rhythm in the *fu* is sustained until a cohesive paragraph of verse is formed. Irregularity, however, rather than the predictability of an unchanging form adhering to fixed poetic principles, seems to characterize the *fu*.[27] It is often diffuse and discursive rather than gathered and focused.

Moore's poems, similarly, rove from site to site, animal to animal. This kind of all-inclusive seeing is the poetic 'pictorial' expression, or in Stephan Oettermann's terms the ' "symbolic form" ', of 'a specifically modern, bourgeois view of nature and the world'. This panoramic viewing in her poems has a didactic purpose similar to the panorama itself, as 'both a surrogate for nature and a simulator, an apparatus for teaching people how to see it'.[28] There remains an amusing, if slightly disturbing,

---

[24] Marianne Moore, 'Feeling and Precision', in *Predilections* (New York: Viking, 1955), 3.
[25] RL, p. 269 in Moore's copy.   [26] Watson, *Early Chinese Literature*, 268.
[27] Waley, *The Temple and Other Poems*, 15.
[28] Stephan Oettermann, *The Panorama: History of a Mass Medium* (New York: Zone Books, 1997), 7, 12.

migratory insistence in Moore's continuous poetic journeying to relocate the subject, for which the reader is not forewarned by either logic or expectation. The *fu* often indulges in this kind of seemingly undisciplined natural roaming as well. Historically, *fu* often observe the unpredictability and inexplicability of contemporary situations. Jia Yi's (*c*.200–168 BC) *fu* contain examples of these, as does 'Encountering Sorrow' (*Li Sao*), putatively authored by Qu Yuan.[29] Historically speaking, the *fu* has accommodated combinations of verse and prose, functioning as an elastic framework for an expository description of nature in addition to a sometimes confrontational, epigrammatic *luan* or conclusion.[30] Both the *fu* and Moore's poems share a preoccupation with natural subjects, and combine features associated with both verse and prose. Interestingly, as Hellmut Wilhelm notes, 'the term *fu* has been quite aptly translated as "prose-poetry"', and has over time been classified with first poetry and then prose genres.[31]

NATURALIZING THE EXOTIC

Moore returns in many of her poems, and in particular to those having to do with Chinese subjects, to what is rare and even exotic in nature and in natural depictions in art, assembling an inventory of the uncommon. The *fu*, likewise, developed a preoccupation with such *rarae aves* as unicorns, giraffes, hummingbirds, parrots, peacocks, and other unique animals and bizarre plants.[32] As Arthur Waley has observed of an early *fu*:

In the reign of the Emperor Ho of the latter Han dynasty, an attempt was made by influential citizens of Ch'ang-an to get the court moved back from Lo-yang to Ch'ang-an. The historian and poet Pan Ku, who had no desire to migrate to the west accordingly wrote his famous *fu*, *The Two Capitals*, in which, after a stranger from the west has described the wonders of Ch'ang-an, its temples, palaces, zoological gardens and aviary . . .[33]

[29] David R. Knechtges, 'Two Studies on the Han Fu', *Parerga*, 1, Seattle: University of Washington Far Eastern and Russian Institute (1968), 14.
[30] Frankel, *The Flowering Plum*, 3.
[31] Hellmut Wilhelm, 'The Scholar's Frustration: Notes on a Type of *Fu*', in John K. Fairbank (ed.), *Chinese Thought and Institutions* (Chicago: University of Chicago Press, 1957), 310.
[32] Waley, *The Temple and Other Poems*, 18.   [33] Ibid. 17.

From the *Chuci* poems to the Han dynasty *fu* there is a distinct predilection for exotic animals and landscapes. Burton Watson, in describing probable reasons for the unfamiliarity of many great *fu*, could easily be describing a version of Moore's 'method' of acquiring arcane knowledge of strange and sometimes lost species when he wrote:

Several of the great *fu* writers, among them Ssu-ma Hsiang-ju, were also lexicographers, and it has been suggested that they composed their poems with a brush in one hand and a dictionary in the other. Perhaps the literary men of the day made a kind of game of collecting the names of odd trees, minerals, birds, or what not, which they then worked into their compositions . . . Since the purpose of the poem obviously is not to convey scientific data, but purely to build up a fabric of rich and exuberant verbiage . . .[34]

Another excellent example of this kind of abundantly descriptive *fu* is Ssu-Ma Hsiang-ju's 'The Shang-lin Park'.[35] Accuracy in these panoramic *fu* was not a first priority and certainly succeeded suasion as a literary imperative. Moore amasses and assembles similar foreign, imaginal material from her wide reading and explorations into Chinese art and mythology. Her approach is panoramic in terms of the breadth and variety of subject-matter but is, at the same time, concerned with the particularity and vital accuracy of her observations as well. She acclimatizes the reader to the fantastic imaginary world of Chinese symbology by treating the magical with familiarity, making it material and palpable. She tries to cull from an imaginary experience of the exotic a tangible translation of the fabulous.

The influences Moore seems to have absorbed from the *fu*, both in terms of structure and subject-matter, are distributed widely throughout her work and can be found in poems written both early and late in her career. That she includes descriptions of the natural opulence of exotic plant and animal life in her poems may also be due in some measure to her abiding interest in science and biology since her undergraduate days at Bryn Mawr. Also the interrelationships between the human and the natural were central to both the Confucian and Taoist traditions,

[34] Watson, *Early Chinese Literature*, 271.
[35] In Cyril Birch (ed.), *Anthology of Chinese Literature* (Harmondsworth: Penguin, 1967), 164–75.

philosophies which Moore studied and referred to in her prose
and poetry over the course of her writing career. Moreover, as
Hans Frankel has observed, 'it is in keeping with the conventions of the *fu* genre to devote an entire poem to a plant species
or some other natural object or phenomenon'.[36]

'Snakes, Mongooses, Snake Charmers, And The Like' (1922)
is a good example of a poem with a *fu*-style ending: 'The passion
for setting people right is in itself an afflictive disease. | Distaste
which takes no credit to itself is best.' In these final lines, Moore's
prose verse falls away and is replaced with standard verse, further
demarcating the change in emphasis and address which accompanies it. The ending contains references to 'that exotic asp and
the mongoose', uniting the *luan* and exotic animal imagery which
characterize the *fu* in a single poem. The poem, however, does
not allude to specifically Chinese symbology and it would seem
that Chinese references appear for the most part in poems which
do not contain axiomatic final refrains like the *luan*.

An exception to this may be found in 'Elephants', a long
paean to 'the Socrates of | animals' whose processional dignity
and massive restraint in captivity, '—a life prisoner but recon-
ciled', reminds the reader again of the wisdom of an ancient
survival, of what has remained from a more glorious and fitting
past, to take up without tribute or gratitude the life of submis-
sion and captivity. Courtly *fu*, in honour of elephants given as
gifts, survive from the T'ang dynasty.[37] It is possible that Moore
was aware of these precedents, but, in any case, her poem revives
the form, subject-matter, and impetus of the T'ang poets. Interestingly enough, an early manuscript version of 'Elephants' sur-
vives among Moore's papers, which reveals that it arose from
a descriptive prose piece barely differing from the final poem.[38]
Prose rhythms are seemingly established by a prose rendering of
'Elephants' which precedes the poetic version. The elasticity of
the *fu* can be witnessed in these successive manuscript stages as
prose is transformed into 'poetic essay'.

During the imperial seventh and eighth centuries of the
T'ang, the elephant was commonly thought of as a token of

[36] Frankel, *The Flowering Plum*, 5.
[37] Edward H. Schafer, *The Vermilion Bird: T'ang Images of the South* (Berkeley
and Los Angeles: University of California Press, 1967), 225.
[38] RL I:01:41. Published in *Marianne Moore Newsletter*, 5/2 (Fall 1981), 12–13.

vassalage.[39] Moore's choice of this image to embody her feelings
about restraint ('Amenable to what, matched with him, are gnat
| trustees, he does not step on them') is appropriate in this con-
text. In many ways the elephant in this poem mirrors the cause
of those lost or misplaced qualities of Chinese art which, as I
discuss in another chapter, she finds revived in the work of Henry
James. Here, however, lament overshadows restored hope even
as ward and warden are seen as interchangeable roles.

> His held-up foreleg for use
> as a stair, to be climbed or descended with
> the aid of his ear, expounds the brotherhood
> of creatures to man the encroacher, by the
> small word with the dot, meaning know—the verb bùd.
> These knowers 'arouse the feeling that they are
> allied to man' and can change roles with their trustees.

(from 'Elephants')

The elephant is thought by the Chinese to be an animal with
exceptional moral standards and riding upon one (*qi xiang*)
symbolizes happiness (*ji xiang*).[40] Another uncollected poem,
'Diligence Is to Magic as Progress Is to Flight' (1915), explores
the use of the elephant for the 'substance' of speed rather than
the 'semblance' of it.

> Speed is not in her mind inseparable from carpets.
> Locomotion arose
> In the shape of an elephant, she clambered up and
> chose
> To travel laboriously . . .

In 'Melancthon' (1919), originally titled 'Black Earth' (1918)[41],
Moore encloses herself in elephant skin ('This elephant skin | which
I inhabit') and gathers 'spiritual poise' and protection from it:

> Will
> depth by depth, thick skin be thick, to one who can see no
> beautiful element of unreason in it?

[39] Schafer, *The Vermilion Bird*, 226.
[40] Wolfram Eberhard, *Chinese Symbols: A Dictionary of Hidden Symbols in Chinese Life and Thought*, trans. G. L. Campbell (London and New York: Routledge & Kegan Paul, 1986), 94.
[41] Moore, 'Black Earth', *The Egoist*, 4 (Apr. 1918), 55.

Under the T'ang dynasty, the Chinese learned elephant legends from South Asians who advised them to take elephant skins with them on ocean voyages to protect themselves from the fearful *kau* dragons.[42] These insights tend to corroborate an initial reading of the poem rather than reveal disguised or hidden meanings.

Marianne Moore, in poems like 'Critics and Connoisseurs' and 'Nevertheless' (1943), exposes intimate linkages between natural and human experience which allow her to draw upon an order in nature to show us the ways by which we might restore order to human experience. Sometimes these frank, preceptive comments are situated within the poem, but we frequently find them visually set apart at the end of the poem, not necessarily as a separate stanza with a distinctly different syllabic arrangement, but as a question in another, penetrating, tone. The final lines of 'To A Giraffe' (1963) are a particularly good example of a poem which separates and indents the *luan* and alters both its syllabic arrangement and rhyming conventions. When writing about free verse in her article 'The Accented Syllable', Moore opined that 'so far as free verse is concerned, it is the easiest thing in the world to create one intonation in the image of another until finally one has assembled a bouquet of vocal exclamation points'.[43] The change of tone in which she addresses the reader, accompanied by the visual change of stanzaic pattern, often approximates to the requirements of the *luan* of the *fu*.

It is certainly possible that Moore derived this particular model from the *fu*-style poem which places its incisive, truistic statement, sometimes in the form of a question, at the end of the poem. Often, as I have pointed out, these gnomic utterances are separated either stylistically or visually from the text of the poem. Moore was undoubtedly acquainted with Ezra Pound's early translation of Li Po's[44] *fu*-style poem entitled 'Leave-Taking Near Shoku' which appeared in *Cathay* in 1915. This and other Chinese *fu*-style poems would have been included in anthologies[45] and certainly on the colophons of Chinese paintings, translations

---

[42] Schafer, *The Vermilion Bird*, 225.

[43] Moore, 'The Accented Syllable', *The Egoist*, 3/10 (Oct. 1916), 152.

[44] Li Po (701–62) was one of the foremost T'ang dynasty poets.

[45] See e.g. Arthur Waley's *The Temple and Other Poems* and *One Hundred and Seventy Chinese Poems* (London: George Allen & Unwin, 1946).

of which have appeared in art-historical works from that period, and Moore was an avid reader of these texts.

In 'Critics and Connoisseurs', Moore uses her observations of swans and ants to ask us to reflect upon the parallels between the posturing of the swan and the ant's transporting a useless burden. Animated nature is seen as replete with both an activity and a constancy which reflect human behaviour. We can distinguish between the changes of tone in this poem and notice that the last stanza functions very much like a *luan*.

> What is
> there in being able
> to say that one has dominated the stream in an attitude
> of self-defense;
> in proving that one has had the experience
> of carrying a stick?

The linear arrangement of these lines within the last stanza separates them graphically as a symmetrically expanding and collapsing shape, calling attention to its distinct difference of address and import. As in 'O To Be A Dragon', lineation in Moore's poems often echoes the spatio-temporal relationships within the poem as well.

This typographical sequestration is crucial to Moore's poetry, because for her the stanza becomes the poetic unit rather than the line. With the *fu* as well, as I have pointed out, the poetic unit comprised a coherent paragraph of verse. The separations between stanzas in Moore's work utilize space and distance as pauses within lines of verse, deliberately retarding the progress of the poem in much the same way that her compounds condense meaning and increase the pace of reading and referring. Marjorie Perloff has commented upon the source and importance of the visual presentation of poems of this kind, citing William Carlos Williams's poems as 'a verbal text to be *seen* at least as much as to be heard'. She emphasizes that 'the typographical lay-out of the page was not a sideline, some sort of secondary support structure, but a central fact of poetic discourse'.[46] It is interesting to note in Moore's poems how the *luan* are presented, how the typographical format is utilized to enhance a change in

---

[46] Marjorie Perloff, *The Dance of the Intellect: Studies in the Poetry of the Pound Tradition* (Cambridge: Cambridge University Press, 1985), 105.

tone and mood or the ways in which it serves to camouflage what becomes a suprising and abrupt ending. The transition between Moore's exotic collocation of natural facts and the moral application they arrive at make this Chinese poetic technique particularly well suited to her simultaneous affinity for a seemingly self-multiplying detail and the didactic imperative which she extracts from it.

MORAL SUASION AND THE *LUAN*

The preceptive *luan* of the *fu* ensured an ethical dimension to each of the poems written according to this model. For Moore, this feature of the *fu* accommodated her almost Puritan tendency to moralize. Even the poetic illustrations which determinedly progress toward these ethical distillations in her poems resemble a kind of moral fable or sermon. This quality of her poetry is not suprising given her Christian background and clerical family ties. Puritanism exerted a powerful and lasting influence on American sensibilities. That Moore treats natural facts as emblems, as symbolic of some profound underlying truth, is typically Puritan and, consequently, very much American as well. The panoramic descriptions in her *fu*-style poems similarly display her willingness to interpret the physical world as a series of moral signs. American poets have traditionally been described as experimenters and preachers. Moore's use of the *fu* and its *luan* shows that, even when employing this foreign and archaic technique, she still fulfils each of these expectations.

Even when compared with Li Po's *fu*-style poems, Moore's poems are often more explicit in conveying, through their *luan*-like epigrams, what she has gathered from her penetrating study of animals and plants. She points, through incisive questions and conclusions, to what it is she wants her audience to ponder, a movement from apprehension towards reflection which typifies meditative verse. 'Aphorism', she writes in 'Ichor of Imagination' (1937), 'is one of the kindlier phases of poetic autocracy.'[47] Her messages are distilled and pointed, and provide a moving contrast to the harmless and benign natural subjects that illustrate

---

[47] Marianne Moore, 'Ichor of Imagination', in *Predilections*, 128.

her aphorisms. In viewing human affairs in natural terms, using the natural scene as a point of departure for reflections and meditations on life, Moore entwines the subject and import of her poems, presenting her 'truths' as if they were as unassailable as the natural emblems which convey them.

In 'Peter' (1924), the unidentified, slippery animal spurs observations upon what distinguishes the human and the natural:

> Profound sleep is not with him a fixed illusion.
> Springing about with froglike accuracy, with jerky cries
> when taken in hand, he is himself again;
> to sit caged by the rungs of a domestic chair
> would be unprofitable—human. What is the good of hypocrisy?

'He' is admired for neglecting to display his ability to talk and, as if justifying his behaviour to an imaginary audience, Moore anticipates and rebukes the critic with axiomatic justification: 'He can talk but insolently says nothing. What of it? | When one is frank, one's very presence is a compliment.' What applies to animals is equally valid and unilaterally applicable to both man and nature. Moore highlights this as a sign, not of mankind's separation from nature or natural laws, but of an acknowledgement that when man is relieved from natural duties associated with self-preservation, has escaped from the exigencies of survival, he will lapse. Only man has the luxury, and perhaps the audacity, to engage in 'unprofitable' behaviour. The adage Moore ends with is neutral, 'one', and has a kind of pan-creationist applicability.

In other poems, like 'The Monkey Puzzle' (1925) and 'Snakes, Mongooses, Snake Charmers, And The Like', we again find something very similar to the *luan* of the *fu*, with the terse, preceptive phrase withheld until the end. 'Bowls', too, with observations about Chinese lacquer carvings and magazine publishers, uses analogies between the artistic and the natural world ('the pins planted in wild duck formation', 'like the ant and the spider | returning from time to time to headquarters') to pare her message down to a distilled, proverbial utterance: 'since he who gives quickly gives twice | in nothing so much as in a letter.' This particular poem reveals the way in which Moore extracts the wisdom which governs the natural world and finds its consonant reiteration in natural depictions in art. It displays a consistent trait within American poetry to read nature, and in Moore's case natural depictions as well, as though it were comprised of moral facts. The American landscape has traditionally been conceived as a text that could be read, as if the terrain itself was capable of disclosing moral truths and certainties. Many of Moore's poems simultaneously represent natural (animal and vegetative) and human truths as if they were commensurate or identical. Even the behaviour of animals, of which she was a dedicated student,[48] is offered up as a moral paradigm. Moore recognizes a seminal truth borne out by the patterns of growth and behaviour in nature and rediscovers a version of it in Chinese *objets d'art* and collectors' curios, nature having found thereby its adequate imitation in art.

Short epigrams can often be found both within and at the conclusion of Moore's poems, and many of them offer classical, generic advice. In addition to those previously mentioned, these are some typical examples which appear at the end of poems and function as *luan*:

> Don't be envied or
> armed with a measuring rod.
>
> ('His Shield', 1944)
>
> Because the heart is in it all is well.
>
> ('The Web One Weaves of Italy', 1954)
>
> Certainly the means must not defeat the end.
>
> ('Values In Use', 1956)
>
> Great losses for the enemy
> can't make the owner's loss less hard.
>
> ('Tippoo's Tiger', 1967)

These unsentimental *luan* or endings resemble the Confucian *Analects* (*Lun Yu*, c.500 BC) in their cryptic fragmentariness which testifies to an often profound incompleteness or under-statement. Moore's library contains a 1938 copy of *The Analects of Confucius* translated by Arthur Waley and heavily annotated. Literary modernism itself was intrigued by, almost fetishized,

---

[48] Moore's library and files of clippings and notes are littered with texts on animals (particularly ones devoted to animals about which she writes, e.g. elephants) and references to animal behaviour and locomotion, in addition to detailed accounts of the differences between members of the same species and how they developed in different countries and climates.

the fragment. The *Analects* themselves are, like the Bible, the transmitted words of disciples, and Confucius clarifies the difference between his writings and authentic authorship when, in the *Analects*, he remarks: 'I transmit but do not innovate. I trust and devote myself to the study of the ancients.'[49] Ezra Pound corresponded with Moore about this in a letter dated 29 January 1952: 'if the esteemed ed eggregia Marianne will merember [*sic*] that Kung did not claim invention but transmission only'.[50] ('Kung' is a transliteration of the first syllable of the Chinese pronunciation of the name which those unfamiliar with Chinese know as 'Confucius'.) The poetic terseness characteristic of these epigrams indicate that they were intended to be, as Stephen Owen has observed, 'indices of some depth held in reserve'.[51] Moore's epigrammatic endings, while finding justification and explication in the text of her poem, likewise promote savouring and reflection. Owen reminds us that one of the most forceful characteristics of the fragment is its 'concentration of value'. Because the fragment implicates something more than itself', he notes, 'it often seems to possess qualities of repleteness and intensity'.[52] Moore discloses her fragmentary sayings with the manner and brevity which declare them to be such, forming a nexus through which the reader can thread multiple plausible meanings and interpretations. As with the elliptical techniques Moore uses, she relays the immediacy of her often imaginary encounters with nature through a vigorously phrased, fragmentary presentation. Her natural emblems become vehicles for the conventional truth of the moral traditionalist. Moreover, this continual movement from proliferation to compression, from a demand for accuracy and detail on the one hand and the impulse to find an ethical imperative in discrete phenomena on the other, is also a distinctly Emersonian strategy. Inevitably, too, Moore's poetics, like Emerson's, is prone to imbalances, when exempla and moral are not adequate to one another.

[49] Confucius, *Lunyu zhenyi* (The Analects with Exegesis), (ed.) Liu Baonan in vol. i of *Zhuzi jicheng* (Collection of Classics), 7:1, 134. Cited and trans. by Zhang Longxi in *The Tao and the Logos: Literary Hermeneutics, East and West* (Durham, NC and London: Duke University Press, 1992), 13.

[50] RL V:51:01.

[51] Stephen Owen, *Remembrances: The Experience of the Past in Classical Chinese Literature* (Cambridge, Mass. and London: Harvard University Press, 1986), 69.

[52] Ibid. 73.

As I have pointed out, Marianne Moore's *fu*-inspired poems often have didactic and authoritative messages and sometimes follow a somewhat reasoned 'argument' supported and illustrated by observations of natural and familiar phenomena. The reader may feel the focus of the urgings of persuasion or that a lesson is being pressed home. In Moore's poems this often takes the form of a dialogue engaged in with an absent subject. An excellent example of this may be found in 'Critics and Connoisseurs' where the poem elaborates upon the natural illustrations which accompany several preceptive observations: 'There is a great amount of poetry in unconscious | fastidiousness', the poem begins, and explores the undeterred concentration which characterizes the efforts of a child to make a puppy stand on its wobbly legs. Following a description of a feeding swan in Oxford, Moore again translates natural into human significance: 'I have seen this swan and | I have seen you; I have seen ambition without | understanding in a variety of forms.' It is the final query, to which I called attention earlier, which arrives at an all-embracing question. 'What is | there in being able | to say that one has dominated the stream in an attitude | of self-defense; | in proving that one has had the experience | of carrying a stick?' Moore fastidiously gathers the filaments of an insistent, connected argument, pursuing throughout the poem a single, elaborated strand of meaning. The confident mottoes with which she finalizes so many of her poems further display the surety of a singular point of view.

Another good example is 'The Monkey Puzzle' where Moore hovers between nature and art ('A conifer contrived in imitation of the glyptic work of jade and | hard-stone cutters'), sifting through the attributes of plant and animal life by examining those places where they meet and where divisions between them break down: 'this pine-tree, this pine-tiger, is a tiger, not a dog'. Plants and animals meet and merge and are translated and appraised for 'society', given a correspondence in 'this bypath of curio-collecting'. 'The Monkey Puzzle' narrows the focus of these observations, finally, to light upon, among other things, what separates man and nature from God: 'we prove, we do not explain our birth'. Moore scales the intricate network of phylae and genera and interpolates those to which she has no access—explanations and justifications for natural and human existence, life's meaning and mystery, she acknowledges, exceed 'our' capabilities. Like natural phenomena, 'we' are facts.

It is certainly possible that Moore found in the origins of the *fu* an appropriate form for her disquisitive poetic forays. While it remained a highly malleable technique, the *fu* retained aspects of its suasive origins. Arthur Waley cites a source for this:

> Though at any rate in the Han dynasty the *fu* was used for almost every kind of poetic purpose—lyrical, narrative, reflective and satirical—yet it is, I think, true to say that at all periods it tends to show one characteristic intimately connected with its origins: the *fu* was originally a spell. In its purely magical form it is derived from the hymns by the recitation of which the priests of Ch'u compelled the gods to descend from Heaven and manifest themselves to their worshippers. In its second form it is an incantation [e.g. Qu Yuan's *Nine Hymns*] addressed to an earthly god, the poet (not by argument nor even by rhetoric, but by a purely sensuous intoxication of rhythm and language) entices to a particular act of worship . . . by the same exploitation of word-magic, the poet sought to influence the decisions of his sovereign in purely secular affairs.[53]

While Marianne Moore's poems show little evidence of a shamanistic intent to cast magical spells upon her reader or to induce a kind of Dionysian euphoria to bring about changes of opinion, her work does exhibit hortatory traits and purposes which are expressed in the *fu* style.

Burton Watson has discussed elements of debate which many *fu* genre poems share, and several of Moore's poems, particularly 'Critics and Connoisseurs', resemble this aspect of the *fu*. Watson cites the famous *fu* of Sung Yu (fl. *c.*275), *The Wind*, and observes that 'the poem is actually in the form of a debate, a form so often used in the *fu* that some scholars have even attempted to derive the *fu* genre from the florid debates and speeches of the diplomats and rhetoricians of the Warring States period.'[54] Often, however, the moralistic message is not as available as it is in the *luan*, and there are many instances of *fu* in which no didactic purpose exists or where the *luan* appears as an afterthought or quaint adage. Moore's 'Elephants' provides a good example of the latter: 'Who rides on a tiger can never

---

[53] Waley, *The Temple and Other Poems*, 16–17.
[54] Watson, *Early Chinese Literature*, 263.

dismount; | asleep on an elephant, that is repose.' Here we find
a homily which leaves behind much of the subtle wisdom and
pregnant observation expressed within the poem. One of the
challenges presented by both the early *fu* and Moore's poems
lies in determining which poetic aims the author considered most
important to a particular poem and which ancillary. The blend
of admonishment with respect to purely descriptive elements often
helps to expose the poet's hierarchy of concerns.[55]

We can determine, even from this brief discussion, that Moore
did not imitate the *fu*, but more likely appropriated certain
essential features from this ancient model in its formative stages
and incorporated them in very different and original ways into
her poetry throughout her lifetime. Wai-lim Yip has drawn a
connection between the '*flight* or excursion theme' in the Ch'u
songs (where the *fu* originated) and the epistemological search-
ings we find in Western verse, both yielding similar discursive,
explanatory methods.[56] Moore's musings upon the workings of
the imaginal and natural world she encounters encompass both of
these Western and Eastern themes or quests. It would seem that
efforts to firmly locate the origins of poetic influence in Moore's
work are not in every instance clearly or solely attributable to
single, unalloyed sources.

She seems, in fact, to have borrowed features from the *fu* which
did not outlast its history as a living, literary subgenre. As Burton
Watson has noted:

Some poets, in the manner of Jia Yi, used the *fu* form to pour out
their private thoughts and feelings; others employed it to describe a
particular object—a tree, a bird, a musical instrument. But many of the
fu continued to be on the same grand scale . . . and to concern themselves with public functions, hunts, sacrifices, or descriptions of the
capital . . . In time, however, the *fu* developed new styles, adopted new
themes, and was imbued with new life and inspiration.[57]

Moore's poems assimilate certain tendencies in choice of subject-
matter and format which we find particularly prevalent in early

[55] Watson, *Early Chinese Literature*, 269.
[56] Wai-lim Yip, *Chinese Poetry: Major Modes and Genres* (Berkeley, Los
Angeles, and London: University of California Press, 1976), 73.
[57] Watson, *Early Chinese Literature*, 284. The spelling of Jia Yi's name has been
converted from the Wade–Giles to the Pin Yin transliteration system for the sake of
conformity.

fu poems such as those described above. These examples from the early stages of the development of the *fu* are much like the ones we find appearing in translations published early on in her career (for example Pound's translation of 'Leave-Taking Near Shoku' and translations from the *Chuci*). Moore's *fu*-inspired poems share several distinctive features with Han dynasty *fu* in particular. Early in the Han, the *fu* emerged as a literary genre and quickly dominated literary expression for several important reasons.[58] Chief among these was the *fu*'s recognized suitability as a literary vehicle to voice veiled criticism or criticism 'by indirection'.[59]

In Chapter 1, I discussed the presence of the orientalist critique as a prominent feature of both English and American writing in Chinese styles. The *fu* was particularly appropriate as a didactic tool for this kind of project. The suasive qualities of the *luan*, or coda, coupled with the less confrontational, understated criticism of certain descriptive observations of the main 'text' of the *fu* (through implied comparison or the overt praise of qualities in nature which man does not share) create for Moore a rhetorical combination evidently suited to the preoccupations of her poetry. These critical and instructive effects of her *fu*-inspired poems are likewise achieved by means of the same literary procedures as those of the Han dynasty *fu*, namely quotation and display. As Hellmut Wilhelm observes:

From the very beginning it was endowed with certain features which have remained characteristic of this genre down to the present. Among them are its rather strict prosodic pattern, in rhythm as well as rhyme, its tendency to quote abundantly from earlier literature, especially the classics, its often highly sophisticated language, its general inclination to display the author's learning, and its wide use of metaphor and symbolism.[60]

The by-product of the use of the *fu* as an inspirational model was a prescriptive justification for Moore's already well developed tendency to display the spoils of her eclectic reading practice through quotation and exposition. A later chapter will analyse in greater depth the meaning of this degree of citation and

---

[58] Wilhelm, 'The Scholar's Frustration', 310.
[59] Ban Gu, *History of the Former Han* (*Han-shu*, *I-wen-chih*, pp. 58b–59a), cited and trans. Hellmut Wilhelm in 'The Scholar's Frustration', 313.
[60] Wilhelm, 'The Scholar's Frustration', 310.

enumeration. What is important to establish here is that the *fu* supplied Moore with a model which permitted her the range and scope to display her vast collection of exotic literary curios and a Chinese literary antecedent from which to launch her subtle critique of modernity. For, finally, it is contemporary facts to which Moore directs her readers' attention, and this consistent feature always overrides the idiosyncracy of her methods, lending primacy to the enduring moral agency of her poems in keeping with the prerogatives of American poetry. 'It is perhaps beside the point to examine novel aspects of successive phases of poetic expression, inherited poetry having been at one time new, and new poetry even in its eccentricities seeming to have its counterpart in the poetry of the past—in Hebrew poetry, Greek poetry, Chinese poetry', she wrote as early as 1926; 'that which is weak is soon gone; that which has value does, by some strange perpetuity, live as part of the serious continuation of literature.'[61]

---

[61] Moore, ' "New" Poetry Since 1912', in William Stanley Braithwaite (ed.), *Anthology of Magazine Verse for 1926* (Boston, Mass.: B. J. Brimmer, 1926), 179, and *CPR* 124.

5
Habits of Privacy, Habits of Thought

The Chinese have been idealists, and experimenters in the making of great principles; their history opens a world of lofty aim and achievement, parallel to that of the ancient Mediterranean peoples. We need their best ideals to supplement our own—ideals enshrined in their art, in their literature and in the tragedies of their lives.

We have already seen proof of the vitality and practical value of Oriental painting for ourselves and as a key to the Eastern soul. It may be worth while to approach their literature, the intensest part of it, their poetry, even in an imperfect manner.

> (Ernest Fenollosa, *The Chinese Written Character as a Medium for Poetry*)

'THERE MUST BE EDGES'

The *fu* technique was not only an original and unique 'find' among many Modernist excavations of foreign poetic models (for example, the haiku), it also provided Marianne Moore with a format with which to reinvent the verse forms which she had inherited. By adopting the *fu* style, Moore was able to retain certain attributes of traditional verse to which she still held some allegiance while, at the same time, resisting some of the more drastic contemporary trends which poets such as Ezra Pound were endorsing. While Imagism and Pound's ideogrammic method were finding adherents among early twentieth-century poets, Moore embraced another Far Eastern model which suited both her descriptive and didactic purposes. However, her adaptation of the *fu* technique permitted the application of some of Imagism's imperatives, namely dispensing with ordinary syntax and connectives. F. S. Flint's clarion call in 1913 to 'use absolutely no

word that did not contribute to the presentation[1] articulated
what was already a poetic premiss for Moore. This particular
dictate of Imagism was embodied in her concern for exactitude,
precision, and restraint. Apart from anomalous poems such as
' "Avec Ardeur" ' (1963) and 'To Victor Hugo of My Crow Pluto'
(1961), whose attenuated spareness is extreme in the context of
her entire poetic *œuvre*, Moore did not abide by Imagism's severe
and stringent principles in her compositions. In 'A Few Don'ts
for Imagists',[2] Pound wrote that a 'true poet is most easily distinguished from the false when he trusts himself to the simplest
expression and writes without adjectives'. Moore eschews excess
and the unnecessary and is always striving for linguistic parsimony
while continuing to concretize images, often with numerous and
unusual adjectival clues. She does, however, limit and sometimes
dispense with the ordinary connective tissue of poetry and prose,
embedding her descriptions within commas and quotation. The
result of this compression is a series of juxtaposed but independent verbal blocks, and the variety and disparity of each of
these segments lends her poems the abbreviated, pared quality
sought by so many poets whose 'excisions' were more pronounced.
Moore's poems offer an alternative method to Pound's 'direct
treatment of the "thing" '[3] by achieving a directness and direction
through an assembly of myriad exempla before proffering a con-
densed statement which unifies the import of her observations.
The strategies she learned from Chinese sources enabled her to
resist the proscriptions of Pound's directives without preventing
her from arriving at similar results. The *fu* technique permitted
Moore the descriptive latitude to display her meaning before
acknowledging it, and was only one device, among many, which
she located in Chinese poetry and language.

However, Moore was indebted to Pound for introducing Chinese
sources as a repository of models for writing, for it is unlikely
that her adoption of the *fu*, which she was drawn to independ-
ently, would have occurred had not the more general interest in

[1] F. S. Flint, 'Imagisme', *Poetry,* 1/6 (Mar. 1913).
[2] From Moore's summation of 'A Few Don'ts' in her commentary on Pound,
entitled ' "Teach, Stir the Mind, Afford Enjoyment" ', published in *Predilections* and
CPR 447–52.
[3] Ezra Pound, 'A Retrospect', in *Literary Essays,* (ed.) T. S. Eliot (London: Faber
& Faber, 1954), 3.

Chinese language and literature been established through Ernest
Fenollosa and, later, Pound. But Moore also adopted features
of the Chinese language and incorporated them into her poetry in
ways which departed from Pound's principles and were sometimes at variance with his instructive guidelines. These borrowings, in addition to her use of the *fu* technique, provided her with
the means to subvert conventional poetic practice as well as to
resist the pressures of contemporary trends and movements in
poetic circles. The procedures of Chinese language and its lack
of syntactic demand would have been easily discernible in translations, many of which Moore owned and read, as has been noted
in earlier chapters. Arthur Waley's and Ezra Pound's contribu-
tions alone account for many volumes of available translations
of verse from the earliest Chinese sources onward.[4]

The results of Moore's contact with these works can account
for a variety of different features of her poetry. An unusual poem
among them is 'O To Be A Dragon' which exhibits a range of
poetic traits which resemble the Chinese language. 'O To Be A
Dragon' soars and imaginatively expands just as its improbable
'If' places the poem from the outset in a context of unreality. It
is a poem of immediate imaginal experience ('If I, like Solomon
...') in which, without speaking in another voice through
quotation, we are linked with an ancient biblical past and an
unearthly, unpredictable heavenly power. The ellipses lend the
poem qualities of the fragment which is one of the more distinctive
features of Chinese literature. The poem is thereby riddled with
lacunae, disjunctive openings in the fabric of the text through
which we link with both the future, in the symbol of the dragon,
and with the past, 'like Solomon'. In the abiding presence of
space in this poem, historical time and memory are deposed and
replaced with longing, myth, and legend. The Chinese language
is also tenseless, and the temporal relation between 'events' is
established contextually, which lends a quality of indeterminacy
to Chinese writing before an order can be established. Often there
remains, as in 'O To Be A Dragon', more than one interpretive
possibility to a sequence of Chinese characters and, in many of
Moore's poems, she captures that temporal dispersion and lack
of certainty.

[4] See e.g. Waley's *Translations from the Chinese* (New York: Knopf, 1919).

Though it is unlikely that Marianne Moore was very familiar with Chinese words and idioms[5] (although she did use a Chinese word in a lay fashion in 'Nine Nectarines'), we can note some similarities with Chinese syntax in 'O To Be A Dragon'. Ellipsis and flexibility are two immanent attributes of a Chinese language characterized by disjunctive grammar and a lack of connectives. Absence of tense likewise leads words in Chinese to be only loosely committed to one another. These features allow for a certain degree of syntactical ambiguity and open up even the most rudimentary associations (for example cause and effect) to interpretation. Wai-lim Yip has described the scope and range of meanings which these features of Chinese language allow:

This syntactic freedom promotes a kind of prepredicative condition wherein words, like objects in the real-life world, are free from predetermined closures of relationship and meaning and offer themselves to us in an open space. Within this open space we can move freely and approach words from various vantage points to achieve different shades of the same aesthetic moment. We are given to witness the acting out of objects and events in cinematic fashion and stand, as it were, at the threshold of various possible meanings.[6]

When these freedoms are adopted in Moore's poems, a piling up of details results and the relation of her observations becomes obfuscated. The reader is thus loosed from syntactical moorings into a defamiliarized world. Moore's syllabic verse also forms a link with the Chinese language, in which each character (or word, in Classical Chinese) is a single syllable, and verse is composed according to the number of characters per line, making the syllable the prosodic vehicle for all poetry written in Chinese. 'I tend to write in a patterned arrangement, with rhymes', she wrote in 1938, 'stanza as it follows stanza being identical in number of syllables and rhyme-plan, with the first stanza.'[7] 'Moore's

[5] In her reading notebook from 1907 to 1915 (RL VII:01:01), Moore exhibited some knowledge of Chinese verse at least in translation, when she noted of Lawrence Housman's 'The Chinese Lantern' that it resembled 'whimsical pseudo Chinese'.

[6] Wai-lim Yip, *Diffusion of Distances: Dialogues between Chinese and Western Poetics* (Berkeley, Los Angeles, and Oxford: University of California Press, 1993), 30.

[7] In William Rose Benét and Norman Holmes Pearson (eds.), *The Oxford Anthology of American Literature* (New York: Oxford University Press, 1938), 1319, and *CPR* 644. This is certainly a verifiable summary of Moore's technique for, in poems such as 'When I Buy Pictures' and 'The Labors of Hercules', where there is no stanzaic arrangement, the syllabic counting is abandoned.

idiosyncratic isosyllabism emerges as a dominant system for her, providing the pattern of rises, turns, and landings of her particular Emersonian stairway of surprise', John Hollander wrote; 'her isosyllabism, with its manner of framing English verse and its partitions of written language, correspond in the mixture of familiarity and strangeness with her segmentations . . . of nature.'[8] Her independence of the fixities of ordinary grammar and syntax also reflects a similar pliancy in the Chinese language. Chinese is an uninflected language with neither fixed syntax nor any identifiable grammar as such.[9] William Carlos Williams remarked upon the undistracted adherence and faithfulness to thought processes which Moore's technique allows:

Nor is 'thought' the thing that she contends with. Miss Moore uses the thought most interestingly and wonderfully to my mind. I don't know but that this technical excellence is one of the greatest pleasures I get from her. She occupies the thought to its end, and goes on—without connectives. To me this is thrilling. The essence is not broken, nothing is injured. It is a kind hand to a merciless mind at home in the thought as in the cruder image.[10]

Moore abandons joinery by aligning successive thoughts and observations, in her own voice and in quotation, to form an uninterrupted, inviolate sequence of compact messages. 'I have a mania for straight writing', she wrote, 'however circuitous I may be in what I myself say of plants, animals, or places.'[11] Her lacunary syntax, brought about by excision and ellipsis, is carefully premeditated, and provides a source of poetic depth and resonance by enabling her to impart the immediacy of a perception without subjecting it to causal and logical strictures.

Emily Dickinson also disliked the connective, and abandoned it in the interests of intensity. Moore's poetry, as was pointed out in an earlier chapter, owes much to Dickinson's influence. Both poets utilized the hyphen or dash as a means to maintain

[8] John Hollander, 'Observations on Moore's Syllabic Schemes', in *Marianne Moore: The Art of a Modernist* (Ann Arbor, Mich. and London: UMI Research Press, 1990), 84.
[9] In Chinese there are no verb declensions, no copulae, and no number indicated with nouns without modifiers (i.e. no plurals).
[10] William Carlos Williams, 'Marianne Moore (1931)', in *Selected Essays of William Carlos Williams* (New York: New Directions, 1969), 126.
[11] Marianne Moore, 'Idiosyncrasy and Technique', in *A Marianne Moore Reader* (Berkeley: University of California Press, 1958), 509.

the poetic line 'unbroken',[12] and Moore observes in Dickinson's poetry the kind of precision and restraint to which she aspired. 'Study which she bestowed on her poems related only to a choice of words that would sharpen the meaning', she wrote in her essay 'Emily Dickinson' (1933); 'an element of the Chinese taste was part of this choiceness, in its daring associations of the prismatically true.'[13] This sensitivity to language may have been what motivated Harriet Monroe, the editor of *Poetry*, to call Dickinson an 'unconscious and uncatalogued *Imagiste*'.[14] Certainly Moore was aware of the extra-lexical power of Dickinson's spare, laconic verse. 'It was hers to make words convey "more than the sum of their meanings laid end to end"', Moore's essay continues, 'and to attain splendor of implication without prefatory statement, for her conciseness was as extreme as her largess.'[15] Jeanne Kammer has made connections between this kind of writing and the social protection which the role of the enigmatic eccentric afforded the female poet. 'This shared impulse to compressive speech may arise in part from habits of privacy, camouflage and indirection encouraged in the manner of the gently-bred female.'[16] This subtle interplay of introversion and class throws an interesting light upon what unites these two poets beyond their use of linguistic compression, and shows that the 'Chinese' qualities of their writing may stand in for a common stance with respect to the world around them. The redolence of Dickinson's verse is partly reliant upon what Moore terms her 'Chinese taste', and derives from their shared grammatic impeccability, the way that, in each poet's work, nuance is very precise and strictly maintained. The absence of excessive connective 'tissue', and the compression which results, is in Moore's poetry more pronounced. This is largely due to

[12] 'I sometimes ended a line with a hyphen, expecting the reader to maintain the line unbroken (disregarding the hyphen)', she remarked in 1965; 'I have found readers misled by the hyphen, mistaking it as an arcane form of emphasis, so I seldom use it today'. Voice of America Poetry Series, published as *Poetry and Criticism: Response to Questions Posed by Howard Nemerov* (Cambridge, Mass.: Adams House and Lowell House Printers, 1965), and *CPR* 588.

[13] From *Poetry*, 41 (Jan. 1933), 219–26, and *CPR* 292.

[14] Harriet Monroe, 'A Review of Emily Dickinson's *The Single Hound*', *Poetry* (Dec. 1914).

[15] *CPR* 293.

[16] Jeanne Kammer, 'The Art of Silence and the Forms of Women's Poetry', in Sandra M. Gilbert and Susan Gubar (eds.), *Shakespeare's Sisters: Feminist Essays on Women Poets* (Bloomington, Ind. and London: Indiana University Press, 1979), 156.

her careful, though also somewhat humorous and playful, use of compound nouns, a feature which is part of Moore's own 'Chinese taste'.

We can see that this kind of abbreviation operates within poems which feature compound nouns, some of which extend to as much as five words together or six words in tandem pairs as in 'Elephant-ear-witnesses-to-be' and 'half-dry sun-flecked stream-bed', both of which appear in the poem 'Elephants', or 'owl-and-a-pussy- | both-content | agreement' from 'Propriety' (1944) and 'the sand-brown jumping-rat—free-born' from 'The Jerboa' (1932). This method of compression could be attributed to Moore's acquaintance with the nature of the Chinese character, or ideogram, itself, which sets up paratactical relations,[17] or juxtapositions of two or more things, nouns standing in for generalized concepts. Certainly these extended compounds appear in poems written after the initial appearance of Fenollosa's 'The Chinese Written Character as a Medium for Poetry'.[18] An alternative source can be located in Chinese poetry, for it becomes obvious upon looking at any number of *fu* that, as Burton Watson observes, 'though common enough in other types of poetry and prose, [descriptive binomial compounds] are particularly numerous in the *fu*, helping to give them their musical, rhapsodic air.'[19] Moore's constructions, unlike the ideogrammic technique, do not set images side by side to invoke an unstated relation. If anything, she articulates and presses home her messages and seems to find satisfaction in the stating and registering of explicit observations. She is not given to Pound's evocation of 'luminous detail'[20] and sudden insight.

[17] 'Parataxis': placing of clauses etc., one after another, without words to indicate co-ordination or subordination. From Greek *para* meaning 'beside', 'beyond', 'wrong', 'irregular', and *taxis* meaning 'arrangement', from *tasso*. Opposite of 'hypotaxis', or 'to arrange under', which designates a dependent construction or relation of parts with connectives.
[18] Ernest Fenollosa, 'The Chinese Written Character as a Medium for Poetry', (ed.) Ezra Pound *Little Review*, 6/5–8 (Sept.–Dec. 1919).
[19] Burton Watson, *Early Chinese Literature* (New York and London: Columbia University Press, 1962), 262.
[20] Pound discusses the 'luminous detail' in a series of essays entitled 'I Gather the Limbs of Osiris', in *Selected Prose 1909–1965*, (ed.) William Cookson (New York: New Directions, 1975). An earlier mention of this idea can be found in a 1901 letter from Pound to William Carlos Williams. See *The Selected Letters of Ezra Pound*, (ed.) D. D. Paige (New York: Harcourt, Brace, 1950), 90–1.

Her compounds appear to be derived from observations of the use of word-pairings in Chinese poetry. The Chinese use similar linguistic devices to form compounds of nouns, adjectives, and verbs by joining, for example, two near-synonyms (for example *shan-shui*, meaning 'mountain(s) and water(s)' or 'landscape'). Metaphorical near-synonyms and near-antonyms are combined to form collective or abstract ideas. These methods, which Moore utilizes throughout her poetry, are ones which find counterparts in the formation of poetic phrases and ideas in Chinese.[21] Indeed, Moore herself allies these attributes to Chinese syntax in her essay 'Feeling and Precision'. 'Instinctively we employ antithesis as an aid to precision', she writes, 'and in Arthur Waley's translation from the Chinese one notices the many paired meanings—"left and right"; "waking and sleeping"; "one embroiders with silk, an inch a day; of plain sewing one can do more than five feet".'[22]

This technique of combining words and phrases without connectives in what often results in an analogical configuration recalls William Carlos Williams's observation about Moore's poems when he refers to 'their cleanliness, lack of cement, clarity, gentleness'.[23] The suggestiveness of the unaided nouns, adjectives, and verbs in tandem permits ambiguity, and introduces potential meanings. In the juxtaposition of two words (and often several more in Moore's case) we can observe in both Chinese and English that, as Hans Frankel notes, 'it is left to the reader (or listener) to determine whether AB means "A plus B" ... or "of the several meanings of A, the one which coincides with B" ... or "the common denominator of A and B" ... or "the total entity of which A and B are constituents" ... or "the abstract concept suggested by the concrete instances A and B" '.[24] Though Moore consistently arrives at the particular relation she wishes to evoke, she deliberately exploits the potential for a variety of possible interpretations to cohere before ascertaining the meaning she intends. Of course, we can find examples of compound nouns in, for example, 'The Seafarer' (translated by Ezra Pound

[21] Hans Frankel, *The Flowering Plum and the Palace Lady: Interpretations of Chinese Poetry* (New Haven and London: Yale University Press, 1976), 1.

[22] *Sewanee Review*, 52 (Autumn 1944), 500, and CPR 397.

[23] Williams, 'Marianne Moore (1925)', in *Imaginations*, (ed.) Webster Schott (New York: New Directions, 1970), 312.

[24] Frankel, *The Flowering Plum*,145.

in *Ripostes*, 1912; also reprinted with *Cathay*, 1915), though not to the extent that they occur in Marianne Moore's poetry. The Anglo-Saxon term 'kenning', or 'the particulars by which the subject is known', may best describe the traditional metaphorical processes which produced compounds such as 'whale-path', 'sword-hate', 'doom-gripped', 'mood-lofty', 'care-wretched', 'flesh-cover', and 'life's-blast' in 'The Seafarer'.[25] 'Chinese poetics', as Hugh Kenner has remarked, 'go back to the roots of English in a more than philological way.'[26] The five- and six-word compounds of Moore's mentioned above, however, belie the notion that an early Anglo-Saxon text is their source and point rather to the influence of Ernest Fenollosa's 'The Chinese Written Character as a Medium for Poetry' (1919) and the availability of both literal and 'poetic' translations of Chinese poetry.[27] This is further supported by a notation in her earliest reading notebook (1907–15) that 'there are butterflies wh [*sic*] are called in Chinese, flying leaves'.[28]

Moore's paratactical constructions extend beyond her use of compound nouns, informing the shape and proximity of nearly all the components of her verse. As Margaret Holley aptly notes, this underlying method helps to create and maintain a hesitation and uncertainty which reinforces the effect of her aphoristic *luan*:

Moore's parataxis—her listing of facts, ideas, sayings, propositions of constantly shifting sorts—is an empirical procedure that stops short of induction. Its particulars are not being marshalled toward a general conclusion, for such conclusions are already adopted as particular items themselves. The inconclusive nature of this strategy serves to keep inquiry and uncertainty alive in the teeth of the poem's useful surface of categorical, single-minded statements.[29]

This strategy is strengthened in those poems which feature supernatural creatures, or animals whose status as real or imaginary is

[25] Ezra Pound, *Collected Shorter Poems* (London: Faber & Faber, 1952), 76–9.
[26] Hugh Kenner, *The Poetry of Ezra Pound* (Lincoln, Nebr. and London: University of Nebraska Press, 1985), 140.
[27] Among her library holdings is a poem book by Tao Yuan-Ming (365–427), translated into Italian by Margherita Guidacci as 'Poema per la Bellezza della sua Donna' (Milan: Vanni Scheiwiller, 1962).
[28] RL VII:01:01, notation no. 105.
[29] Margaret Holley, *The Poetry of Marianne Moore: A Study in Voice and Value* (Cambridge: Cambridge University Press, 1987), 103.

indeterminate. In an earlier chapter, we also saw how imagery of exotic or strange animals served much the same purpose in defeating any effort on the part of the reader to finally establish the claims being made on reality.

Moore may have been drawn to paratactical strategies by her study of other subjects besides Chinese poetry. Her undergraduate training in biology may have instilled a scientific approach to her own poetry, developing into a technique of evaluation and reflection which approximated to the comparative and factual basis of the ideogrammic method. Pound described the laboratory conditions under which poetry must be examined in *The ABC of Reading*: 'The proper METHOD for studying poetry and good letters is the method of contemporary biologists, that is careful first-hand examination of the matter, and continual COMPARISON of one "slide" or specimen with another.'[30] Employing direct observation as a means of formulating general laws, Pound advocated gathering this kind of particular 'fact' as evidence from which to draw conclusions by induction. Laszlo K. Géfin notes the breadth of Pound's application of this method and the structure it provided for his ideas about poetry:

Pound insists on the existence of close ties between this aspect of the new science, i.e., axioms emerging from observation, and the new art because he sees science (natural science as well as the *sciences humaines* of psychology, anthropology, and archaeology) as the foundation of the new *forma mentis*, validating—because it links them to the processes of nature—the emergence of nonlogical nontransitional modes in literature, painting, sculpture, cinema, and music.[31]

This kind of detailed observation and comparison is also typical of Moore's poetry and is accomplished in several ways. William Carlos Williams describes the process of her poetic method in terms which evoke both the domestic and scientific aspects of her procedure:

Miss Moore gets great pleasure from wiping soiled words or cutting them clean out, removing the aureoles that have been pasted about them or taking them bodily from greasy contexts. For the compositions which

[30] Ezra Pound, *The ABC of Reading* (London: Faber & Faber, 1951), 17.
[31] Laszlo K. Géfin, *Ideogram: History of a Poetic Method* (Austin, Tex.: University of Texas Press, 1982), 32.

Miss Moore intends, each word should first stand crystal clear with no attachments; not even an aroma. As a cross light upon this, Miss Moore's personal dislike for flowers that have both a satisfying appearance and an odor of perfume is worth noticing. With Miss Moore a word is a word most when it is separated out by science, treated with acid to remove the smudges, washed, dried and placed right side up on a clean surface . . . It may be used not to smear it again with thinking (the attachments of thought) but in such a way that it will remain scrupulously itself, clean perfect, unnicked beside other words in parade. There must be edges. This casts some light I think on the simplicity of design in much of Miss Moore's work.[32]

Clearly Pound's and Moore's scientific 'methods' have much in common; both treat words as singular entities, as individual 'specimens' whose relations with other words are not pronounced, but examined. Williams's description calls attention to the peculiar clarity and unattached quality of Moore's language, an arranging of linguistic components 'slide' by 'slide'. But she remains decidedly at a remove from her descriptions, both in the singularly visual quality of her images and by the fact that her subjects are themselves never examined at first hand. Her poems are at variance with what Williams, another practitioner of the ideogrammic method, has written about the matter of art. 'Art can be made of anything,' he wrote, 'provided it be seen, smelt, touched, apprehended and understood to be what it is— the flesh of a constantly repeated permanence.'[33]

But certain aspects of the Chinese ideogram do prevail in Moore's poems, though not those that Pound looked to for his 'latent structure', invisible idea or unseen form.[34] The integration of several separate pictographic components within the ideogram into a cluster of meanings is captured in linear terms by Moore's extended circuitry and arranged progression of words. For even when these clusters of compound nouns are not joined by hyphenation, Moore achieves the same filmic effect through the omission of some prepositions and articles as in 'The Pangolin':

---

[32] Williams, 'Marianne Moore (1925)', *The Dial*, 78/5 (May 1925); repr. in Williams, *Imaginations*, (ed.) Webster Schott (New York: New Directions, 1970), 317–18.
[33] Williams, *Selected Letters*, (ed.) John C. Thirlwall (New York: McDowell, 1957), 130.
[34] For his discussion of these ideas, see Ezra Pound, *Guide to Kulchur* (London: Faber & Faber, 1938), 152.

'strongly intailed, neat | head for core, on neck not breaking off, with curled-in feet'. Hans Frankel similarly observes that in the Chinese case, 'the advantages of this procedure are many: it makes for brevity and force (letting the facts speak for themselves), it involves the reader in the thought process, it dispenses with normal restrictions of logic, chronological sequence, orderliness, and the like, and it leaves room for multiple meanings'.[35] Moore captures and establishes phonetically what is visually secured by pictographic forms like the Chinese character. The reader, in encountering these compounds, becomes an imaginative participant, repeatedly restoring to these sequences a unity and meaning often based upon the variety of compositional interactions among individual words which Frankel outlined above.

Moore's strings of compound words share with the Chinese character[36] and the ideogrammic method the ability to record the simultaneous, disconnected impressions which constitute our perception of the world. She creates in these isolated instances short cinematic interludes within her poems which counteract the attenuation of the ability of ordinary language to relate the complexity of experience. It frees her temporarily, as we saw in an earlier chapter that imaginary creatures do, from the constraints of a static point of view by introducing at intervals a hybridization of perspective. Word-groupings of this kind likewise demand a continuously reflexive referential process which suspends any immediate or instinctive apprehension until a unity within the compound can be perceived. These linguistic devices continually alter the pace and the direction of the poem, disturbing the reader's expectations. Walter Sutton observes that the 'reflexive reference', common to both the ideogram and the 'image' or auditory field, is analogous to Coleridge's 'willing suspension of disbelief', a conscious state of suspended judgement.[37] Here we find links with Romantic poetry, reflourishings in the twentieth century of ideas conceived in the early nineteenth century.

[35] Frankel, *The Flowering Plum*, 145.
[36] Moore's library contains a copy of Rose Quong's *Chinese Wit, Wisdom, and Written Characters* (New York: Pantheon, 1944).
[37] Walter Sutton, 'The Literary Image and the Reader', *Journal of Aesthetics and Art Criticism*, 16/1 (Sept. 1957), 115.

MODES OF COLLOQUY

In addition to Moore's utilization of compound nouns, her poems likewise often reveal no sense of time or temporal progression. This is augmented by the absence of human subjects in her descriptions, there being no person to whom these mostly visual impressions are appearing. James J. Y. Liu observes that the lack of tense in Chinese also adds to the Chinese poet's ability to present timeless scenes from no particular point of view. He notes that this sense of timelessness and universality is further enhanced in Chinese poetry by the frequent omission of the subject of a verb. Liu gives as an example the following quatrain by Wang Wei (701–61):

> Empty mountain not see people
> Only hear people talk sound
> Reflected light enter deep forest
> Again shine green moss upon

The reader is made to feel the presence of nature as a whole, in which, Liu observes, 'the mountains, the human voices, the sunlight, the mosses, are all equals'. Such omissions of the subject permit the poet not to intrude his own personality upon the scene, 'for the missing subject can be readily identified with anyone, whether the reader or some imaginary person'.[38]

Again, similar results can be ascribed to aspects of Chinese language and poetry found in poems like Moore's 'The Labors of Hercules', 'Smooth Gnarled Crape Myrtle', and 'Like a Bulwark' (1948). A timeless, ethereal quality inhabits portions of each of these poems and is brought about by the deliberate exclusion of named or assigned subjects, inviting participation by the reader who must continually speculate upon their identities. In 'The Labors of Hercules', the poem operates as a kind of public list, an indictment of contemporary social reality, a set of tasks which are set out as humanly impossible to fulfil. The futility which the poem presumes eliminates any intended audience, as if the energy and impetus which generate the poem are exhausted by the attempt to register the frustration of modern

---

[38] James J. Y. Liu, *The Art of Chinese Poetry* (London: Routledge & Kegan Paul, 1962), 40–1.

life and circumstances. In 'Smooth Gnarled Crape Myrtle', there is a detached quality and a deliberate lack of address, as if the phrases commit themselves to no one, are indifferent to who might encounter them. The lines feel anonymous, historically uncommitted, seem to have no desire for witness. And in 'Like a Bulwark', the reader is cut off from the import of this attempt to bind the impressions and qualities of an unnamed person to the image of a bulwark. It is as if the reader is unwittingly privy to an all too private, too proximal response, positioned so close that there is no distance within which to bring these observations into some human relation, no opportunity to configure the strong emotional address.

These means of excluding human subjects, in an attempt to prevent the intrusion of the author's 'personality', to democratize man and nature, or to shun the reader's access, enable Moore to preserve her 'habits of privacy'.[39] Wai-Lim Yip comments on the ability of Chinese poetry to focus on discrete visual events, much as Moore's does:

The success of the Chinese poets in authenticating the fluctuation of concrete events in phenomenon, their ability to preserve the multiple relationships in a kind of penumbra of indeterminateness, depends to a great extent on the sparseness of syntactic demands. This freedom allows the poet to highlight independent visual events, leaving them in coextensive spatial relationships. And this language, this medium for poetry, would not have become what it is without the support of a unique aesthetic horizon—the Chinese concept of the loss of self in undifferentiated existence—ordained by centuries of art and poetry.[40]

Perhaps these self-effacing techniques, rather than promoting 'the loss of self', work instead to call attention to the demonstrable efforts she expends to disguise the active presence of an inventor of such unlikely verse. At the same time, these numerous devices of linguistic compression—ellipsis, compound nouns, quotation and sentence embedding, omission of personal pronouns and connectives—all convey a desire to withdraw, to be exempt, to write with immunity.

To a certain extent, these effects result from Moore's 'imagistic' techniques. She eliminates so-called 'narrative' in much of her

---

[39] From a comment by Jeanne Kammer quoted earlier in this chapter.
[40] Wai-lim Yip, *Diffusion of Distances*, 47.

poetry, any discernible progression of ideas being the culmination, rather than the gradual assimilation, of gathered correspondences between images and phrases. T. S. Eliot supplies some explanation of this method of imagistic writing in the preface to his translation of St-John Perse's *Anabase*:

Any obscurity of the poem, on first readings, is due to the suppression of 'links in the chain', of explanatory and connecting matter, and not to incoherence or to love of cryptogram. The justification of such abbreviation of method is that the sequence of images coincides and concentrates into one intense impression of barbaric civilization. The reader has to allow the images to fall into his memory successively without questioning the reasonableness of each at the moment; so that, at the end, a total effect is produced. Such selection of a sequence of images and ideas has nothing chaotic about it. There is a logic of the imagination as well as a logic of concepts.[41]

The final coincidence, or 'total effect', of images is reliant upon a suspension of reason and ordinary logic. William Carlos Williams, writing specifically about Moore's poetry, confirms the underlying precision and exactitude required of her writing when he explains its almost mathematical basis in 'the geometric principle of the intersection of loci: from all angles lines converging and crossing establish points', and that 'apprehension perforates at places, through to understanding—as white is at the intersection of blue and green and yellow and red'.[42] Williams's description also calls attention to the inevitability of Moore's poetic process, its order and outcome as predictable as the succession of colour in a spectrum, as fundamental as white is to the relation and progression of colour itself. 'It is this white light that is the background of all good work', he concludes.[43] The exclusion of human subjects, in addition to logical and syntactic connectives, establishes a degree of freedom in Moore's poems similar to that of the T'ang dynasty poet, Wang Wei, quoted above. In 1968, Moore reviewed a collection of T'ang dynasty poems by Hsüeh T'ao (or Hung Tu, 768–831), the most famous woman poet of the T'ang dynasty.[44] Hsüeh T'ao's verse resembles that of Wang

---

[41] T. S. Eliot, preface to *Anabase* (London: Faber & Faber, 1959), 8.
[42] William Carlos Williams, 'Marianne Moore (1925)', in *Imaginations*, 309.
[43] Ibid.
[44] Moore's dust-jacket remarks on Mary Kennedy, *I Am a Thought of You: Poems by Sie Thao (Hung Tu)* (New York: Gotham, 1968).

Wei in that, as in much Chinese poetry, human subjects are either omitted or evoked obliquely through inference. This poem is a good example:

> The Moon
> The crescent, tiny as the curtain hook;
> The fan, woven on the Han loom, is round.
> The slender image, its nature, to gain fullness—
> Where else on earth is this seen?[45]

Even with the translator's insertion of verbs and prepositions to interpolate the meaning in English, it is evident that no human subject is mentioned, and that the poem's original structure has four characters per line, most of which are nouns and adjectives. 'Just as Chinese painters avoid restricting their paintings to one perspective', Wai-Lim Yip has noted of the absence of personal pronouns in Chinese poetry, 'the Chinese poet refrains from restricting the poetic state to only one participant.'[46]

Moore is often mentioned in studies of Imagism. Her poems appear in Imagist anthologies from the early twentieth century;[47] later volumes include her poems as examples of Imagist verse.[48] Certainly, the poems included in such works are not representative of her poetry as a whole. They tend to offer poems published when Imagist techniques were being experimented with by a considerable number of poets (c.1915–25), while even earlier poems by Moore already displayed a loyalty to certain Imagist imperatives, and these continued to pervade her work until late in her writing career. The concepts of Imagism, as Bram Dijkstra has pointed out, were 'self-evident for the poets in the Metropolitan area', where the visual arts were already influenced by Imagism's theories several years before Flint and Pound articulated them in *Poetry*. 'Even in America, in *Camera Work*', Dijkstra writes, 'this goal was being stressed as early as 1909.'[49]

---

[45] Hsueh T'ao, 'The Moon', trans. Eric W. Johnson, in Wu-chi Liu and Irving Yucheng Lo (eds.) *Sunflower Splendor: Three Thousand Years of Chinese Poetry*, (New York: Anchor, 1975), 190.

[46] Wai-lim Yip, *Diffusion of Distances*, 36.

[47] Moore contributed three poems to the 'special Imagist number' of *The Egoist* (May 1915).

[48] See e.g. Peter Jones (ed.), *Imagist Poetry* (Harmondsworth: Penguin, 1972).

[49] Bram Dijkstra, *Hieroglyphics of a New Speech: Cubism, Stieglitz and the Early Poetry of William Carlos Williams* (Princeton, NJ: Princeton University Press, 1969), 24.

Several Imagist strictures are similarly dependent upon the classical writings attributed to Longinus (c.AD 213–73), namely his *On the Sublime*. In this essay, Longinus discusses the role of 'images', or 'actual mental pictures' (a term used by Pound), and how they may be brought 'vividly before the eyes of your audience'.[50] Another passage explains how 'connecting particles' flatten and dissipate emotion in writing.[51] Moore mentions Longinus' writings on two occasions in 'Feeling and Precision'.[52] Clearly the wide range of sources that conspired to create Imagism can no doubt account for Moore's having employed some of its tenets in verse that preceded its debut. However, some of Moore's poems do adhere to all of the Imagist guidelines (for example 'He Made This Screen', 1909, and 'To a Chameleon', 1916[53]), and could be said to expose the more austere instances of her poetic 'method'. One reason for the claim that Moore was a practitioner of Imagism is that the movement was, above all, a set of poetic ideals which few of its adherents achieved. The principles which constituted Imagist practice are also characteristics of 'good' poetry generally and continue to inform the creation of verse which is not in other respects Imagist. 'Partly because of the kind of poetry she wrote at this time, but also partly because she was championed by Aldington (Poetry Editor of *The Egoist*) and associated in some ways with H.D. and Pound', Charles Molesworth has pointed out, 'Moore was to be thought of as an Imagist poet for many years.'[54]

The shortcomings and faults of both the several Imagist manifestos (by F. S. Flint and Ezra Pound[55]) and the poetry they inspired were highlighted in subsequent years by former Imagists such as John Gould Fletcher, who blamed Imagism

---

[50] Cassius Longinus, *On the Sublime*, trans. W. Hamilton Fyfe, Loeb Classical Library 199 (Cambridge Mass.: Harvard University Press; London: Heinemann, 1982), 171 (section 15).

[51] Ibid. 192–3 (section 21).

[52] Moore, 'Feeling and Precision', *Sewanee Review*, 52 (Autumn 1944), 499–507, and *CPR* 396–402.

[53] 'To a Chameleon' also appeared as 'You Are Like the Realistic Product of an Idealistic Search for Gold at the Foot of the Rainbow'.

[54] Charles Molesworth, *Marianne Moore: A Literary Life* (New York: Athenaeum, 1990), 112.

[55] F. S. Flint's 'Imagisme' and Pound's 'A Few Don'ts by an Imagiste', both published in the March 1913 issue of *Poetry*. Also Pound's prefaces to *Some Imagist Poets* (1915) and *Some Imagist Poets* (1916).

for not allowing its devotees to 'draw clear conclusions about life and to force the poet to state too much and to deduce too little—to lead its disciples too often into a barren aestheticism which was, and is, empty of content'.[56] But this is one of the points at which most of Moore's poetry diverges from the imperatives of Imagism. While she dispenses with connectives and human subjects, Moore clings to the moral and the didactic, as is evident in poems like 'The Labors of Hercules' and 'In Distrust of Merits' (1943), among others. Her poems which employ the *fu* technique, discussed in an earlier chapter, are committed to moral conclusions, or *luan*, which reduce her visual perceptions to some kernel of aphoristic wisdom or advice. Her departures from Imagism, then, seem to amend the movement's weaker features. Moore's freedoms from syntax and subject augment the focus and power of her verse because they are tied to a cautionary moral vision. Much like the austerity and discipline which her poems exude, she balked at the kind of 'freedom' which led Imagism's adherents to excess and a kind of emptiness. 'Poetry merely descriptive of nature as such, however vivid, no longer seems to me enough', continued Fletcher; 'there had to be added to it the human judgement, the human evaluation.'[57]

Moore's presentation of images, moreover, never subscribes to the dynamic quality endorsed by Pound when he defined the Image as 'that which presents an intellectual and emotional complex in an instant of time'.[58] But her process can be seen as genuinely ideogrammic in certain respects, particularly in the manner in which she effectively groups pictures together to form a constellation of static visual representations of natural subjects. Moore supplies a series of static descriptions by offering natural images, usually of animals, which are deliberately acquired from sources in art. Robert Pinsky has discerned this in her style. 'Her poems suggest the tact and authority of a scholar in a room rather than in the field', he writes; 'the rhythm of autocracy, reticence, and asseveration in the poems confirms the sense that Moore is studying a static

---

[56] John Gould Fletcher, *Life is My Song* (New York: Farrar & Rinehart, 1937), 213–14.
[57] Ibid.   [58] See Pound, 'A Few Don'ts', and 'A Retrospect', 4.

representation.'[59] 'Those of us who do not spend time in bogs, near ponds, or by streams, where water plants abound and gnats, newts and spiders hatched out', Moore admitted, 'may be obliged to console ourselves with frogs and toads in replica.'[60] These depictions represent, therefore, a verbal tableau of initially visual images, images which are prevented from coming to life because they are acknowledged as not being live. Moore creates an orchestrated reticulation of still life, moving between static tableaux which she never attempts to reanimate. This process focuses the reader's attention on the verbs which she does use, always maintaining the predominant mood in the active, present tense, as in 'Smooth Gnarled Crape Myrtle':

> A brass-green bird with grass-
> green throat smooth as a nut springs from
> twig to twig askew, copying the
> Chinese flower piece—businesslike atom
> in the stiff-leafed tree's blue-
> pink dregs-of-wine pyramids
> of mathematic circularity; one of a
> pair

The descriptive present tense maintains the illusion that there is activity here, that the 'brass-green bird' is springing, the redbird alighting, and the 'legendary white-eared black bulbul' singing. A dynamic quality is thereby set in motion between images when their correspondence is reflected upon as the poem progresses. But the reader experiences a stasis, an arrest, when it is disclosed that these creatures are 'one of a | pair' or 'usually a | pair', that there is no adequacy between art and life.

When the nature she represents doesn't come from art, it usually has a similarly still source, as in, for example, 'An Octopus', where her subject is a frozen replica:

[59] Robert Pinsky, 'Marianne Moore: The Art of a Modernist Master, a Symposium', in Joseph Parisi (ed.), *Marianne Moore: The Art of a Modernist* (Ann Arbor, Mich. and London: UMI Research Press, 1990), 118.

[60] Moore, 'Of Beasts and Jewels', *Harper's Bazaar*, 97 (Dec. 1963), 82–9, and *CPR* 573.

An Octopus
of ice. Deceptively reserved and flat,
it lies 'in grandeur and in mass'
beneath a sea of shifting snow-dunes;
dots of cyclamen-red and maroon on its clearly defined
                                        pseudo-podia
made of glass that will bend—a much needed invention—
comprising twenty-eight ice-fields from fifty to five hundred
                                        feet thick,
of unimagined delicacy.

Oddly, this poem locates deception in its own metaphorical conceit, in the reserved and flat ice which inspires the 'octopus'. There is no necessity in nature here, but rather a necessity of 'invention' to the 'pseudo-podia', the false tentacles of this sea animal, which technology has made unimaginably delicate through artifice.

Still in other poems, Moore's sources are written texts whose provenance is carefully noted, as in the first stanza of 'Sea Unicorns and Land Unicorns':

with their respective lions—
'mighty monoceroses with immeasured tayles'—
these are those very animals
described by the cartographers of 1539,
defiantly revolving
in such a way that
the long keel of white exhibited in tumbling,
disperses giant weeds
and those sea snakes whose forms, looped in the foam, 'disquiet
                                        shippers.'

Not only are these unicorns imaginary, their appearance is recorded on antiquated maps, another source in drawing and art. Quoting the cartographers' description of these ' "mighty monoceroses with immeasured tayles" ' accentuates the historical remove as well as the wonder which these enormous beasts inspired. Again, a static quality is indirectly conveyed by this belated source, while the reader is simultaneously seduced by the currency of the description.

Another means of distancing her poems from their subjects is achieved by Moore's acknowledgement of sources in reportage or hearsay, as in 'Rigorists' (1940): ' "We saw reindeer | browsing," a friend who'd been in Lapland, said: | "finding their own food".' In poems like 'Elephants', the reader is alerted by the poem's notes to the fact that the 'data utilized in these stanzas, [is] from a lecture-film entitled *Ceylon, the Wondrous Isle* by Charles Brooke Elliott'. It is possible to view this kind of citation as a means of democratizing her poems, as creating the impression that, while her subjects are exotic and foreign, Moore herself encounters them at travelogues or in a widely available magazine or newspaper. In 'The Arctic Ox (or Goat)', a short epigraph inserted between the title and text asserts that the poem was 'derived from "Golden Fleece of the Arctic," by John J. Teal, Jr., who rears musk oxen on his farm in Vermont, as set forth by him in the March 1958 issue of the *Atlantic Monthly*'. This is an unusual bibliographic gesture even for Moore,[61] and yet the intrusion upon the poem's sanctity situates its concerns in the contemporary and promotes an exigency to her plea for animal rights. 'If you fear that you are | reading an advertisement, | you are', she concludes the poem, 'If we can't be cordial to these creatures' fleece, I think that we deserve to freeze.' And, finally, in 'The Pangolin', a note to the poem citing ' "Pangolins" by Robert T. Hatt, *Natural History*, December 1935', works to denaturalize the exuberant detail and unhindered familiarity found in the text itself. So that when a poem itself does not disclose a second-hand source in art or literature, these extra-textual compendia alert the reader to sources outside of nature, renditions or interventions by other authors between the living source and Moore's poems.

This is not to say that there are no poems by Moore whose subjects are not observed first-hand (as they are in 'Bird-Witted', 1936) but, in addition to the role that memory already inevitably plays in the construction of a poem, the poetic utterance is more often belated and cannot be temporally coextensive with perception. In other ways, however, Moore establishes a reciprocity with the reader by repeatedly concretizing her second-hand images. In 'Snakes, Mongooses, Snake-Charmers, and the Like', 'the essentially Greek, the plastic animal all of a piece from

---

[61] The only other epigraph of this kind appears in ' "Keeping Their World Large" ' (1944).

nose to tail' has become one of the 'products of the country in which everything is hard work', where 'the only positive thing about it is its shape'. In this poem, purpose and use ('for what was it invented?'), a consistent preoccupation of Moore's, relocate the imaginal within our human purview by transforming what we may have thought was a snake—'Thick, not heavy, it stands up from its traveling-basket'—into plastic form. She draws upon the close-at-hand and somewhat rarefied, pictorial models of the mysterious here, just as she appropriates another author's description of the animals in quotation. The second-hand is dismantled, rearranged, and reassembled, always at one remove from any direct experience of nature; the surfaces of paintings, porcelain, and plastic become the landscape within which nature darts, swims, and crawls.

Borrowed speech intensifies the unfamiliarity of Moore's verse; it resists, perhaps intentionally, the reader's efforts to constantly synthesize the disparate language of a broad range of disciplines. And Moore's own language opposes rather than assists the reader, subverts any attempt to find a common linguistic platform from which to negotiate quoted material. Her allegiance is always to her personal methods of craftsmanship, and she deploys rather than employs language, sometimes in a mildly aggressive or at least an armoured manner, abetting co-opted prose, often at the price of clarity. These lines from 'Novices' (1923) are a particularly apt example of this:

> Accustomed to the recurring phosphorescence of antiquity,
> the 'much noble vagueness and indefinite jargon' of Plato,
> the lucid movements of the royal yacht upon the learned
> scenery of Egypt—
> king, steward, and harper, seated amidships while the jade and
> the rock crystal course about in solution,
> their suavity surmounts the surf—
> the willowy wit, the transparent equation of Isaiah, Jeremiah,
> Ezekiel, Daniel.

And in 'Voracities and Verities Sometimes Are Interacting' (1947) her references undermine and defy ready comprehension: 'the elephant's "crooked trumpet" "doth write" '; and Moore claims to be 'under obligation' to a book she is reading. Evidently Moore does not actually think that the reader 'know[s] the one', for she notes below the poem 'Tiger-book: Major James Corbett's *Man-Eaters of Kumaon*', a singular instance where a footnote appears with the text of a poem rather than appended at the back of the volume. A letter from Ezra Pound to Harriet Monroe of January 1915 situates this kind of writing with respect to Imagist principles:

Objectivity and again objectivity, and expression: no hindside-beforeness, no straddled adjectives (as 'addled mosses dank'), no Tennysonianness of speech; nothing—nothing that you couldn't, in some circumstance, in the stress of some emotion, actually say. Every literaryism, every book word, fritters away a scrap of the reader's patience, a scrap of his sense of your sincerity. When one really feels and thinks, one stammers with simple speech; it is only in the flurry, the shallow frothy excitement of writing, or the inebriety of a metre, that one falls into the easy—oh, how easy!—speech of books and poems that one has read.[62]

While Moore is hardly Tennysonian, many of her poems do call her 'sincerity' into question, and certainly there are not many poems which use language that the reader would 'actually say'.

Even the overtly demotic speech, as has been pointed out in an earlier chapter, is arranged in such a way that while the words are familiar they are never beholden to the idiomatic or the vernacular. Moore writes about baseball, American history, and small towns and yet her speech is profoundly un-American. Her odd yokings of literary and colloquial expression seem idiosyncratic and contrived, particularly when compared to American poets such as William Carlos Williams. An early poem by Moore, 'To Be Liked By You Would Be a Calamity' (1916),[63] begins with a quotation from Thomas Hardy: ' "Attack is more piquant than concord," ' and continues in the language of fencing—'I can but put my weapon up, and | Bow you out.' Again in this poem, she demonstrates that her language is neither contemporary nor indigenous. While the choice of words maintains the period conceit of the formal duel (a type of combat reserved for upper-class Europeans of another century), these lines betray the dated, obtrusive quality which inheres in so much of her poetry. Each poem is bound to another time, another discourse (historical, scientific, palaeontological, literary, etc.), none of which are her own, or ours. When she writes about personal exchanges, her tropes seem to impersonate, rather than relate, speech. Robert Pinsky writes about the artificiality of Moore's address and notes that, particularly in 'To Be Liked By You Would Be a Calamity', Moore shows that she can 'write in the mode of colloquy without writing colloquially'. 'That is, address and something like exchange take place, but not vocally, and not in words much like any conversational language of twentieth-century America', Pinsky continues, 'but an exchange imagined in the terms of another century.'[64] The interiority and self-address of Moore's poetry is unusually combined with components of the ideogrammic method and Imagist principles to form a highly personal style and a complicated, and somewhat ambivalent, response to the variety of verse forms to which she was attracted. This often bewildering mix of the demotic and the arcane, the spare and the excessive, contributes to the peculiar strength and, at the same time, the obvious limitation of her poetry.

Moore was sufficiently aware of the operations of Imagist verse to imitate it in a response to Pound's translations of T'ang dynasty poetry. She demonstrates a familiarity with Pound's poem 'Li Po' (701–62) by transcribing it thus in the following entry from her reading notebook of 1907–15:

> Pound—Li Po. Epitaph
> and Li Po also died drunk
> He tried to embrace a moon
> In the yellow river[65]

Similarly, a poem written in March 1915, and not published during her lifetime, exposes a wry humour in this self-conscious foray into Imagist verse:

> *Ezra Pound:*
> 'Frae bank to bank, frae wood to wood I rin.'
>   The rinning that you do,
>   Is not so new
>   As it is admirable.
>   'Vigor informs your
>   SS Shape' and ardor knits it.

[64] Robert Pinsky, 'Idiom and Idiosyncrasy', in *Poetry and the World* (New York: Ecco Press, 1988), 48.
[65] RL VII:01:01, Notebook 1250/1, notation no. 113.

> Good Meditatio
> And good Li Po;
> > And that page of Blast, on which
> > Small boats ply to and
> > Fro in bee lines.   Bless Blast.[66]

But Moore espoused her own unique methods for creating verse and held fast to her writing 'habits' throughout her writing career. T. S. Eliot, in his introduction to Moore's *Selected Poems* (1935), refers to her as a 'descriptive' poet, and probably even the most complicated of her processes of compression are subordinated to that over-arching aim. 'Don't be descriptive',[67] Pound instructed poets in his usual dogmatic manner, 'the gulf between evocation and description . . . is the unbridgeable difference between genius and talent.'[68] Yet Moore proceeded to devise a descriptive procedure which attempted to bridge that gulf, and she looked to Chinese models to fortify her efforts. Aphoristic form (the *luan* of the *fu*), compression, ellipsis, and condensation, as Stephen Reckert observes, 'correspond to certain habits of thought, feeling, and expression that are historically . . . associated with the East'.[69]

[66] RL I:01:49. Published in the Marianne Moore Newsletter, 3/2 (1979), 5.
[67] From 'A Few Don'ts by an Imagiste'.
[68] Ezra Pound, 'The Later Yeats', in *Literary Essays*, 380; first appeared in *Poetry* (May 1914).
[69] Stephen Reckert, *Beyond Chrysanthemums: Perspectives on Poetry East and West* (Oxford: Clarendon Press, 1993), 231.

6

Precision, Perspective, and the
Harnessing of Silence

What is more precise than precision? Illusion.
(Marianne Moore, from 'Armor's Undermining
Modesty', 1950)

REPLICATING NATURE

Marianne Moore, like William Carlos Williams and Henry James, wanted in her youth to become a painter.[1] Her poems display a penetrating and attentive visual sense augmented by a sensitivity to colour[2] and the proximal relations and interactions of the various subjects in her compositions. Painterly verbiage appears repeatedly throughout her poetry and prose, with particular references alluding to matters of style and execution in Chinese art and art generally. Books on oriental rugs and carpets, Chinese bronzes, Chinese theories of art, museum bulletins on Chinese stele and prints, as well as gallery and auction catalogues on Chinese porcelains, jades, bronzes, textiles, fans, pottery, and sculpture make up a significant portion of Moore's library holdings.[3]

---

[1] Jean Garrigue, *Marianne Moore*, Pamphlets on American Writers 50 (Minnesota: University of Minnesota Press, 1965), 8.

[2] For example, 'the Chinese vermilion of the poincianas' in 'People's Surroundings' (1922), and the exposed colour of ancient Chinese punctilio in 'Bowls' (1923).

[3] Examples include Stanley Reed, *Oriental Rugs and Carpets* (New York: Putnam's, 1967); *Master Bronzes* (Buffalo: Albright Art Gallery, 1937); Lin Yutang (trans.), *The Chinese Theory of Art* (London: William Heinemann, 1967); *Metropolitan Museum of Art Bulletin*, 19/4 (New York, 1924); *Metropolitan Museum of Art Bulletin* entitled 'The Treasure of Luhan' (Dec. 1919); Anderson Galleries (New York) catalogues of the Veitch Collection (Nov. 1927), the Print Collection of Norman James (Nov. 1928), and European and Oriental Sculpture (Dec. 1928); Bourgeois Gallery (New York) pamphlet, with Moore's annotations, for Exhibition of Early Chinese Paintings and Sculptures (Nov.–Dec. 1922); Metropolitan Museum of Art pamphlet for special exhibition, Costumes from the Forbidden City (Mar. 1945).

Even Moore's early reading notebooks are full of details and art-historical information about such subjects as the Chinese method for painting the sides of porcelain vessels,[4] the Chinese affinity for bold colours, and their 'excellent good taste'.[5] An entire file, labelled 'Chinese Art', includes a Boston Museum of Fine Arts picture book publication entitled *Animals in Paintings from Asia* (1965) illustrating Chinese paintings from the eleventh, twelfth, and thirteenth centuries as well as museum postcard illustrations of a range of Chinese art spanning from the Shang dynasty (began *c.*1523 BC) to the Ch'ing dynasty in the nineteenth century. Moore's personal library, then, holds material covering the entire history of Chinese art and dates from the very beginning of her writing career. The range of understanding she displays about Chinese art-historical styles and classifications varies from that of the curio-collector to that of the informed academic. Moore's abiding fascination with curios of all kinds reveals her interest in retrieval and display. Evidence of this is found in her revival of many aspects of the *fu* (which means 'display') form discussed in an earlier chapter. This sense of recovery also extends, in many cases, to Chinese art objects and to perspectival principles in Chinese painting. Moore's impulse to look to the past and to an ancient civilization is crucial to her search for examples adequate to her demands for art and is part of her ongoing valuation of art and its relation to nature.

Examples of Moore's treatment of nature as a curiosity abound. 'The Camperdown Elm' is a poem which seems to offer a sincere appeal on behalf of this cavity-riddled elm, although it ends on a note which distances Moore from the detailed description of the tree's outward appearance and inner cavities: 'It is still leafing; | still there. *Mortal* though. We must save it. It is | our crowning curio'. Moore assays her subject for the Brooklyn residents whom she addresses, appealing to their instinct and desire for exhibition and show. Such displays depreciate this otherwise commendable civic gesture rather like the displays of curio-collectors, reflect, in a spectacular and somewhat undignified way, upon the collector. Or, perhaps, she satirizes in this last line those who view nature as valuable only to the extent that it excites wonder and

[4] From a notebook dating from 1907–15.
[5] RL VII:01:01. From a notebook dating from 1916–21.

awe in those that behold it. Moore's files include four versions
of her review[6] of Mai-Mai Sze's *The Tao of Painting*, in which
Sze observes that early Chinese tree cults were founded on 'the
symbolization of life and death', hollow trees being especially
meaningful since 'emptiness was interpreted as being filled with
spirit'.[7] Moore may wax eulogistic about the elm in this way to
highlight the enterprise, and contrast the spiritual significance of
the tree with its 'mortal', precarious existence. She clarifies her
stance, however, by unequivocally pronouncing her estimation
of the relative values of art and nature in an early poem, 'The
Monkey Puzzle':

> A conifer contrived in imitation of the glyptic work of jade and
> hard-stone cutters,
> a true curio in this bypath of curio-collecting,
> it is worth its weight in gold

Here we find an articulation of value in art, even if it is nature
imitating art, as it acquires status as 'a true curio', or as a curio
finds a market value in gold. Moore's uncompromising terms are
sarcastic and sharp, unwavering in their brutal stock-taking of
what art is and who appreciates it. The status of works of art
and nature as curios concerns Moore throughout her work, the
theme occurring as early as 1915 in 'Diligence Is to Magic as
Progress Is to Flight',[8] where she establishes elephants as 'not
curios', but 'prosaic necessities'.

In 'Smooth Gnarled Crape Myrtle', too, animals appear in
'pairs' just as the reader realizes that possibly the birds are not
alive but are painted figures upon the surface of an unspecified
objet d'art. As Bonnie Costello has pointed out, 'this play of
priorities is always alive in Moore's verse . . . At the simplest
level', she writes, 'objects in nature remind her of images she
has already seen in art—the pangolin [from 'The Pangolin'] is
"Leonardo da Vinci's replica".'[9] Unlike 'The Camperdown Elm',
'Smooth Gnarled Crape Myrtle' is a masterpiece of illusion
which endlessly plaits unverifiable observation in terms which

    [6] RL II:6:12.
    [7] Mai-Mai Sze, *The Tao of Painting* (Princeton, NJ: Princeton University Press,
1963), 88.
    [8] *The Egoist*, 2 (1 Oct. 1915), 158.
    [9] Bonnie Costello, *Marianne Moore: Imaginary Possessions* (Cambridge, Mass.
and London: Harvard University Press, 1981), 210.

are intrinsically uncommitted to either art or life. We find the
bird is 'one of a pair' or 'on the | hyacinth-blue lid', nature some-
times verifying art and art copying nature.

> A brass-green bird with grass-
> green throat smooth as a nut springs from
>   twig to twig askew, copying the
> Chinese flower piece—Business-like atom
>   in the stiff-leafed tree's blue-
>   pink dregs-of-wine pyramids
>   of mathematic
>   circularity; one of a
>   pair . . .

Nature, like the 'columbine-tubed trunk' of the elephant, is
deceptive; its trunk is unexpectedly 'delicate', an 'at will heavy
thing'. 'Art is unfortunate', she concludes in 'Smooth Gnarled
Crape Myrtle', it doesn't have the option to vary its aspects,
cannot exceed itself, be other than what it is at any one time.

   Moore's method of examining nature and art through keen
observation of each uses some of the guiding principles of
montage.[10] Words ordinarily used to describe nature are inter-
spersed with the vocabulary of art, and the profusion of uncertainties which surrounds these mixtures of language is mimicked
by the various perspectives, or 'shots', which she 'takes' of her
subjects. Close-up 'shots', in which only a bird is revealed, often
seem to situate the subject in nature, sometimes springing from
'twig to twig askew', while 'long shots' restore the surroundings
of the bird, which is then exposed as having been painted on
the surface of a lid or vase. This kind of irregular succession
of long and close-up 'shots' is one of two principle strategies of
montage within an individual scene. The other, which entails a
succession of detailed shots of distinctly different, discrete subjects, is a strategy Moore employs in poems like 'Critics and
Connoisseurs'. Perhaps this is what Alicia Ostriker is referring
to when she comments upon Moore's 'videolike cuts'.[11] And yet,

---

[10] Moore was an avid filmgoer, as the film programmes and reviews of dozens
of foreign films (for the most part French) in her files attest. See RL, Vertical File:
'Film, Feature Film—Foreign'. This file includes programmes and reviews of Akira
Kurosawa's films.
[11] Alicia Ostriker, 'Marianne Moore, the Maternal Hero, and American
Women's Poetry', in Joseph Parisi (ed.), *Marianne Moore: The Art of a Modernist*
(Ann Arbor, Mich. and London: UMI Research Press, 1990), 51.

like Chinese poems, which, as Wai-lim Yip has pointed out, often operate 'pictorially rather than semantically',[12] Moore's successive 'shots' do not constitute a linear development:

> the objects coexist as in a painting, and yet the mobile point of view has made it possible to temporalize the spatial units . . . Unlike film, however, which often focuses on events to be strung together with a story line, the cinematic movement here reproduces the activities of the perceiving act of an intense moment, the total consciousness of which is not completed until all the visual moments have been presented— again, as in a classical Chinese painting.[13]

Moore employs the cinematic qualities of Chinese poetry and painting to achieve her own poetic ends. For her, these filmic manoeuvres[14] almost always have nature and art in view while man stands behind the viewer as a reference, or latent bene-ficiary, of her eclectically sought wisdom.

The variety of her exotic subjects, like the panoramic views embraced by the *fu* discussed in an earlier chapter, are exposed by a roving cinematic gaze. Sergei Eisenstein describes this successive ocular movement when he observes that 'the whole picture cannot be grasped entirely by the eye *all at once*, but in *sequence*, as if pouring out of one independent subject into another, out of one fragment into the next; that is, it appears before the eye as a stream of separate depictions (shots!) mer-ging into one'.[15] As we will see, this 'panning' from view to view in Moore's poems has much in common with Chinese painting. The abrupt impact of successive 'collisions' of observation, often depicted in her verse encased in the cells of quotation, is an aspect of montage. It is Eisenstein's notion that montage is created through 'collisions', and that 'from the collision of two given factors *arises* a concept',[16] or 'a new quality'[17] is produced by that juxtaposition. He goes on to explore what constitutes a

---

[12] Wai-lim Yip, *Diffusion of Distances: Dialogues between Chinese and Western Poetics* (Berkeley, Los Angeles, and Oxford: University of California Press, 1993), 45.
[13] Ibid.
[14] See Rudolph Arnheim, *Film* (London: Faber & Faber, 1933), 101.
[15] Sergei Eisenstein, *Nonindifferent Nature*, trans. Herbert Marshall (Cambridge: Cambridge University Press, 1987), 238.
[16] Eisenstein, *Film Form*, (ed.) and trans. Jay Leyda (London: Dennis Dobson, 1951), 37.
[17] Eisenstein, *The Film Sense*, trans. Jay Leyda (London: Faber & Faber, 1943), 14.

collision and finds that certain 'cinematographic' conflicts exist within the frame, among which are conflicts of graphic direction and depth.[18] As this discussion progresses it will become clear that these conflicts of direction and depth are what function in the formation of Moore's poetic topography. Her texts appear as screens on which are projected 'frames' of images. The discrete nature of these images, various and unconnected as they seem, calls attention to the cinematic procedure of her poetry. The poems inaugurate with each successive image cluster a simultaneous presentation of image and process—the praxis of this procedure becomes part of the operation of the poems themselves. It also makes possible the relative surprise of learning that the natural subjects in one image are later found to be decoratively embossed or part of a painting.

Man's place or value with respect to nature is depicted in many of Moore's poems as minute and incidental. She muses upon nature's wisdom and what its lessons can teach mankind; man remains the audience for, and recipient of, this informing advice. This subtle redirection of focus and concern from man to nature, and a nature replicated in art, is a strategy which Moore shares with Chinese landscape painting from its early beginnings (on silk, clay shards, and lacquer boxes) in the Chou dynasty.[19] Laurence Binyon called attention to this aspect of Chinese painting, so unlike the Western tradition of landscape painting, when he wrote that 'we are accustomed to regard landscape subjects as external to ourselves, but to the Chinese painters this world of nature seemed a more affecting way of shadowing forth the manifold moods of man than by representing human figures animated by those moods'.[20]

It is very clear that Moore's acquaintance with Chinese art filtered into her poetic compositions as well. *Poems* (1921), an early collection of her verse, includes a short poem entitled 'He Made This Screen'.[21] While not explicitly concerned with a Chinese work of art, the poem describes the subject-matter

[18] Ibid. 39.
[19] Michael Sullivan, *The Birth of Landscape Painting in China* (London: Routledge & Kegan Paul, 1962), 17.
[20] Laurence Binyon, *The Flight of the Dragon* (London: John Murray, 1911), 29.
[21] Originally published in 1909 in *Tipyn O'Bob*, 6 (Jan. 1909), 2–3 and again in *Marianne Moore Newsletter*, 5/1 (Spring 1981), 19.

typical of Chinese screens. The elements which the artist introduces are, like the material of a screen, proven resilient to the
ravages of the elements, chosen and placed 'here' and 'there',
purposefully arranged in a stable, premeditated configuration.
There is a deliberate quality as well to the way in which the artist
is reintroduced by Moore in the poem, as he so consciously places
figures on a screen of sturdy wood, a common substance not
precious like silver or fragile like coral. The sea is 'uniform like
tapestry', made a convention or symbol by its execution. The
single opening in this description follows the 'dragon circling
space—', where a dash allows this one imaginal element to soar
in motion, unsteadied by any pattern, unlike the sea or the still
tree, bower and passion-flower. Here, the artist is the subject of
the poem, and it is a particular screen, 'this' screen of the title,
which Moore has chosen to bring to the reader's attention. She
examines the artist through his expression; it is a study of placement and juxtaposition, of choices made. The gait and pace of the
poem imitate the movement of the visual scanning of the screen,
the 'here' and 'there' of looking at paintings and designs, as our
attention is guided from the foremost to the less significant. 'As
a poet what distinguishes you, do you think, from an ordinary
man?', Moore was once asked in a questionnaire. 'Nothing', she
replied, 'unless it is an exaggerated tendency to visualize.'[22]

'Black Earth' (1918),[23] is one of the first of Moore's to use the
word 'patina', a term ordinarily used in reference to the blue and
green salts which form a fine layer on the surface of bronzes
and other ageing articles. This word is often used in descriptions
and discussions of ancient ritual bronze vessels and bells of
which the Chinese were prolific craftsmen, particularly during
the Shang and Chou dynasties. Ezra Pound was interested in
these vessels and wrote about their architectonic influence on
Gaudier-Brzeska's sculpture, particularly *The Boy with a Coney*
(1914), in the *Egoist* of March 1914. By reading this and other
art historical works on early Chinese art, Moore would have
become familiar both with the descriptive language of ancient
vessels and with the blue and green patinas which cover all of them.
Among lines excised from a manuscript version of ' "A Tiger" ',

[22] Moore, 'Answers to an Enquiry', *New Verse*, 1 (Oct. 1934), 16, and *CPR* 674.
[23] Also entitled 'Melancthon' and collected in *Poems* (1921).

Moore included a quotation about an ancient bronze with a blue and green patina, which featured what is most likely a *t'ao t'ieh* mask, which is a stylized Chinese dragon face.[24] Indeed, a News Bulletin and Calendar (1955) from the Worcester Art Museum in her library files includes an article on Chinese jades in addition to photos of Chou dynasty dragon and fish pendants and a scrolled scabbard ornament.[25]

Moore's poems derive more than a historical vocabulary from Chinese art. Some poems adopt a visual resemblance to the Chinese hanging scroll and acquire many of its attributes in the process. This similarity is not as unusual for the Chinese as it is in the West, because the arts of poetry and painting are intimately allied in China, being created with the same materials, both brush and ink and identical types of scroll.[26] The inherent relationship between literature and painting was more clearly established in the East where, as A. Owen Aldridge noted, 'the study of Chinese literature traditionally involves the study of painting, calligraphy and seal-carving'. Pictorial imagination in poetic works was extolled in Chinese literary criticism texts, and poetry, painting, and calligraphy were deemed closely related arts and referred to as the 'three perfections'. A couplet current during the Northern Sung dynasty distils the Chinese feeling about the equivalence between the art of poetry and the art of painting: 'A poem is a picture without form, a picture a poem in form.'[27] 'In the West, the concept of the resemblance between painting and poetry was accepted as commonplace from classical times until the late eighteenth century when Lessing pointed out an essential difference', Aldridge explains, 'that poetry describes consecutive action while sculpture portrays special relations confined to a particular moment of time'.[28] Moore renewed that unity among these arts which always continued to exist in China. As Bonnie Costello

[24] RL I:04:37.   [25] RL Vertical File: Chinese Art.
[26] Susan Hilles Bush, *The Chinese Literati on Painting* (Cambridge, Mass.: Harvard–Yenching Institute Studies 27, 1971), 23.
[27] The couplet comes from Kuo Hsi's chapter entitled 'Ideas or Motives for Painting' ('Hua I') in *Lin Quan Gao Ji* (The Great Message of Forests and Streams), trans. in Osvald Sirén, *The Chinese on the Art of Painting* (Peiping: Henri Vetch, 1936), 49.
[28] A. Owen Aldridge, foreword to John J. Deeney (ed.), *Chinese–Western Comparative Literature Theory and Strategy* (Hong Kong: Chinese University Press, 1980), p. xiii. Aldridge is referring to G. E. Lessing's *Laocöon: An Essay upon the Limits of Poetry and Painting* (1766).

has claimed, she conceived of the moral situations which drive her poems 'pictorially' before developing them sequentially.[29]

'To Victor Hugo of My Crow Pluto' from *Tell Me, Tell Me* (1966) resembles the hanging scroll format, being one of a couple of Moore's poems which include a series of narrow, episodic stanzas arranged vertically.[30] Similar stanzaic arrangements are found in early poems by William Carlos Williams such as 'The Locust Tree in Flower' (1933) and 'To A Mexican Pig-Bank' (1935) (both from *An Early Martyr and Other Poems*, 1935), and in 'It is a Living Coral' (1924) (*Collected Poems*, 1934) and 'Perpetuum Mobile: The City' (from *Adam and Eve and the City*, 1936), all from the first half of his writing career. James Cahill has written that the Chinese short hanging scroll 'is designed to be hung on a wall, completely exposed, so that the entire composition may be viewed at once'.[31] This is true of shorter scrolls, but many famous extant scrolls (for example Tao Chi's early Lohan scroll[32]) are far too long to hang and were meant to be viewed horizontally in portions, as one end was unravelled and the other slowly rolled up, 'from right (*yang*) to left (*yin*) . . . revealing a view of nature in a manner equivalent to the unfolding processes of nature itself'.[33] Water, mist, and willowy trees create 'space cells' which provide a temporal dimension.[34] The long Chinese scroll painting represents a journey, a process of visual discovery which relies upon continual movement through the scroll as it is alternately unravelled on one side and rolled up again on the other. Discussing these long folded scrolls, Mai-Mai Sze wrote that 'as the eye travels from one scene to the next, the sequence in space introduces the element of time'.[35] Each portion of a long scroll, with this method, would never be seen twice with the same 'frame' unless deliberately unrolled to fixed points. Interestingly, the Chinese describe film as a series of 'electric shadows' (*tièn-ying*) and cinema as an 'electric shadow scroll'.[36]

[29] Costello, *Marianne Moore*, 202.   [30] See also ' "Avec Ardeur" ' (1963).

[31] James Cahill, *Chinese Paintings: XI–XIV Centuries* (London: Elek, 1961), 4.

[32] Tao Chi was born under the late Ming dynasty (1368–1644) and was active as a painter during the early Ch'ing dynasty (1644–1911).

[33] Sze, *The Tao of Painting*, 91.

[34] 'Space cell' is a term given currency by the art historian Ludwig Bachhofer.

[35] Sze, *The Tao of Painting*, 91.

[36] Victor H. Mair, *Painting and Performance: Chinese Picture Recitation and its Indian Genesis* (Honolulu: University of Hawaii Press, 1988), 58.

Separate 'views' were often painted in succession on the long scrolls, dividing the sequence up into smaller 'scenes'. We can look at 'To Victor Hugo of My Crow Pluto' and 'Occasionem Cognosce' (1963),[37] for example, and see these vertical poems, sometimes with two-line stanzas, as visual and experiential versions of the unravelling of a scroll, or as parallel columns of Chinese characters, which would have appeared on the colophons of any scroll. In fact, Moore's 'Occasionem Cognosce' was printed as an honorary edition in 1963 in parallel columns, with the first and final stanzas arranged at the top and bottom between them, creating the effect of a scroll or banner and setting off the final stanza as a chant or congregational response: 'Nothing mundane is divine; | Nothing divine is mundane.' This particular typographical layout lends the poem an uninterrupted continuity of lineation which is not alien to the traditional appearance of poetic texts in Chinese. As James J. Y. Liu has pointed out, 'actually, in traditional editions, Chinese poems are not printed in separate lines but continuously'.[38]

Among the visual strategies which the scroll and ideogram share are discrete presentation (the frames of the scroll always changing with each unravelling) and discontinuity. The vertical arrangement of both imposes a narrative control over the pace and speed of the reader/viewer's movement from image to image, which Moore refers to in 'Blue Bug'.

> speeding to left,
>   speeding to right; reversible,
> like 'turns in an ancient Chinese
>   melody, a thirteen
>   twisted silk-string three-finger solo.'
>   There they are, Yellow River-
> scroll accuracies
>   of your version
>   of something similar—polo.

Clearly, Moore's familiarity with Chinese scrolls was such that she was capable of making references to a specific type of scroll which depicted characteristic scenes of the larger rivers in China.

---

[37] 'Occasionem Cognosce' first appeared in *New York Review of Books*, 1 (31 Oct. 1963), 19. This poem appeared as ' "Avec Ardeur" ' in *CP*.
[38] James J. Y. Liu, *Essentials of Chinese Literary Art* (Belmont, Ca.: Wadsworth, 1979), 28.

These scrolls typically show, often in minute detail, the daily concourse of boats and fishermen, as well as the trade and social
gatherings along bridges and banks, and they provided ample
opportunity for the artist to exhibit painterly accuracy. Scrolls
of this type display phenomenal powers of observation in the
depiction of individual faces, gestures, and movements found in
each of hundreds of tiny figures. Moore has, in this metaphor,
found a precise and unassailable expression. It is, however, highly
specialized and certainly inaccessible to the uninformed reader.
Even more than the art-historical vocabulary, this scroll reference,
as well as the mention of ancient Chinese music and performance
('three-finger solo') which precedes it, betray the connoisseur.
Other kinds of Chinese scrolls dating from the T'ang dynasty,
called 'picture scrolls' or *chuan-pien*, accompanied a type of
oral storytelling, a genre of Chinese vernacular narratives, which
were comprised of popular didactic tales. These *pien-wen*, or
'transformation texts', were discovered at the turn of the century
and derived from the promptbooks of Buddhist monks for giving
lectures and sermons.[39] The pervasive moral quality of Moore's
poetry and the didactic *luan* of the *fu*, discussed in an earlier
chapter, may indicate that the visual and instructive aspects of her
poetry were modelled on these both secular and religious sources
as well. Moore offers no notes to 'Blue Bug' at all. This is a particularly good example of the ways in which Moore's annotations
inexplicably fail to disclose certain kinds of information and
yet, at other times, offer in plenitude information which robs an
initial reading of its original meaning.

The precision and accuracy found in the Chinese river scrolls
are qualities which Moore finds in much of Chinese art, including painting ('Blue Bug'), lacquer carving ('Bowls'), enameled
porcelain ('Smooth Gnarled Crape Myrtle'), carved glass
('People's Surroundings'), and tiles ('Critics and Connoisseurs').
In 'Critics and Connoisseurs', however, Moore begins: 'There
is a great amount of poetry in unconscious | fastidiousness.'
'Certain Ming | products, imperial floor coverings of coach- | wheel
yellow' are satisfactory, but a child's efforts to right a tottering
newborn animal deserve more admiration. The Ming dynasty,
renowned for its exquisite artisanry, here furnishes Moore with

[39] Mair, *Painting and Performance*, 1.

a conscious counterpart to the 'poetry' of the child's untaught efforts to school nature in the habits of domestication. She forms a hierarchy of value here, as elsewhere, which establishes nature's fastidiousness as superior to man's, natural accuracy as preferable to artistic precision. In 'Logic and "The Magic Flute"' as well, 'the magic flute and harp | somehow confused themselves | with China's precious wentletrap', precise musical instruments becoming indistinguishable from an elegant, usually white, marine animal's shell. Flights of stairs and musical scales in this poem display the natural accuracy and genius of producing successive intervals of sound. A Chinese shellfish here embodies not only the exactness of its natural form, but also the 'precious' value and estimation which China accords it.

The 'flights of marble stairs' may also refer to the precisely spaced marble stairs of the Forbidden City in Beijing, where the accuracy of their placement causes a percussive echo of any sounds made while standing on spots marked on particular marble slabs. The sonic relationship which exists between these marble staircases in the Forbidden City and the source of the reverberated sound reflects the precise, natural intervals found in marine shell chambers and imitated in musical instruments. Moore may well have been aware of these unusual Chinese staircases, as her reading notebook entry of 14 March 1916 includes notes about the architecture of the Temple of Heaven in the Forbidden City.[40] Her interest in the Chinese imperial family, who at that time were incarcerated within the Forbidden City's walls, is revealed in a reference included among her notes to 'Half Deity' in *What Are Years* (1941).[41] The note cites an interview with the former and last emperor of China by Edmund Gilligan (*New York Sun*, 1 December 1934), entitled 'Meeting the Emperor Pu Yi', and Pu Yi's remark: 'It is not permitted . . .' 'Half Deity' speaks of the butterfly:

> . . . though some are not
> permitted to gaze informally
> on majesty in such a manner as she
> is gazing here . . .

[40] RL: Reading Notebook (1916–21), entry no. 41 (14 Mar. 1916).
[41] This poem was not included in *CP*. The footnote referred to here appears on p. 51.

These lines emphasize the natural democracy of the animal world, and this is one of the very small number of poems where gendered animals appear, and one of only two in which the animal is expressly female.

This is an instance among many which exposes the deferred meanings that enrich initially unremarkable quotations throughout Moore's poems. By referring to sources outside the poem, she provides the reader with an exact context for what has become, by this process, a symbol or cipher within the poem. In the footnote quoted above which concerns her Chinese referents, the reader can observe the importance of these disclosed sources, which cast another, either new or enhanced, meaning upon these borrowed lines and upon the poem as a whole. They provide, as well, the sometimes overwhelming bibliographical complexity of a text which becomes laden with sources so disparate as to defy the imagination. The quotations ceaselessly move along a continuum of meaning, between their functions as words in the poem and their enhanced importance as references to additional texts. This process is redoubled through the textual exchange that is implied. As Margaret Holley remarks, Moore, like other Modernists, brought

a certain literal intertextuality into the foreground of poetry by recognizably quoting and paraphrasing other sources. On the one hand, this procedure has an effect of preserving the past by setting the new work into the context of its forebears; on the other hand, it has the effect of dismantling prior whole texts and of separating a fragment from its original context, exchanging its old field of meaning for a new one. Quotation thus gives the poem a double relation to the tradition from which the fragment was lifted.[42]

The imaginative associations suggested by the annotations subtly pervade the reader's experience of the poems as well, the notes working as a refining process for the ideas which Moore presents in the poetic texts.

This unique poetic referential process may be allied with spatial principles found in Chinese landscape painting, which presents layers of landscape elements in a non-linear perspective, progressively occluding portions of mountains, rivers and hills, and thereby creating a spatial depth. In much the same way that

---

[42] Margaret Holley, *The Poetry of Marianne Moore: A Study in Voice and Value* (Cambridge: Cambridge University Press, 1987), 16.

the Chinese arrange landscape elements, Moore may be seen to spatially model poetic tracts along perspectival principles. Her ability to accomplish this is highlighted by a comment by Richard Sieburth about the fact that the art of quotation 'involves shifting the emphasis from language as a means of representation to language as the very object of representation . . . To quote is thus to adduce words as facts, as exhibits, as documents, to lift them out of context, to isolate them, to make them self-evident', he wrote.[43] Moore's quotations are not only lifted out of context, but can be seen as raised topographically in their enclosed self-containment as dislodged and relocated portions of another text laid upon the pocked surfaces of her poems. The pages of the poems can therefore be revisualized as typographically modelled constructs.

BETTER GOVERNANCE OF THE EMOTIONS

This literary topography has precedents in Chinese poetry in the *fu*. Liu Xie (*c*.465–522), in his chapter 'Elucidation of *Fu*' (*Quan-fu*),[44] in the most comprehensive work in traditional Chinese literary criticism, describes these qualities of the form:

The *fu* was derived from poetry
And developed into several different forms.
In describing objects and picturing appearances
The richness of its patterns is like that of carving and painting;
It casts lustre over the dull,
And paints what is vast and immense in language that has no limitations.
In style, its ultimate achievement is beauty under control,
And its language is the result of the cutting out of weeds.[45]

The patterning of carving and painting finds literary equivalents both in the *fu* and in Moore's poetry. Control and spareness are part of Moore's creed—the 'weeds' the connective tissue which she dispenses with by paring away linguistic elements which prevent her phrases from being hard-edged, codified, and exact.

[43] Richard Sieburth, *Instigations: Ezra Pound and Rémy de Gourmont* (Cambridge, Mass. and London: Harvard University Press, 1978), 121.
[44] Moore's library files contain a copy of a review of the book in which this chapter appears, entitled 'Quintessence of Chinese Literature', from the *Times Literary Supplement*, 4 Dec. 1959.
[45] Liu Xie, *The Literary Mind and the Carving of Dragons*, trans. Vincent Yu-Chung Shi (Hong Kong: Chinese University Press, 1983), 95–6.

'I myself . . . would rather be told too little than too much', she writes in 'Humility, Concentration and Gusto' (1949), 'a poem is a concentrate'.[46] The integrity of Chinese art lies, for Moore, in the simplicity of its portrayal; the spiritual qualities of the invisible which it evokes allow nature to retain its orchestrated mystery. Moore implies that humankind can participate in that mystery by renouncing the selfhood which precludes assimilation into the natural world. 'A Chinese "understands | the spirit of the wilderness"', she writes in 'Nine Nectarines', 'It was a Chinese | who imagined this masterpiece.' In the introduction to *A Marianne Moore Reader* she refers to 'the Tao being a way of life, a "oneness" that is tireless; whereas egotism, synonymous with ignorance in Buddhist thinking, is tedious'.[47] Mai-Mai Sze's book on Chinese painting mentions that 'in connection with the Taoist emphasis on *wu wei* (outer passivity and inner activity), there is an aspect of the dragon that should be mentioned, namely, the power of restraint'.[48] Moore values restraint, and this is nowhere more evident than in her poem 'O To Be A Dragon'. The dragon is Moore's imaginal counterpart in this poem about the exercise of power, how to both unleash it and grow 'immense', and to rein it in and control it.

Moore's syllabic metre, so closely tied to Chinese poetics, is likewise a product of these imposed constraints which she places upon her verse and which become imperatives of her composition. David Perkins has noted the deliberate and enforced unnaturalness of syllabic verse:

Its function in English seems primarily to negate accentual scansion and allow the prose rhythm to move forward and receive first emphasis. For the poet, syllabic meter may serve more personal needs. One easily learns to think in blank verse, for example, and to a lesser degree in other traditional meters also. Thus, for most poets the metrical aspect is partly unconscious. But syllabic meter can never become habitual. The syllabic line presents itself to the poet as an external form that must be filled consciously.[49]

[46] Moore, 'Humility, Concentration and Gusto', *Grolier Club Gazette*, 2 (May 1949), 289–300, and *CPR* 422.
[47] *A Marianne Moore Reader* (New York: Viking, 1961), p. xiv.
[48] Sze, *The Tao of Painting*, 83.
[49] David Perkins, *A History of Modern Poetry: From the 1890s to the High Modernist Mode* (Cambridge, Mass. and London: Harvard University Press, 1976), 558.

Control such as this defies rather than complies with the original impetus of ancient poetry as an unbridled expression of emotion through chant or song. Syllabic verse does not have a metric source which follows the rhythm of music, dance, or incantation. Moore's consistent need to control the emotional source of her poetry through unnatural metre may be a way of expressing the intensity of that emotion. 'Governance of the emotions and impassioned perceptiveness seem to me "the artist" ', she said in her interview with Howard Nemerov, 'every day it is borne in on us that we need rigor,—better governance of the emotions'.[50] There is little tolerance here for the involuntary or spontaneous sources of ancient verse.

This kind of 'governance' pervades Moore's artistic ideas about poetic discourse and expression. 'Governance', from the Old French 'gouvernance', indicates not only 'the controlling action, power or manner of governing', but 'the state of being governed'. It also carries with it the meaning of 'discreet or virtuous behavior and wise self-command'. 'So art is but an expression of our needs', Moore wrote in conclusion to an essay entitled 'Feeling and Precision' (1944), 'is feeling, modified by the writer's moral and technical insights.'[51] As she makes an orchestrated onslaught upon the creative text the writer, like the surgeon, must be aware that 'precision is both impact and exactitude'.[52] And in the prose essay 'Profit is a Dead Weight' (1963), Moore quotes Confucius in her discussion of cynicism: 'If there be a knife of resentment in the heart, the mind fails to attain precision.'[53] Technique becomes allied with morality, to become restraint at the behest of exactitude. Perhaps that is why Darlene Erickson has described Moore as 'fanatic about using the exact word'.[54] The typographic text itself is shown to betray a writer's moral candour: 'One notices the wholesomeness of the uncapitalized beginnings of

[50] Moore, *Poetry and Criticism: Response to Questions Posed by Howard Nemerov* (Cambridge, Mass.: Adams House and Lowell House Printers, 1965), and *CPR* 592–3.

[51] Moore, 'Feeling and Precision', in *Predilections* (New York: Viking, 1955), 11, and *CPR* 402.

[52] Ibid. 4.

[53] Moore, 'Profit is a Dead Weight', in *Tell Me, Tell Me: Granite, Steel, and Other Topics* (New York: Viking, 1966), 21, and *CPR* 569.

[54] Darlene Williams Erickson, *Illusion is More Precise than Precision: The Poetry of Marianne Moore* (Tuscaloosa, Ala. and London: University of Alabama Press, 1992), 219.

lines', she writes in 'Feeling and Precision'.[55] Moore's correctives
link a writer's method with a writer's wisdom, self-involvement
belies sagacity. She wrote as early as 1927 that 'literary "neatness"
implies a certain decorum of manner as of matter'.[56] A version
of these ideas has been expressed in Liu Xie's *The Literary Mind
and the Carving of Dragons* when, in 'An Exegesis of Poetry'
(*Ming-shi*) he writes that 'poetry means discipline, disciplined
human emotion'. 'The single idea that runs through the three
hundred poems in the *Book of Poetry* is freedom from undisciplined thought', he continues; 'the interpretation of poetry as
disciplined human emotions is in thorough agreement with this
observation.'[57] Moore's quotations sometimes provide the kind
of distance from emotion which complies with these strictures
on discipline. A. Kingsley Weatherhead offers insight into the ways
in which she uses quotations as 'a means of controlling feeling,
like the elaboration of an image or the proliferation of new ones'.[58]
In some ways we can view Moore's use of quotation as a means
of distraction, as a device behind which she can speak to her
reader/listener in another voice without having to take credit for,
or acknowledge, their disclosure or sentiment as her own.

Just as Chinese landscape painters used clouds and mists
to mask the borders and transitional areas between the layers
of landscape elements,[59] Moore encases borrowed language in
quotation which substitutes for, and masks the interposition of,
often somewhat alien, 'anti-poetic', textual material. The con-
tours of her 'primary' poetic language and that of her 'secondary',
appropriated poetic material are established on separate textual

---

[55] Moore, 'Feeling and Precision', 7, and *CPR* 399.

[56] Moore, 'Comment', *The Dial*, 82/3 (Mar. 1927), 267, and *CPR* 178.

[57] Xie, *The Literary Mind*, 61.

[58] A. Kingsley Weatherhead, *The Edge of the Image* (Seattle and London: University of Washington Press, 1967), 83.

[59] See e.g. such paintings as *Clear Weather in the Valley* by Tung Yuan (*c.*1000), *Hills and Trees in Mist* by Mi Fei (eleventh century), *Ch'iao and Hua Mountains in Autumn* by Chao Meng-fu (thirteenth century). In 'A Father's Instructions', Kuo Hsi suggested that 'if you want to show the height of mountains, they will appear high if half hidden midway by cloudy forms, but not so if completely exposed': 'A Father's Instructions' (dated 1080), in Yutang, *The Chinese Theory of Art*, 79–80. Wang Wei (699–759), who established the principles of atmospheric perspective in the eighth century, wrote in *Formulas for Landscape*: 'The lower parts of hills are blocked off by clouds, rocky bluffs are blocked off by streams. Building structures are blocked off by trees and pathways are blocked off by men' (quoted in Yutang, *The Chinese Theory of Art*, 39).

'planes', the quotations lifted from the text to form another, elevated register. Moore's 'planes', as William Carlos Williams has pointed out about the disposition of her word units, 'remain separate, each unwilling to group with the others except as they move in the one direction'.[60] Since its beginnings, landscape painting in China has utilized clouds and mists to obfuscate difficult transitional areas, placing either discrete, clear-edged clouds or dissolving mists between mountains which then seem to recede and become indistinct. As noted above, this layering or overlapping of mountains, for example, functions as the primary method of establishing perspective. Rudolph Arnheim has written about this technique as a means of establishing depth: 'Overlapping is particularly useful in creating a sequence of visual objects in the depth dimension when the spatial construction of the picture does not rely on other means of perspective . . . this was observed even in antiquity.'[61] When we view Moore's poems as a textual and visual raising and lowering of poetic 'planes', we can see that the principles of overlapping which Chinese landscape painting has relied upon for centuries are similar to the ones which Moore uses in creating her poetic landscapes. Arnheim describes the importance of visually contiguous elements such as these when he writes:

The space-building role of superposition in Chinese landscape painting is well known. The relative location of mountain peaks or clouds is established visually by overlaps, and the volume of a mountain is often conceived as a skeleton of echelons or slices in staggered formation. The complex curvature of the solid is thus obtained through a kind of 'integral' based on the summation of frontal planes.[62]

Moore's poems which contain multiple quotations are likewise 'staggered' by demanding to be 'read' on alternating textual planes, and a tension set up as the reader moves between and traverses textual levels. This kind of multiple perspective was originally used to witness a landscape from all vantage-points at once, to capture simultaneously many compositional axes, or establish what Wai-lim Yip has called a 'total environment':

[60] William Carlos Williams, *Imaginations*, (ed.) Webster Schott (New York: New Directions, 1970), 146.
[61] Arnheim, *Art and Visual Perception: A Psychology of the Creative Eye* (Berkeley and Los Angeles: University of California Press, 1974), 250.
[62] Ibid. 251.

Therefore, the viewer is not restricted to seeing the scene from one static location *selected* arbitrarily by the painter. The viewer revolves, as it were, with the multiple perspectives available for viewing. In order to preserve this flexibility, the Chinese painter sometimes makes use of an emptiness that is at the same time a space of thingness, such as mists and clouds, to diffuse the distances, or manipulates the curving lines of mountains or other natural objects to camouflage the change of perspectives, subtly returning freedom of mobility to the viewer.[63]

It is not surprising that Moore's poems seem to acquire features which resemble the topographic assemblage of Chinese landscape painting. Ancient Chinese records suggest that painting developed out of the drawing of maps and, as Mai-Mai Sze has observed, '*tu* (map or plan) is a term still used in reference to certain kinds of pictures'.[64] The keys to Moore's maps use the conventions of natural metaphors. One finds in her poems, as with Chinese painting, a predominance of subjects found in nature. It would seem that she instinctively shared a belief in one of the fundamental unities expressed in Chinese philosophy. The Chinese philosopher 'understood the continuity of the universe; he recognised the kinship between his own life and the life of animals and birds and trees and plants', Laurence Binyon wrote, 'and so he approached all life with reverence, giving each existence its due value'.[65]

Moore's familiarity with the history of Chinese landscape painting can be seen in her repeated references in poems like 'Nine Nectarines' to the 'blue and green' style in Chinese painting: 'Fuzzless through slender crescent leaves | of green or blue or | both, in the Chinese style'. In Chinese art this style refers to landscapes from the T'ang dynasty onward which were painted predominantly with blues and greens.[66] Blue mountains and green trees lend the landscapes an imaginary, surreal quality. These were landscapes of pure enchantment whose colouring displayed affinities with the cave paintings of Tunhuang, the famous repository of Buddhist art.[67] Other indications that Moore was well acquainted with Chinese painting can be found in book

[63] Yip, *Diffusion of Distances*, 32.   [64] Sze, *The Tao of Painting*, 36.
[65] Binyon, *Flight of the Dragon*, 26.
[66] For example, during the Sung dynasty, Chao Po-chu's famous *The Emperor Ming Huang's Journey to Shu*.
[67] René Grousset, *Chinese Art and Culture*, trans. Haakon Chevalier (London: Andre Deutsch, 1959), 231.

reviews like the one of Louise Wallace Hackney's *Guide-Posts to Chinese Painting*, which reveals a detailed knowledge of Chinese painting techniques, imagery, and history. Moore writes that Hackney is 'as attentive as the author could wish one to be, to the "ideals and methods" of Chinese painting, to "influences and beliefs reflected in it," and the influence exerted by it'.[68] The same issue of *The Dial* (at that time edited by Moore) includes two 'Chinese-style' poems in English, 'Of Tung-Ting Lake I am Reminded' by Kwei Chen and 'Hang Fu' by Elizabeth Coatsworth.[69] She also mentions in her annotations to 'Novices' (1923) an auction of Chinese *objets d'art* which provoked 'that tinge of sadness about it which a reflective mind | always feels, | it is so little and so much'.[70] Moore regularly read and saved the Chinese art auction notices, museum pamphlets, and bulletins as well as gallery programmes of the exhibitions she attended. In an essay entitled 'Well Moused, Lion', she refers to Tu Mu's lyric criticism on Chinese painting,[71] in reference to Wallace Stevens's *Harmonium* (1923), a collection which includes the poem 'Six Significant Landscapes', whose opening lines evoke a classical Chinese character and setting as the first of its six significant land-scapes.[72] In addition to the Chinese river scrolls and technical art-historical vocabulary discussed earlier, Moore's references to scholarly texts such as Mai-Mai Sze's *The Tao of Painting* in her notes provide ample evidence that she had an advanced understanding of Chinese art history and connoisseurship. Additionally, her foreword to Lancaster's *Prospect Park Handbook* quotes the Chinese painter and theorist Kuo Hsi, whose essays on Chinese painting have been widely known and often quoted by painters and scholars from the time they were written.[73]

Chinese landscape perspective, unlike Western perspective, has traditionally not been established from a human vantage-point, but from sustained heights not always corroborated by what can be seen from particular, existing mountain viewing points.

---

[68] Moore, 'Briefer Mention', *The Dial*, 84 (Apr. 1928), 345.
[69] Ibid. 314 and 328.
[70] From Arthur Hadyn's article in *Illustrated London News* (26 Feb. 1921).
[71] See Moore, 'Well Moused, Lion', in *The Dial*, 76 (Jan. 1924), 84–91, and *CPR* 91.
[72] See Wallace Stevens, *Collected Poems* (London: Faber & Faber, 1955), 73–5.
[73] *CPR* 609–10.

Imaginal landscapes, too, are most often painted from a seemingly airborne point of view. Raphael Petrucci has commented upon this kind of isometric perspective:

Chinese perspective . . . was evolved in an age when the method of superimposing different registers to indicate different planes was still being practised in bas-reliefs. The succession of planes, one above the other, when codified, led to a system totally different from our monocular perspective. It resulted in a perspective as seen from a height. No account is taken of the habitual height of the eye in relation to the picture. The line of the horizon is placed very high, parallel lines, instead of joining at the horizon, remain parallel, and the different planes range one above the other in such a way that the eye embraces a vast space . . .[74]

Western central perspective, conversely, is a manifestation of the humanist individualism of the Renaissance.[75] Moore's poetry is evidently taken up with ways of seeing, and Albrecht Dürer[76] and Leonardo Da Vinci,[77] both important theorists on perspective in painting, are mentioned several times in her work.[78] The principles of linear perspective construction, known to the Greeks and Romans, were rediscovered by Filippo Brunelleschi (1377–1446) and codified by the humanist architect Leon Battista Alberti in *Della pittura* (On Painting, 1435), a work dedicated to Brunelleschi. Brunelleschi understood the concept of a single vanishing-point, towards which all parallel lines drawn on the same plane appear to converge, as well as the principle of the relationship between distance and the diminution of objects as they appear to recede in space. The imitation and execution in drawing and painting of linear perspective had to be reasoned out, learned through precise measurement. Rudolph Arnheim critically observed that 'symbolically, such a centered world suits a hierarchical conception of human existence . . . It would hardly fit the Taoist or Zen philosophies of the East', he wrote, 'which express themselves in the centerless continuum of the Chinese

[74] Raphael Petrucci, *Chinese Painters*, trans. Frances Seaver (New York, 1920), 29–30; cited in Grousset, *Chinese Art and Culture*, 248.

[75] Arnheim, *Art and Visual Perception*, 294.

[76] Albrecht Dürer (1471–1528), author of *Treatise on Measurement* (1525).

[77] Leonardo Da Vinci (1452–1519), author of *Treatise on Painting* (1518), and the first to define atmospheric or 'aerial' perspective.

[78] See e.g. Moore's review of an exhibition of prints by Dürer and his contemporaries at the New York Public Library in *The Dial*, 85 (July 1928), 89–90, and *CPR* 203–4.

and Japanese landscapes shaped by isometric perspective.'[79] The influence of Taoist and Chan Buddhist philosophies upon Chinese landscape painting is discussed in Mai-Mai Sze's book, *The Tao of Painting*, which Moore mentions in the notes to 'O To Be A Dragon'. Moore's method of treating the textual surfaces of her poems is securely linked to several Eastern philosophical and artistic sources. Moore's sheaf of notes on *The Mustard Seed Garden Manual*, a well-known Taoist treatise on Chinese painting methods translated in Sze's book, include her observation that 'the manual is to me a world of romance—the romance of words'.[80]

However, Moore remains firmly attached to her American surroundings and origin despite these forays into 'oriental' mysticism and her passion for Chinese masterpieces. Her ability to 'see so much without ever leaving home' is part of her wisdom, part of the silent precision in her every execution which can be attributed to so many sources in addition to Chinese ones. The 'sublimated wisdom of China', 'Egyptian discernment', and the 'emotion' of the Hebrew language (from 'England') are all sought in America. Wisdom, discernment, and emotion were clearly in evidence in the work of fellow American artist, Henry James, who Moore felt was one of the few surviving practitioners of precision. 'Perfect diction is not particularly an attribute of America', Moore wrote, 'we have it, however, in the geometrically precise, snow-flaked forms of Henry James.'[81] It is his quoted phrase which she uses to counter the argument presented in 'New York' (1921).

> it is not the atmosphere of ingenuity,
> the otter, the beaver, the puma skins
> without shooting irons or dogs;
> it is not the plunder,
> but 'accessibility to experience.'

She mentions James more than any other single writer in her prose, which includes an essay entitled, 'Henry James as a Characteristic American'.[82] In a letter to Ezra Pound in 1919, Moore wrote that 'Gordon Craig, Henry James, Blake, the minor

---

[79] Ibid. 295.   [80] RL II:06:12, p. xvi.
[81] Moore, 'Briefer Mention', *The Dial*, 80 (May 1926), 444–8, and *CPR* 165.
[82] *Hound and Horn*, 7 (Apr.–May 1934), 363–72, and *CPR* 316–22.

Prophets and Hardy, are as far as I know, the direct influences
bearing on my work.'[83]

Moore's feelings about restraint and precision and all that
they embodied were well established in her early college years
at Bryn Mawr. 'The indispensable thing is *restraint* wh [*sic*] gives
on the one hand simplicity', she wrote in a course notebook of
February 1909, 'by the time you have simplic [*sic*] and restraint
combined you have austerity—that is going to cut out most of our
friends.'[84] Moore may have felt that James was her counterpart
as a writer. 'One might say that Miss Moore is, fragmentarily,
Henry James in pure crystalline form', Randall Jarrell has
remarked.[85] James's particularity was the natural outcome of his
visual imagination, perhaps the result of his own training and
interest in painting. It would seem, from her remarks in an interview with Donald Hall, that Moore recognized this ability to
'see' imaginatively as a link creating their artistic consonances:
'Didn't I write something one time, "Part of a Poem, Part of a
Novel, Part of a Play"? I think I was all too truthful. I could
visualize scenes, and deplored the fact that Henry James had to
do it unchallenged.'[86] Moore fashions links between Henry James
and nature, and later to the Chinese predilection for precision,
accuracy, and, necessarily, restraint.

These possibilities in the execution of a work of art are, along
with 'economy of statement', what Moore tells Hall, 'liberate
—at least have some bearing on—the imagination'.[87] David
Perkins has called attention to the underlying moral imperative
of Moore's emphatic focus on brevity and precision when he
writes that 'her idiom, like her stance generally, is low-keyed,
prosaic, American, and precise'. 'Precision is the master word',
he continues, 'it is the effect and—because it is a moral as well
as a stylistic value and effort—to some degree the meaning of
her poetry. It involves not only accuracy ("certainty of touch")
but also self-discipline.'[88] In several poems, Moore interweaves

[83] RL V:50:06–10. From a letter dated 9 Jan. 1919. Also published in *The
Selected Letters of Marianne Moore* (New York: Knopf, 1997).
[84] RL: 'Imitative Writing Notes', p. 39.
[85] Randall Jarrell, 'The Humble Animal', *Poetry and the Age* (New York:
Vintage–Knopf, 1953), 165.
[86] Moore, interview with Donald Hall, in *A Marianne Moore Reader* (New York:
Viking, 1961), 254.
[87] Ibid. 255.   [88] Perkins, *History of Modern Poetry*, 561.

references to James and the Chinese artist, asserting that they are aware of the need to approach art in this way in order to find the freedom which follows restraint, and the verbal precision which is the natural outcome of a precision of feeling. These lines from 'An Octopus' are a good example of this:

> this fossil flower concise without a shiver,
> intact when it is cut,
> damned for its sacrosanct remoteness—
> like Henry James 'Damned by the public for decorum';
> not decorum, but restraint;
> it is the love of doing hard things
> that rebuffed and wore them out—a public out of sympathy
> with neatness.
> Neatness of finish! Neatness of finish!
> Relentless accuracy is the nature of this octopus
> with its capacity for fact.

James is linked with nature, with the fossil flower, a remnant of what once was alive and damned for the 'sacrosanct remoteness' which critics often pillory him for. Moore offers a corrective to this misconception, tries to explain and make heroic these deeds of restraint and neatness. And again, in the end, she allies James's efforts with those of nature, of the 'nature of this octopus', the nature of the past in the fossilized flower and the struggling, relentless octopus before us now.

Moreover, Moore shares certain 'methods' of articulation with James which are often referred to as the 'Jamesian parenthesis' or aside. Moore's poems often groan with a plodding detail which forces the reader to call up visual embodiments of this abundant material if only to 'place' and organize it, locate or create linkages between images which might reveal or elucidate her meanings. In the work of both writers this makes for what Jean Garrigue has described as 'a kind of brio of the irrelevantly relevant'.[89] In many of the same ways, Moore's poetic texts are arranged, or even built, by means of expression in another 'voice', or with yet another undetermined extratextual emphasis. A. Kingsley Weatherhead discusses a similar effect in James's writing, citing R. P. Blackmur's comment on the extratextual associations that this enables:

---

[89] Garrigue, *Marianne Moore*, 33.

Inverted commas, then, as well as indicating borrowed material, are directing the reader to set the words off from their context and giving them the tonal effect that words similarly enclosed have in Henry James. As R. P. Blackmur says, they 'indicate a special or ironic sense in the material enclosed or as a kind of minor italicization, they are used as boundaries for units of association which cannot be expressed by grammar and syntax'.[90]

Perhaps Moore found this a textual indication of a presiding morality in James which became, in execution, the accuracy and precise detail which she associated with the Chinese artist. She allies 'a James, Miss Potter, Chinese | "passion for the particular" ' in 'Tell Me, Tell Me'. Certainly in her own work, Moore both conceives of the moral 'lessons' in her poems pictorially and executes them with a precision which becomes for her a moral stance. 'A master axiom for all writing, I feel, is that of Confucius: "When you have done justice to the meaning, stop" ', she wrote, 'that implied restraint, that discipline is essential.'[91]

Of course, the notion that there is accuracy of representation implies that there is a 'proper' distance or perspective from which to view things, that something can be 'seen' from a particular vantage-point. Moore lacks James's multiple perspectives on the nuances and subtlety of human interaction and language, his finely graded moral observations, or what Moore calls 'James's odysseys | Of intricate outlook' in 'To A Cantankerous Poet Ignoring his Compeers—Thomas Hardy, Bernard Shaw, Joseph Conrad, Henry James'.[92] There is a certain presumption, authority, and impulse towards mastery in Moore's persistent call to pare down, to arrive at 'what it is'. Nothing is tentative, provisional, or contingent in her poetry; there is no doubt. 'Few poets have as much moral insight as Miss Moore; yet in her poems morality usually *is* simplified into self-abnegation', Randall Jarrell observes. 'Poems which celebrate morality choose more between good and evil, and less between lesser evils and greater goods, than

[90] Weatherhead, *The Edge of the Image*, 83–4, citing R. P. Blackmur, *Form and Value in Modern Poetry* (New York: Anchor, 1957), 227.
[91] Moore, 'Impact, Moral and Technical; Independence Versus Exhibitionism; And Concerning Contagion', in *Harvard Summer School Conference on the Defense of Poetry* (Cambridge, Mass.: Harvard University Press, 1951), 71–6, and CPR 435.
[92] RL I:01:36. This poem was neither published nor dated, but the manuscript has Moore's address at 343 North Hanover St., Carlisle on it and this places it between 1909 and 1916.

life does, so that in them morality is simpler and more beautiful than it is in life, and we feel our attachment to it strengthened.'[93] The distinctly Protestant rigour of her demands for diligence, fastidiousness, and 'neatness' in artistic production may explain her apparent preference for the clarity of a precise moral statement over the murkiness of moral pondering. Her subjects, perhaps because they so often come from art and descriptive accounts of nature, are already morally static or inert, already ordered by the media in which they appear to her.

The boundaries, limits, and restraint in her work account for the sometimes uneven quality of her poetry. Suzanne Clark observes that Moore, like Louise Bogan, 'was severe with her own work, pruning mercilessly, and perhaps giving the critical spirit so large a scope that she curtailed her own productivity, unbalancing the relationship between the critical and the creative'.[94] 'My own revisions are usually the result of impatience with unkempt diction and lapses in logic; together with an awareness that for most defects, to delete is the instantaneous cure', Moore admitted.[95] Moore's artistic process seems to have been haunted by a fear of excess which was apparently not an abiding concern of Henry James. The precision and restraint which both writers arrive at are those of different crafts, though both are meticulous and accurate, and these are qualities that Moore locates in the Chinese art that she studied with such concentration and interest.

Moore's work is formally and informally preoccupied with notions of precision and restraint which find a focal point in a poem entitled 'Silence'. The poem, as is explained in the annotations, expands upon a few comments made by a Miss A. M. Homans: 'My father used to say, "Superior people never make long visits. When I am visiting, I like to go about by myself. I never had to be shown Longfellow's grave or the glass flowers at Harvard".' An additional, and uncited, source for this poem appears in a May 1916 entry in one of her early reading notebooks, where she cites James Prior's *Life of Burke* (1872)

---

[93] Jarrell, 'Her Shield', in *Poetry and the Age*, 183.

[94] Suzanne Clark, *Sentimental Modernism: Women Writers and the Revolution of the Word* (Bloomington and Indianapolis: Indiana University Press, 1991), 107.

[95] Moore, *Idiosyncrasy and Technique* (Berkeley: University of California Press, 1958), and *CPR* 507.

as the source of a reported conversation between Edmund Burke and a friend: 'throw yourself into a coach said he. "Come down and make my house your inn" '.⁹⁶ This is an interesting incidence of one of the 'omissions' which Moore alludes to in her epigraph to the *Complete Poems*, a subject which will be discussed at more length in the next chapter. Despite the disparity between attribution and source, however, the poem's autobiographical implications are evident in Moore's early separation from her father and in the nature of Moore's elaborations on the original quotation. Her version takes on the stalking primitiveness of the cat's appetite and the stoical acceptance of a father's limited feeling. The temporary visits which the father in the poem encourages are presented with a double negative, as if hesitant, at first, to make plain the true implications of his offer: 'Nor was he insincere in saying'.

Moore's father's insanity and his permanent institutionalization before her birth are possible sources for the temporary quality of the idea of 'home' in this poem. In 'Silence', Moore resigns herself to the observation in her simple, unqualified last line that 'Inns are not residences'. The 'father' feels that the 'deepest feeling' shows itself in silence and restraint, which recalls an annotation to Moore's poem 'Marriage' (1923): 'Silence of women—"to an Oriental, this is as poetry set to music".' Silence is a pivotal concept in Chinese thought and in Buddhist philosophy. Moore's attention to this concept and its alliance in her work with notions of restraint (' "The deepest feeling always shows itself in silence; | not in silence, but restraint." ') exposes the degree to which the philosophical and the personal potentially stand in for one another in her poems. As Zhong Longxi has noted:

Qian Zhongshu points out that Sikong Tu's phrase 'without putting down' should be understood as 'without putting down more' or 'without putting down again,' and that the moment of silence . . . or the blank space in Chinese landscape painting, is always framed in words, in lines and colors. It is important to realize the close relationship between silence and its verbal frame; in fact, suggestiveness is nothing but the framing

---

⁹⁶ RL VII:01:01. Reading Notebook of 1916–21. Moore cites James Prior, *Life of Burke* (London: Beel & Daley, 1872). Prior cites 'Townley's Study' (1787) as the source of the remarks.

of silence, the use of words around a center of absence which contains the possibilities of meaning and interpretation.[97]

Restraint becomes a method of achieving silence, and its power in Chinese landscape painting, as in poetry, was recognized by Moore as a means to harness the quiet energy of the reticence and solemnity, the 'deepest feeling', which drives her work.

Her absorption in, and commitment to, maintaining the ideals of precision and restraint is shown in 'Silence' to be authentic and unremitting. 'Silence' conveys a daughter's realization that her father's love is limited and qualified, that there is no safety in it, no residence. The poem comes at the end of *Selected Poems* (1935), endorsing that closure and either preventing the reader from forming the expectations Moore may once have had, or re-enacting their disappointment. Certainly this is a potential source of the remarkable concentration and restraint which Moore exercised in the execution of her poetry. Her poetic interest in silence, precision, and restraint finds a source in personal issues which only rarely surface. The criteria of exactness and 'neatness of finish'—she adds an insistent exclamation mark—emerge as values in her writing from her earliest poems onward. These attributes inhere in Chinese literature and art, offering her a repository of intermediary emblems with which to encode her dialogue on these subjects. Moore scavenged widely in the culture of the Far East and culled potent metaphors for the concerns which compelled her to write. She interposes a vast number of Chinese references to ensure that her readers would 'stumble upon' the 'sublimated wisdom of China'.

[97] Zhang Longxi, *The Tao and the Logos: Literary Hermeneutics, East and West* (Durham, NC and London: Duke University Press, 1992), 171–2, citing Qian Zhongshu, *Tan yi lu* (Discourses on Art) (Beijing: Zhonghua Shuju, 1980), 414–15, referring to Sikong Tu (837–908) *Shipin jijie* (Twenty-four Moods of Poetry), (ed.) Guo Shaoyu (Hong Kong: Shangwu, 1965).

7
Quotation, Curio-Collecting, and the Privileging of Detail

Every book is a quotation; and every house is a quotation out of all forests, and mines, and stonequarries; and every man is a quotation from all his ancestors.

(Ralph Waldo Emerson, 'Plato, or the Philosopher')

There is no pure originality. All minds quote. Old and new make the warp and woof of every moment.

(Ralph Waldo Emerson, 'Quotation and Originality')

If man takes any step, exerts any volition, initiates anything, no matter what, it is law of fate that another man shall repeat it, shall simply echo it.

(Ralph Waldo Emerson, journal entry of 1867–8)

IMAGINARY POSSESSIONS

Moore's efforts to translate the peculiarities of Chinese poetry and painting into a personal method of writing can be seen as an attempt to interpret America through a poetic reconciliation with an alien world and its curiosities. Her use of the *fu* technique, Chinese perspectival principles, symbology, and philosophy all indicate that she looked to the Far East for models and ideas with which both to resist logic and contemporary trends in poetry, and to embrace the enduring nature of an ancient civilization and the clarity of its decisive moral framework. Ironically, this process has much in common with the efforts of medieval and Renaissance explorers and collectors to incorporate foreign lands, including America itself, into domestic commerce, to confer legitimacy on 'home' by assembling representations of 'abroad'. Moore's compilations of arcane information from scholarly texts as well as popular journals and newspapers can, therefore, be read as a kind of colonial gesture to glean from the world's resources a store of images and facts with which to both assess and confirm her estimation of America. The sometimes overwhelming profusion of detail gleaned from these different kinds of texts also reveals a prototypically American avidity for culture, which often seems to translate into accumulation rather than discrimination. Her interest in forming this kind of collectanea is exposed by the evident similarities between her poetry, early literary miscellanies, and the curiosity cabinets of Renaissance collectors. Her attraction to the marvellous in Chinese myth and symbology, in particular, re-enacts a European colonial tradition of collecting and cataloguing the wonders of the new in order to ascertain similarities between local and foreign cultures. She addresses a long-held perception of America's provisional nature with respect to established nations and ancient cultures through her repeated efforts to isolate China's superior qualities and then to find reflections of them 'at home'.

Similarly, an examination of Moore's methods for acquiring, stockpiling, and deploying observations and images gleaned from Chinese sources should illuminate the process by which she legitimizes certain kinds of learning and knowledge which appear in her verse. This activity is also one of the many strategies she employs in her attempt to create an impersonal poetry, to eliminate subjective feeling, and maintain privacy as a kind of defence or shelter. Moore's repeated use of quotations from every conceivable source, in addition to her lengthy poem notes, highlights her instinct for salvage and the careful husbandry of her scholastic spoils. Moore began quoting other sources in two early poems which appeared in *The Egoist* of October 1915, continuing and extending this practice throughout her career. She even made alphabetical indices for the quotations found in her writing notebooks. But however successful her poems are, there are evident risks attached to inventing an idiom which, in Jean Baudrillard's words, 'forfeits all value for others'.[1] As a collector of the exotic, unusual, and unfamiliar, Moore's eclectic procedure further distances her from her audience and allows her to indulge her predilection for independence from both her reader and the world.

---

[1] Jean Baudrillard, 'The System of Collecting' in John Elsner and Roger Cardinal (eds.), *The Cultures of Collecting* (London: Reaktion, 1994), 24.

The cabinet of curiosity had its heyday between the sixteenth and eighteenth centuries, and her methods for selecting and hoarding information and substitute representations of the rare have much in common with the kinds of collection formed during this period. 'Moore's collector's approach is very much in the tradition of late sixteenth- and early seventeenth-century prodigious troves, such as Walter Cope's "wonder-cabinet" ', Jeredith Merrin observes, 'which was said to include an embalmed child, a unicorn's tail, a flying rhinoceros, and a sea mouse.'[2] Merrin also notes that Sir Thomas Browne's *Pseudodoxia Epidemica* (Vulgar Errors) of 1646 is an example of the literary miscellanies with which Moore's poetry shares an appetite for unusual detail. The titles of several of Moore's poems are nearly identical to chapters found in Browne's 'literary menagerie'— 'Of the Basilisk', 'Of the Oestridge' (the first sentence of which reads 'The common opinion of the Oestridge . . . conceives that it digesteth Iron'), and 'Of Unicornes hornes'.[3] Moore's fondness for these seventeenth-century compendia could also explain the very dated quality of some of her poems' syntax and speech, discussed in earlier chapters.[4] Also, Browne's book is not cited as a source for those of her poems which use these particular animals as subjects, a fact which corroborates her admission in the epigraph to her *Complete Poems* that 'omissions are not accidents'.

Moore's penchant for promoting natural facts and phenomena to the status of cultural objects reflects the medieval conception of the coextensivity of natural and man-made objects. Medieval curio collections, as Anthony Alan Shelton notes, 'did not even distinguish between objects found in nature (natural curiosities) and those made by exceptional craftsmen (artificial curiosities)'.[5]

---

[2] Jeredith Merrin, *An Enabling Humility: Marianne Moore, Elizabeth Bishop, and the Uses of Tradition* (New Brunswick, NJ and London: Rutgers University Press, 1990), 18.

[3] Sir Thomas Browne, *Pseudodoxia Epidemica: or, Enquiries into Very many received Tenents, And commonly presumed Truths. By Thomas Browne Dr. of Physick.* (London: printed by T. H. for Edward Dod, 1646).

[4] This is apparent in her prose writing as well. Donald Hall records that Moore found the sermon's antique sentence structure 'appealing' when she studied seventeenth-century imitative writing at Bryn Mawr. See Donald Hall, *Marianne Moore: The Cage and the Animal* (New York: Pegasus, 1970), 19.

[5] Anthony Alan Shelton, 'Cabinets of Transgression: Renaissance Collections and the Incorporation of the New World', in John Elsner and Roger Cardinal (eds.), *The Cultures of Collecting* (London: Reaktion, 1994), 182.

Likewise, Moore does not appear to discriminate between these two categories in her poetic treatment of natural curiosities from the Far East and Chinese *objets d'art*. Chinese precision and restraint in executing a range of artistic tasks from lacquer painting ('He Made This Screen', 1909) to acrobatics ('Blue Bug', 1962) are similarly indistinguishable from the evidence of those qualities in art in Moore's non-hierarchical display of the incomparable and rare. And in her emblematic use of exotic animals, marvellous beings, and foreign wonders, Moore strives to derive from these 'natural' creatures and 'artificial' crafts a series of moral tenets which, the poems imply, are drawn from qualities to be found in the farthest corners of the world and which inhere even in the most remote varieties the animal kingdom can offer. The categories of nature, man, and man-made are all undifferentiated and subordinate to Moore's moral promotions. The *fu* with its *luan* endings, as was discussed in an earlier chapter, is an example of a Chinese poetic model perfectly suited to this procedure of moral extraction from the exotic and the peculiar.

A similar impulse to discern immanent qualities in nature that could provide a template for more universal meanings was felt by early collectors of curiosities. Shelton points out that French encyclopedic collectors were known as *curieux*, 'because of their passion for, and commitment to, seeking deeper knowledge of the workings and nature of the universe, and a fuller, perhaps grander, picture of the totality of creation'.[6] To be 'curious' is not only to be 'eager to learn' and 'inquisitive', but also to be 'minutely careful'. Moore's attention to detail in her poems, to the 'echidna and echinoderm' of the hedgehog in 'His Shield', for example, as well as her need to cite and explain her many quotations, unmistakably links her poetic process with a European tradition of collecting. Like the medieval and Renaissance collector's retrieval of strange booty from unvisitable sites (the deep sea) and foreign lands, Moore's poetic practice is appropriative, and has led Bonnie Costello to call her a 'kleptomaniac of the mind'.[7] Her obvious enthusiasm not only to learn but to display that learning, additionally exposes the connections

---

[6] Ibid. 181, citing K. Pomian, *Collectors and Curiosities: Paris and Venice, 1500–1800* (Cambridge University Press, 1990), 58–9.

[7] Bonnie Costello, *Marianne Moore: Imaginary Possessions* (Cambridge, Mass., and London: Harvard University Press, 1981), 5.

between 'curious' and 'curiosity'. 'Curiosity' is both 'strangeness' and 'a desire to know' and, for the curiosity collector, a need to possess or exercise some authority over the conspicuous and the strange. Certainly Moore's habit of indexing her vast collection of copied quotations (filling some nineteen notebooks) betrays her desire to command them as knowledge and facts. As with her emblematic references to a wide variety of animals and objects, she fills her poems with quotations which are offered as if they were pregnant with other meanings, if not in their original contexts, then in the ones she creates for them. It is remarkable that these disparate components of her poetry are all meant to exemplify or corroborate the larger, and usually moral, statements she is drawn to make, much as if they proceeded from deduction or argument. This feature of her poetry is also reminiscent of medieval and Renaissance collections and the ends they were supposed to serve. 'A large part of the justification for collections in the Renaissance', Shelton explains, 'was borrowed from medieval scholasticism, its ideas concerning the innate meaning of things and the nature of revelation, and its vision of the relationship between the microcosm and macrocosm.'[8]

Moore's library also holds a copy of the *Historie of Foure-Footed Beastes* (1607) by Edward Topsell, which she cites in an issue of *The Dial* in reference to dragons.[9] Given that this book is mentioned by her at an early stage in her writing career, and that she studied seventeenth-century literature as an undergraduate at Bryn Mawr, it is reasonable to conclude that Moore made a conscious and early decision to resurrect and embrace Renaissance ideas of the immanence of the divine in the mundane, as well as the insistent optimism this necessitates and is meant to encourage. And her urge to collect has been identified as a preoccupation from an earlier era as well. Suzanne Clark describes Moore's sensibility as 'premodern' with 'a passion for miscellany that is seventeenth-century'.[10] But some of these characteristics can also be attributed to Moore's Protestant background, her proximity to the clergy, and her familiarity with sermons. She did read Lancelot Andrewes at Bryn Mawr, and yet the construction of her verse displays a wider acquaintance with methods of

[8] Shelton, 'Cabinets of Transgression', 58–9.
[9] Moore, 'Comment', *The Dial*, 83 (Aug. 1927), 178, and *CPR* 187.
[10] Clark, *Sentimental Modernism*, 120.

writing sermons. Much of an earlier chapter was devoted to an examination of the way that Moore's poems resemble Puritan sermons and prompt books. In her collection and use of quotation, however, she can be seen to share certain practices with early biblical commentators. 'Moore's characteristic incorporation of quotations into her verses owes something to a similar use of quotations in the work of Protestant biblical commentators', Andrew J. Kappel explains, 'as her remark on her notes to her quotations suggests: "take probity on faith and disregard the notes" . . . her attitude toward nature, as God's second book, is recognizably Protestant, especially in its attention to animals.'[11] These sources for her collecting instincts, and her use of animals as emblems of the divine, are most likely just a few of many. 'Moore was fascinated by the use of quotation in poetry, criticism, and sermons and often marked passages in books or newspapers that discussed this technique', Celeste Goodridge observes, '[her] aesthetic preference for the part over the whole also explains in part why quotation is so important to her.'[12]

Moore's collection of facts and quotations for her poetry also reflects a Modernist interest in 'found objects' and collage. This is one way of coming to terms with the very disparate and dispersed references in her poems, which retrieve a seemingly inexhaustible quantity of material from every kind of source and historical period (for example, Ming tombs, ancient Chinese bronzes, the peach *yu*). Her assembly of these oddments of information resembles what John Hollander refers to as certain 'devices of quotational mosaic'. Hollander offers some potential early models for Moore's method for displaying her vast collection of detail when he goes on to note that *cento* is a medieval practice where a poem is created out of various arrangements of half-lines from Virgil. He also mentions *capricci*, in which the poet occasionally uses borrowed lines.[13] While neither of these models could adequately account for Moore's sequences of often

---

[11] Andrew J. Kappel, 'Notes on the Presbyterian Poetry of Marianne Moore', in Patricia C. Willis (ed.), *Marianne Moore: Woman and Poet* (Orono, Maine: University of Maine Press, the National Poetry Foundation, 1990), 50.
[12] Celeste Goodridge, *Hints and Disguises: Marianne Moore and her Contemporaries* (Iowa City: University of Iowa Press, 1989), 22, 25.
[13] John Hollander, 'Marianne Moore: The Art of a Modernist Master, A Symposium' in Joseph Parisi (ed.), *Marianne Moore: The Art of a Modernist* (Ann Arbor, Mich. and London: UMI Research Press, 1990), 120.

unrelated observation and detail, it is possible that an initial impulse for her preservation and display of quoted material is the result of her familiarity with the kinds of poetic practice to which Hollander refers. There is an abiding sense that Moore is not only gathering quotation and fact, but that she is engaged in the salvaging and restoration of idiosyncratic detail which is part of an eclectic and very personal display. Sandra M. Gilbert has observed about her poem, 'Marriage' that 'the collage of quotations that Moore has constructed persistently supports her own pose as a bemused researcher'.[14] The Chinese artefacts and Chinese mythological material she uses in her poems fulfil this function as well, because they represent unusual moments when the reader must refer to her appended notes, or indeed use other resources, to understand her meaning. It is these instances which reinforce the impression that Moore's allusive method works to install her as the initial authority both on her poems and on the even larger amounts of reference material to which they refer.

Her collages of seemingly unrelated description and quotation are further problematized by the reader's unavoidable assumption that the poems cohere in some fashion, or have an intended meaning. The moral statements which often conclude Moore's poems are, in many cases, not connected in any perceivable manner to the stanzas that precede them and, therefore, do not function as conclusions or reassuring clues as to the import of the poem as a whole. The poems' notes explain so many things— sources, citations, snippets of conversation—in a 'nearly neurotic desire for exact record-keeping and documentation',[15] according to Daniel L. Guillory, and yet there is often no apparent reasonableness or plausibility to an individual poem. Certainly Moore may have cultivated this tension between the clarity of her smallest observations and the inchoate impression formed by their accumulation. She valorizes marginal or negligible detail while demoting, by contrast, the importance of integrating, rather than serializing, that detail. This kind of arbitrary presentation, though, implies a greater unity—a unity which is somehow assured by the 'format' itself. 'To recognize that the components

---

[14] Sandra M. Gilbert, 'Marianne Moore as Female Female Impersonator' in Parisi (ed.), *Marianne Moore: The Art of a Modernist*, 37.

[15] Daniel L. Guillory, 'Marianne Moore and Technology' in Willis (ed.), *Marianne Moore*, 86.

of a given collage have corporate impact is to acknowledge that they form a systematic ensemble', Roger Cardinal writes; 'it follows that the collage is in fact a collection—by which I mean *a concerted gathering of selected items which manifest themselves as a pattern or set, thereby reconciling their divergent origins within a collective discourse.*'[16] Perhaps it is this reconciliation to which Cardinal refers which seems absent in Moore's verse. Moore's habit of assembling, iterating, reciting and listing precious and uncustomary pieces of information, added to her busy efforts to catalogue and cite, call attention not so much to her poems themselves but to the activity and effort of them. They resemble the masterpieces of a proud archivist, a showcase of authorized detail—and of difference—being accompanied by a class-related phenomenon of refinement. She sees her quoted passages, in John Hollander's analysis, 'as potential pieces of her own discourse . . . quotations, private scriptural allusions, or citations from a vast bible of ordinary discourse'.[17] Moore seems confident of the legitimacy of her strategy of incorporation, which refuses to grant priority either to speech or to the written words which replace it. Her dilemma becomes not which kind of borrowed speech or text to choose, but how to synthesize appropriated material and whether to supply attributions. 'Orientalism is after all', Edward Said reminds us, 'a system for citing works and authors.'[18]

Moore's poems in this light subscribe to an alternative medieval justification for forming collections, for not all medieval collections relied upon a confirmation of the divine in nature. According to William of Ockham, as Anthony Alan Shelton relates, objects had only a nominal existence, unregulated by the 'mind of God'. These kinds of collection could be arranged without any apparent order between their constituent items. 'For collectors of a nominalist persuasion, what was important were curiosities, rare or near-unique phenomena that were thought to have resulted from some exceptional condition or circumstance.'[19] While Moore

[16] Roger Cardinal, 'Collecting and Collage-making: The Case of Kurt Schwitters' in Elsner and Cardinal (eds.), *The Cultures of Collecting*, 71.
[17] John Hollander, 'Observations on Moore's Syllabic Schemes', in Parisi (ed.), *Marianne Moore: The Art of a Modernist*, 89.
[18] Edward Said, *Orientalism* (New York: Vintage, 1978), 23.
[19] Shelton, 'Cabinets of Transgression', 180.

may have been persuaded by this competing rationale to embrace disorder or randomness, she would have had to consider even the most drab detail 'exceptional' in order for it to qualify for her collection. It is also exceedingly unlikely that a poet who cited 'God and family' as her 'personal panacea'[20] would deny that 'the mind of God' ordered phenomena. In the final lines of an early poem, 'When I Buy Pictures', written in 1921, she makes an overt statement about the immanence of the divine in things: 'it must be "lit with piercing glances into the life of things"; | it must acknowledge the spiritual forces which have made it.' Interestingly, it is in a poem about collecting, about 'imaginary' possession, in which she lists what she demands of 'pictures'. Her stipulation that what she collects 'must be "lit with piercing glances into the life of things"' is, as the poem's notes disclose, quoted from A. R. Gordon's *The Poets of the Old Testament*.[21] Much more will be said about this poem, but it is pertinent here to notice that Moore does require that 'spiritual forces', whether human or divine, make what she considers to be art and are necessary to the collectible. 'If everything literary were deleted, in which there is some thought of deity, "literature" would be a puny residue', she declared; 'one could almost say that each striking literary work is some phase of the desire to resist or affirm "religion".'[22]

Moore's alternate resistance to, and affirmation of, 'religion' could account for the resemblance to incompatible collecting practices her poetry displays. They may be symptoms of private ruminations, an internal dialogue or debate, about the necessity to impose moral certitude on a prevailing disorder. Or it may be that Moore's method of collecting is an attempt to subvert established norms and categories of writing and borrowing. It is true that 'collecting can also attempt to challenge the norm, and cock a snook at the accepted patterns of knowledge into whose regulative frame the interests and energies of the world have been corralled', as John Elsner and Roger Cardinal have commented: 'outside the boundaries of social recognition arises the myth of the pioneering, the experimental collector whose

---

[20] Moore, 'Marianne Moore', *Esquire*, 58 (July 1962), 99, and *CPR* 679.

[21] Cited as A. R. Gordon, *The Poets of the Old Testament* (Hodder & Stoughton, 1919).

[22] Moore, 'Religion and the Intellectuals', *Partisan Review*, 17 (Feb. 1950), 6–7, 48, and *CPR* 678.

vocation may be to parody orthodox connoisseurship, to challenge the expectations of social behaviour, even to construct a maverick anti-system.'[23] Indeed, in a review of William Carlos Williams's *Collected Poems 1921–1931* Moore hints at her own reasons for amassing and juxtaposing an indiscriminate profusion of unrelated observation when she observes that ' "the senseless unarrangement of wild things," which he imitates, makes some kinds of correct writing look rather foolish'.[24] This kind of subversion, however, imposes its own rules, even if they do advocate change and a kind of anarchy. 'I think she is an autocratic writer', Robert Pinsky has said; 'Moore is very much in charge in the way she quotes and apostrophizes . . . it's somewhat incendiary, is the more explicit dealing with social classes in her writing.'[25] And Alice Ostriker has remarked on the way that Moore's use of quotation is simultaneously a 'gesture of modesty' and a 'gesture of authority'.[26] Whatever the origin, the competition between these conflicting models generates an abiding tension in Moore's poetry which is perplexing if the reader is unaware of, or disinterested in, these potential overtones.

'The object pure and simple, divested of its function, abstracted from any practical context, takes on a strictly subjective status', Jean Baudrillard has noted; 'the result is that all objects in a collection become equivalent.'[27] As a critical manoeuvre, Moore makes the attribution and acknowledgement of source material become a central feature of her poems, whose appended notes often go on for pages and identify even exegetical trifles in order to lend equal textual authority to both a work by Edmund Burke and a casual newspaper article, to set on an equal footing the abstruse and the mundane. 'My observations, as usual, are borrowed', she remarked at an honorary dinner in 1963.[28] And in an early reading notebook for 1907–15, Moore copied the

[23] Introduction to Elsner and Cardinal (eds.), *The Cultures of Collecting*, 3.

[24] Moore, ' "Things Others Never Notice" ', *Poetry*, 44 (May 1934), 103–6, and *CPR* 325–7.

[25] Robert Pinsky, 'Marianne Moore: The Art of a Modernist Master, A Symposium', in Parisi (ed.), *Marianne Moore: The Art of a Modernist*, 109.

[26] Alice Ostriker, 'Marianne Moore: The Art of a Modernist Master, A Symposium', ibid. 110.

[27] Baudrillard, 'The System of Collecting', 8.

[28] Moore, 'Remarks', *Proceedings of the American Academy of Arts and Letters and the National Institute of Arts and Letters*, 2/5 (1963), 280–1, and *CPR* 657.

following remark by Butler Savil: 'as I have said over & over again if I think something that I know & really like ... no matter where, is appropriate, I appropriate it ... A good stealer is ipso facto a good inventor.'[29] This is a telling indication of Moore's method of appropriation, one that is resistant to any orthodox hierarchy or classification—it does not purvey the sanctioned principles of 'taste'. To 'appropriate' is 'to make one's own' and comes from the Latin *proprius*, meaning 'proper' and 'property'. Moore's observations and quotations, her appropriations, are her imaginary possessions, her property. As with her borrowings, she makes it clear in 'When I Buy Pictures' that she does not discriminate between the ordinary and the extraordinary: 'it may be no more than a square of parquetry' or the variegated colour of an artichoke. Savil's remark, this poem of 1921, and her dinner remarks from 1963 also show that her appropriative poetic strategies remained consistent over the course of her writing career.

But this effort to democratize her sources seems not so much a desire as a deliberate, emphatic, and public claim for the availability of her poetry, when it is decidedly not so. There is something very controlling and manipulative about Moore's notes and the unidentified allusions they fail to explain. The implied erudition which they go so far to convey is hardly the kind of concession to 'plain American which cats and dogs can read' which Moore leads us to expect in poems like 'England'. 'The reader thus remains at Moore's mercy, guided by no predictable signs of discursive, logical, or associational continuity', Joanne Feit Diehl asserts; 'the effect of such willful contextualization, whatever its sources, is to create a verbal field that borders upon the impenetrable, proving as deflective as any of those created by her contemporaries.'[30] Moore's non-hierarchical stance toward the boundaries of 'taste' and 'art' is not extended to her readership. It is clear where she positions herself with respect to her audience, and no reader will have read the same motley collection of books, articles, and newspapers to which she refers in her notes. Every reader, then, is among the uninitiated. To this extent, at least, her poems treat readers just as she treats,

---

[29] RL VII:01:01. Notebook 1250/1, entry no. 118. This quotation is attributed to Butler Savil, but the title of a text is not noted by Moore.

[30] Joanne Feit Diehl, *Women Poets and the American Sublime* (Bloomington and Indianapolis: Indiana University Press, 1990), 51–2.

or claims to treat, her collected poetic material—all readers of
Moore become equivalent. In Susan Stewart's terms, 'the forms
of alienation arising from preferences for difficulty and the
exotic as qualities of the modernist text reflect an increasing
distance between the forces of literary production and those
of literature's general consumption'.[31] Chinese and other exotic
elements in Moore's poetry thus serve the same function as
'difficulty'. 'Difficulty' carries with it the meaning 'obscure' which,
in turn, means 'remote from observation' and 'dark'. The preference for the difficult and the exotic are, in a sense, part of
the same inclination. Moore's Chinese borrowings are part of
her collection of the difficult, the remote, and the unobservable.
They are one component in a system which deflects the reader
from her poetry.

An earlier chapter examined the ways in which Moore's poetry
works to sequester her authorial subjectivity by demanding
manners and asserting morals, conveying a need for a genteel
setting for her poems. Chinese artefacts, craftsmanship, and
creatures of marvellous origin are implicated in that effort. Here
we can observe the way that Chinese elements, and perceptions
about Chinese ingenuity and craftsmanship, figure in the more
encompassing project of Moore's vast collection of quotation
and citation. Her passion for particularizing the very visual
observations in her poems and the detailed, scholastic activity of
citation and correct attribution are, for her, distinctly Chinese
preoccupations, some of the tasks which require restraint and
precision. These are the qualities she demanded of her own
writing and revered in the artistry of others. Thus Chinese references in Moore's poetry are part of a system of choosing the
remote, the ancient and the unfamiliar, while what she calls the
'Chinese | "passion for the particular"' in 'Tell Me, Tell Me'
is, as the quotation marks imply, a commonplace or widely
understood attribute, which she adopts as an imperative of her
work. 'She is *the* poet of the particular—or, when she fails, of
the peculiar; and is also, in our time, *the* poet of general moral
statement', Randall Jarrell has remarked; 'often, because of their

[31] Susan Stewart, *On Longing: Narratives of the Miniature, the Gigantic, the Souvenir, the Collection* (Baltimore, Md. and London: Johns Hopkins University Press, 1984), 5.

exact seriousness of utterance, their complete individuality of embodiment, these generalizations of hers seem almost more particular than the particulars.'[32]

And Moore's continual gathering of morsels of observation, fact, and quotation works to legitimate the discrete nature of her aphoristic *luan*. This process not only attempts to valorize the detail as a unit of observation, it also makes claims for the relevance of detailed reading and looking as means of construing meaning. 'To read in detail is, however tacitly, to invest the detail with a truth-bearing function', Naomi Schor has noted.[33] By their steady accretion of parcels of quotation and description, Moore's poems try to assure her reader that the moral truths they arrive at are founded on irreducible observation, on the sturdy components that, she implies, reveal and corroborate indisputable verities. Her method seems to offer the minute and the marginal as guarantors of, rather than threats to, the stability and authenticity of her epigrammatic conclusions. The partial and 'incomplete' quality of Moore's constantly roving description, it seems, is part of an effort to validate her short, truncated, and often seemingly reductive, moral endings. Likewise, the laborious burden of details and lists in her poetry draws attention away from aphoristic statements which are not fully elaborated. 'In terms of technique', Joanne Feit Diehl explains, 'the effect of Moore's enumerative poetics is to deflect the reader from the thread of continuity or the possibility of a continuity existing beyond the proliferation of description'.[34]

This attention to detail as a supposed repository of larger meanings has sources in Far Eastern philosophy. 'To see big within small', a saying common among Sung dynasty painters, is to realize the immanence of all matter.[35] The tradition of Chinese fan painting, for example, is a long-standing artistic recognition of this principle. Fan painting displays both the ability of artists

---

[32] Randall Jarrell, 'Her Shield', in *Poetry and the Age* (New York: Vintage–Knopf, 1953), 172.

[33] Naomi Schor, *Reading in Detail: Aesthetics and the Feminine* (New York and London: Methuen, 1987), 7.

[34] Diehl, *Women Poets and the American Sublime*, 68.

[35] See Osvald Sirén, *Chinese Painting: Leading Masters and Principles*, vol. ii (London: Lund Humphries, 1956), 73. Under the Northern Sung dynasty emperor Hui-tsung (1101–25) the saying, translated literally, was 'a thousand *li* in a square foot of space', the *li* being a Chinese unit of length equal to half of a kilometer.

to create an entire landscape on the open surface of a hand-held fan and the importance of depicting and looking at small subjects, a butterfly or blossom for example, to discern more far-reaching 'truths' about man's place and importance in the phenomenal world. Moore's fascination with detail reflects a non-Western tradition of experiment with scale. In addition to fan painting, the minute detail of Chinese scroll paintings, discussed in an earlier chapter, and the arrangement of Chinese garden views all testify to the subtlety and importance of the particular in Chinese artistic traditions. Japanese *netsuke* is another, and perhaps better known, outcome of the lure of the miniature and the detail in the Far East.

There are times, however, when Moore's reluctance to 'see' on a larger scale can overwhelm a reader buried under the sheer number and disparity of her detailed observations. As Diehl has observed of 'Virginia Brittania' (1935), a poem written fourteen years after 'When I Buy Pictures', 'Moore's lines veer into an ever-accreting descriptiveness where flourishing life coexists with a death-like excess'.[36] These two stanzas from this twelve-stanza poem support Diehl's remark:

> Observe the terse Virginian,
>   the mettlesome gray one that drives the
> owl from tree to tree and imitates the call
>   of whippoorwill or lark or katydid—the lead-
>   gray lead-legged mocking-bird with head
>   held half away, and meditative eye as dead
> as sculptured marble
>   eye, alighting noiseless, musing in the semi-sun,
>   standing on tall thin legs as if he did not see,
>   conspicuous, alone,
>   on the stone-
> topped table with lead cupids grouped to form the pedestal.
>
> Narrow herring-bone-laid bricks,
>   a dusty pink beside the dwarf box-
> bordered pansies, share the ivy-arbor shade
>   with cemetery lace settees, one at each side,
>   and with the bird: box-bordered tide-
>   water gigantic jet black pansies—splendor; pride—

---

[36] Joanne Feit Diehl, *Elizabeth Bishop and Marianne Moore: The Psychodynamics of Creativity* (Princeton, NJ: Princeton University Press, 1993), 80.

> not for a decade
>   dressed, but for a day, in over-powering velvet; and
>   gray-blue-Andalusian-cock-feather pale ones,
>   ink-lined on the edge, fur-
>   eyed, with ochre
> on the cheek . . .

This deathly profusion is somewhat perplexing, given Moore's otherwise stalwart endorsement of personal rigour and her positive affirmation of the value of effort. Certainly it is the effect, rather than the acknowledged subject, of her poetry. This kind of mania for collecting and displaying the spoils of her active book-learning could be seen as another means of alienating her reader, of establishing and maintaining the self-protective distance she seems to have required. In Randall Jarrell's words, 'the most extreme precision leads inevitably to quotation; and quotation is armour and ambiguity and irony all at once—turtles are great quoters'.[37] The stultifying excess to which she was given can also be read as the preservational impulse, as she saw it, behind her poetic tasks. 'When a thing has been said so well that it could not be said better, why paraphrase it?', Moore replied more than once to queries about the many quotations in her poems; 'my writing is, if not a cabinet of fossils, a kind of collection of flies in amber'.[38] And this 'death-like' proliferation of detail is also tied, not only to the sometimes dated quality of her language, but also to the colonial overtones of her catalogue of the marvels of China, examined in previous chapters. As John Elsner and Roger Cardinal point out, 'collections gesture to nostalgia for previous worlds (worlds whose imagined existence took place prior to their contents being collected) and also to amusement'.[39]

FLIES IN AMBER

Moore is quite evidently amused by, if not proud of, the activity and the results of her collecting. 'I fix upon what would give me pleasure in my average moments', she writes in 'When I Buy

---

[37] Jarrell, 'Her Shield', 180.
[38] Moore, foreword to *A Marianne Moore Reader* (New York: Viking, 1961), p. xv, and *CPR* 551.
[39] Elsner and Cardinal (eds.), *The Cultures of Collecting*, 5.

Pictures', 'Too stern an intellectual emphasis upon this quality or that detracts from one's enjoyment'. These lines pinpoint the objectives of Moore's verse and go a long way towards explaining and justifying the procedure of her poetry. Pleasure and enjoyment are part of the amusement both of collecting and of writing poetry. 'The collection is a form of art as play', in Susan Stewart's words, 'a form involving the reframing of objects within a world of attention and manipulation of context.'[40] As in her poem 'Museums' (written between 1918 and 1925), Moore takes a certain pleasure in the display of her curiosities: 'The museum exists | for those who are able to enjoy what they see'.[41] The fact that the sources of her minute observations are almost always mediated or second-hand, from the written records of those who actually experienced them or as they appear on works of art and in photographs, must also be part of her attraction to the inert. The whole of her collecting process, in this light, is also complicit in her efforts to remove herself from the concourse of life, to be aloof and safe. The hermetic world of Moore's poetry, with its myriad animals, insects, and bewildering maze of quotation and citation, is a place of concealment and also an impenetrable shell. 'This is why withdrawal into an all-encompassing object system is synonymous with loneliness', Baudrillard wrote of the collector's world, 'it is impervious to communication from others, and it lacks communicability.'[42] When asked at an early stage in her writing career what she considered to be her weakest characteristic, Moore replied—'unsociability'.[43]

Collecting is, in and of itself, a kind of hobby or at least an activity which has little end other than itself. It is not productive and is, by definition, not involved in exchange—it is an aristocratic, leisure activity. Collecting, in the traditional sense,

[40] Stewart, *On Longing*, 151.

[41] The entire text of 'Museums' (in addition to a draft version) appears in *Marianne Moore Newsletter*, 1/1 (Spring 1977), 8–9. The gloss on the poem (p. 7) by the unspecified editors notes that Moore had written to Ezra Pound on 10 May 1921 about the American literary climate and noted that her current reading included Gilman's *Museum Ideals of Purpose and Method* from which she excerpted ten pages of notes (RL 1250/2).

[42] Baudrillard, 'The System of Collecting', 24.

[43] Moore, 'Confessions: Questionnaire', *The Little Review*, 12 (May 1929), 64, and *CPR* 673.

is both moribund and belated—it is an activity whose goals
are to collate the dead artefacts of life and, in some way, to
return them to another, and always changing, significance at the
boundaries of the present in the collection. As Jean Baudrillard
points out, *'the setting-up of a collection itself displaces real time*
. . . collecting remains first and foremost, and in the true sense,
a *pastime'*.[44] It is, additionally, a pastime which usurps the more
corporate concerns of the museum—it is a closed system and
a repetitious task. 'Throughout her lifetime Marianne Moore
collected, saved, and savored the hard and well-made artifacts
of the world', Daniel L. Guillory has noted; 'in those gestures
of retrieval, in all the crystal and ivory animals perched on her
bookshelves, in every poem she sent out into the world, there
is a subtext, an urging for preservation and collecting, a silent
pleading that turns the world into an open-air museum.'[45]

   In her first version of 'Museums', written between 1918 and 1925
and unpublished in her lifetime, Moore notices that museum
exhibitions can provide 'a commentary upon death that | one
prefers to the cemetery' and that a museum visit is like 'a foregone conclusion'—mourning and memory are here part of the
repetition of visiting a collection. The museum 'exists | for
those who are able to enjoy what they | see, at the time as well
as afterward', she writes, and in a later version concludes that
'one follows a stream, every turning of which is a foregone con-
clusion; it is similarly | that one goes to a museum to refresh one's
mind with the | appearance of what one has always valued.'[46]
'Museums' intimates that Moore's own collecting practices may
aid the retrieval of memory and the exercise of mourning, making
them into constant and repeatable occupations. 'Museums are,
for Moore, a way of concentrating and renewing her relation to
the world', Bonnie Costello notes; 'the qualities of the objects she
describes in this poem are on display everywhere in her work.'[47]
To establish a collection and to display it also makes that activity
accessible, consistent, and fixed. It keeps memory and mourning
at bay ('but there is there'), contained and purposeful, functioning

---

[44] Baudrillard, 'The System of Collecting', 16.
[45] Guillory, 'Marianne Moore and Technology', 90.
[46] Moore wrote at the top of her manuscript of the second draft (RL I:03:11),
'not published and not finished'.
[47] Costello, *Marianne Moore*, 191.

as an endless rehearsal where all time is made simultaneous, where origin and history are replaced by classification. The museum and the experiences it furnishes also sets itself in opposition to modern urban life and its stimulants, yet another instance where Moore's instinct to remove herself from the concourse of contemporary life is in evidence.

She prefers the second-hand, or versions of natural life, to living creatures and acknowledges this when she writes that the carved eternity ape 'without responsiveness or breath, is better than the ac- | tuality contemplating its new fur'. These lines encapsulate Moore's preferences for experience; she needs to be able to make summations, to deal in generic terms, to eliminate the unexpected and the individual—to orientalize. In a way, life must be over in order to draw conclusions from it, or beings must be analysed in groups, or as populations, in order to be accessible. This is why 'mankind' is 'the supreme curio' and not any individual woman or man. 'Curio' is an odd word to use in reference to 'mankind', because it implies not only 'curiosity', as if Moore were not part of 'mankind', but also 'curio-collecting', as if humanity would form the most treasured portion, the 'supreme' find, of her collection. It is clear in 'Museums' that Moore's enterprise of mastery, her compilation of fact, observation, quotation, and detail, is also a search for ways to collect 'mankind'. She attempts this by offering aphorisms, statements that can be applied to humankind as a whole, as a species, alongside her observations about nature. The inclusion of moral epigrams in her poems brings 'mankind' into her collection of still life as the ultimate, prized possession. For Moore, this 'supreme curio' completes so many of her poems, makes the 'cabinet' of each poem, like an early modern collection,[48] a microcosm, a summary of the universe, just as, in museum collections, there are only renditions of the living, samples of the strange, fossils and bones, paintings and porcelain. Moore's poems progress much as if she is wandering in a museum, with

---

[48] James Clifford has noted that in the early modern period the rarity and strangeness of collected objects was prized. A curio cabinet 'jumbled everything together, with each individual object standing metonymically for a whole region or population'. See James Clifford, 'On Collecting Art and Culture' in Russell Ferguson, Martha Gever, Trinh T. Minh-ha, and Cornel West (eds.), *Out There: Marginalization and Contemporary Cultures* (Cambridge, Mass.: MIT Press, 1990), 149.

the details of each exhibit supported by documentation and fact. And just as in a museum, there is no necessary connection between the 'rooms' of her observation. Both the museum and Marianne Moore collect for a reason. As Roger Cardinal has noted, 'there is almost always an intention eventually to place the collage or the collection on display'.[49]

The apparent relish with which Moore identifies and marks her 'found objects' and the fact that the style of her writing remains virtually unchanged over time, show that she remained committed to her particular, repeated methodology. Her undergraduate study of biology has been noted in earlier chapters. John Hollander contends that the particularity of her writing is evident in both its method and format, observing:

the quoted texts are like her poetic elements, her syllables, insects or tiny organs of the natural history of written language; these fascinate her from the early poems on, and at first she begins to prize apart the written organ/organism. This botanizing or lepidoptery extends to the larger formats of poems themselves, I think, and graphic patterns of stanzaic forms, found on pages of books of poetry, await her inclusions and decontextualizations. And so too, to a degree, with her quoted material.[50]

To submit things to an ever more exacting scrutiny, like the increasing magnification of a microscope, is part of Moore's scientific approach to writing. It is something she was aware of in the requirements for collecting she sets out in 'When I Buy Pictures', when she writes that 'it must be "lit with piercing glances into the life of things"'. To 'detail', as the etymological sense of the French *détailler* reveals, is to 'cut in pieces', or in Hollander's terms, 'to prize apart'. Moore's apparent need to look into the life of things, to reduce natural phenomena to their fundamental components, is part of her desire to detail, to list, and to name. This is an orientalist practice in both its scope and concentration. Tejaswini Niranjana makes clear that orientalist discourses, among which poetry is included, 'provided a vast quantity of detailed, meticulously collected information'.[51]

---

[49] Cardinal, 'Collecting and Collage-making', 71.
[50] Hollander, 'Observations on Moore's Syllabic Schemes', 89.
[51] Tejaswini Niranjana, *Siting Translation: History, Post-Structuralism, and the Colonial Context* (Berkeley, Los Angeles, and Oxford: University of California Press, 1992), 72.

Moore's taxonomic interest in naming and classification has already been discussed in previous chapters, but her association of this activity with China has yet to be noted. These lines from 'Tell Me, Tell Me' offer an example of the link she makes:

> It appeared: gem, burnished rarity
> and peak of delicacy—
> in contrast with grievance touched off on
> any ground—the absorbing
> geometry of a fantasy:
> a James, Miss Potter, Chinese
> 'passion for the particular,' of a
> tired man who yet, at dusk,
> cut a masterpiece of cerise—

She locates this 'passion for the particular' as a national characteristic in these lines, a passion shared here by only Henry James and Beatrix Potter. Other poems and prose pieces also attribute this fascination with detail and precision to the Far East and have been examined in earlier chapters. Indeed, Edward Said has characterized orientalism as a 'theory of Oriental detail',[52] the idea of discovery necessarily entailing an act of sustained, highly particularized representation.

However, there is little narrative representation in Moore's poems; they seem like storehouses of accumulated detail with little order or integration among it. As Jeanne Heuving has observed, 'Moore opts for the superfluity and specificity of items, rather than for their schematization.'[53] What claims her attention are the bibelots of the natural and artistic world, which can be anything from any time or place. The 'bibelotization' of nature and art reflects a bourgeois desire for excess—too much of anything from anywhere in the same space. This style is, in Rémy Saisselin's terms, 'an economic and psychological style that at worst might be called the accumulative, or museum style, or, at best, the eclectic'.[54] The centreless profusion of Moore's poetic catalogues has been characterized by Robert Pinsky as 'dizzying,

[52] Said, 'The Problem of Textuality: Two Exemplary Positions', *Critical Inquiry*, 4 (Summer 1978), 712.
[53] Jeanne Heuving, *Omissions Are Not Accidents: Gender in the Art of Marianne Moore* (Detroit: Wayne State University Press, 1992), 109.
[54] Rémy Saisselin, *Bricabracomania: The Bourgeois and the Bibelot* (Rutgers: University of Rutgers Press, 1984; London: Thames & Hudson, 1985), 68.

even inchoate . . . bilious, imaginary, "not-right", animal'.[55] Her method of collecting is idiosyncratic in the extreme and aspires to be seen as distinctive and inimitable. It creates an illusion of a relation between things whose interconnectedness, if there is any, has been occluded. And this is true, not only for her poetry, but also for her prose. 'Her criticism is unsystematic', writes Donald Hall, 'depending upon a juxtaposing of observations and quotations so that an overall impression emerges that could scarcely be called a thesis.'[56] And despite the seeming effort to acknowledge the sources for her poems, to make her method of construction available to the reader, Moore regularly omits citations for some of her quotations, just as her notes often fail to explain the sources of all of her references. Much of this appears almost haphazard at first glance, though Moore warns the reader in her epigraph that her omissions are not accidental.

What this elision of sources signals is difficult to determine. Arthur Versluis has noticed that Ralph Waldo Emerson also often failed to note his indebtedness to certain sources, particularly Eastern ones, and concludes that in doing so Emerson avoided alienating his audience. In Versluis's analysis, this was in keeping with Emerson's belief 'that all particular men or literatures were manifestations, at their best, of universal man and universal literature'. He elided his references in part because he was preparing for an American renascence of the *philosophia perennis*. America could be the new Eden, but the revelation must take place by degrees, the groundwork being laid at every level as it were, from the teaching of karma to the excitation of the intellectual class and the poet. All was fertilization, preparation.[57]

This could be part of Moore's reasoning for domesticating texts of all kinds, for mining and scavenging among history and literature, both lay and professional, to celebrate and encourage the freedom to call upon a plenitude of information and images. Her writing reflects the eclecticism of American culture, what Robert Pinsky has called 'the not-quite melting pot of

[55] Pinsky, 'Marianne Moore: Idiom and Idiosyncrasy', in *Poetry and the World* (New York: Ecco Press, 1988), 51.
[56] Donald Hall, *Marianne Moore*, 135.
[57] Arthur Versluis, *American Transcendentalism and Asian Religions* (New York and Oxford: Oxford University Press, 1993), 74.

imports and appropriations'.[58] It plays havoc with the very notion
of attribution and acknowledgement, in the very way it cites
excessively at times and, at others, refuses to do so. Moore's
use of quotation is more random and offhand than that found
in, for example, either Eliot or Pound. *The Waste Land* and
The Cantos are layered with historical references in the form of
quotations, and yet there is a certain obligation to the perceived
burden of history and a reverence for the past in those poems.
Moore, on the other hand, quotes in a playful, almost defiant,
way. There is a purpose to both her attention and neglect;
omissions are deliberate and premeditated. The epigraph to
the *Complete Poems* alerts her reader to this hidden bibliographic skirmish in her method of composition. The text and
notes to each poem reinforce the impression that this is one
of the central dramas of her work. It is as if she is proving that
she can set things out in detail, she can rummage in history,
pilfer from books and conversations, and yet dispense with the
ordinary regulations of that kind of activity. The process is
one of colonization and also one of independence; it says that
'these sources can be mine' at the same time that it implies that
'they belong to no one'. She shares Emerson's edenic delight
in universal literature and yet, at the same time, shows that she
can control a universe of texts and information. Like so many
aspects of Moore's verse, her quotation practices are both subversive and authoritarian.

To assume, however, that writing is a neutral, referential
medium that invokes objects, that description aspires only to
transcription, is ostensibly not Moore's intention. The exuberant detail and constant quotation in her poems also prove that
the convention and significance of these collected 'objects' have
been altered by their appropriation, and this, too, becomes an
issue of her poetic texts. The assumption could be that what the
quotation signifies in its changed context is something different
from what it says or what it originally meant. Indeed, even a
cursory glance between Moore's poems and their notes shows that
much of her borrowed material functions as borrowed language
more than borrowed context. And Moore's effort to assimilate such an enormous number of details and images can also be

[58] Pinsky, 'American Poetry and American Life', in *Poetry and the World*, 128.

interpreted as a deliberate effort to exhibit just how unassimilable they are. The rivalry often staged through quotation, between 'original' and derivative, is in these poems arrested through the courtesy of citation and through the deliberate variety of types of quoted text. Moore's professed humility seems exaggerated, as she laces her poems with texts whose status reflects upon her own status as an author. The implied democracy of her poems would be more convincing if she alluded to sources from which she had borrowed meaning rather than language, which referred to traditions of thought rather than information. But, as Jeanne Heuving has remarked, Moore repeatedly quotes statements from 'insignificant and anti-poetic sources'.[59]

It is worthwhile noting that she rarely quotes poets or from poetry. One well-documented instance of her 'taking' from another poet involves Elizabeth Bishop. In her memoir of Moore, Bishop describes how 'the bell-boy with the buoy-ball', a phrase from Moore's 'Four Quartz Crystal Clocks', was taken from a story she told Moore in private conversation.[60] Naturally Bishop was disappointed to recognize her own words and find that they did not merit an acknowledgement in Moore's notes, and this was no doubt particularly difficult given Bishop's status as Moore's protégée. Moore seems to have shied away, not only from quoting poets and poetry, but from stating whose influence she had come under in different stages of her writing career. When she was drawn out on this subject, she named writers who seem to have little bearing on her work at all (Thomas Hardy, for instance) and whose books she did not own or keep in her library, while poets like Emily Dickinson, whose writing is in so many ways similar to Moore's, are given little mention in any of Moore's writing. This Dickinson poem, which bears so much resemblance to Moore's 'To A Prize Bird' (1915) and 'The Wood-Weasel' (1942), is an obvious example:

> The rat is the concisest tenant.
> He pays no rent,—
> Repudiates the obligation,
> On schemes intent.

---

[59] Heuving, *Omissions*, 12.

[60] See Elizabeth Bishop, 'Efforts of Affection: A Memoir of Marianne Moore', in *The Collected Prose*, (ed.) Robert Giroux (London: Chatto & Windus, 1984), 141.

Balking our wit
To sound or circumvent,
Hate cannot harm
A foe so reticent.

Neither decree
Prohibits him,
Lawful as
Equilibrium.

Both Dickinson and Moore share a decisive authority with language, display a deliberate modesty in their writing, and were avid readers of the Bible. Both used animals as emblems in their poems to comment upon human nature and acknowledge the spiritual in the mundane. 'Travel why to Nature, when she dwells with us', Dickinson wrote to a friend in 1866, 'Those who lift their hats shall see her, as devout do God.'[61] James J. Y. Liu has even located some similarities to Chinese poetry in Dickinson's verse, in the kind of images she is sometimes drawn to and the evocative simplicity of their arrangement.[62] But Moore mentions Dickinson only in a book review of a collection of her letters,[63] and in passing on two other occasions in her prose. Again, Moore isn't willing to acknowledge the actual influences upon her writing, almost as if she is intentionally diverting attention away from the formative influences on her work.

So that citation, both within and outside her poems, seems systemically organized and, perhaps, distorted or impaired. In a poet who is otherwise so methodical, who strives to be precise, who is dedicated to a system of syllabic counting, it is almost unthinkable that some sort of personal economy of quotation and citation is not at work in Moore's verse. 'Half Deity' provides a good example of Moore's strategic use of a Chinese source which, by the simple act of its citation, opens up avenues of interpretation not available in the text of the poem itself and highlights the way she dismantles sources, to make a subsidiary source in

[61] Emily Dickinson, 'Letter to Mrs. J. G. Holland', in *Selected Poems and Letters of Emily Dickinson*, (ed.) Robert N. Linscott (New York: Doubleday, 1959), 297.
[62] James J. Y. Liu, 'Time, Space, and Self in Chinese Poetry', *Chinese Literature: Essays, Articles, Reviews*, 1/2 (July 1979), 144.
[63] Moore, 'Emily Dickinson', *Poetry*, 41 (Jan. 1933), 219–26, and *CPR* 290–3, where Moore reviews *Letters of Emily Dickinson*, (ed.) Mabel Loomis Todd (New York: Harper, 1932).

citation yield collateral meanings. This half deity is also 'half worm' —a butterfly. After enumerating the unsurpassed varieties of butterfly, the poem introduces a nymph who tries to touch one of the swallow-tail butterflies, but is frustrated in the attempt by the swallow-tail's continuous movement from surface to surface:

> Defeated but encouraged by each new gust
>
> of wind, forced by the summer sun to pant,
> > she stands on rug-soft grass; though some are not
> > permitted to gaze informally
> > > on majesty in such a manner as she
> is gazing here.[64]

The only note for this poem states: 'It is not permitted. Edmund Gilligan: the *New York Sun*, December 1, 1934; *Meeting the Emperor Pu Yi*'. This citation shows that the insect world offers freedoms not always available to humans, yet another example of the emblematic use of animals in Moore's poetry. Actually, 'Half Deity' borrows only two words from Gilligan's article— 'not permitted'—and insignificant ones at that. Evidently, she requires this citation to make her poem be more than the lengthy description of the daily trials and strategies of insect life. The poem thus takes on a parallel significance, reflecting on the unnatural restrictions which imperial life in China imposed. To collect this kind of partial remark also signifies the ease with which Moore uses citation to reduce foreign worlds and customs to the subject of a poem about insects, the majesty of the 'Half Deity | half worm' whom 'We all, infant and adult' have gazed upon.

These lines from another poem, 'Novices', show how citation can simply add information which does not amplify any meaning attached to the borrowed words:

averse from the antique
with 'that tinge of sadness about it which a reflective mind always feels,
it is so little and so much'—
they write the sort of thing that would in their judgment
> > > > > > > interest a lady;

The note to the final quotation reads: ' "The Chinese objects of art and porcelain dispersed by Messrs. Puttick and Simpson on

---

[64] 'Half Deity' first appeared in *Direction* (Peoria, Ill.), 1 (Jan.–Mar. 1935), 74–5, and again in *What Are Years*. It was not included in *CP*.

the 18th had that tinge of sadness which a reflective mind always feels; it is so little and so much." Arthur Hadyn, *Illustrated London News*, February 26, 1921.' Here Moore cites to add names, dates, and the fact that 'the antique' originally refers to Chinese *objets d'art*. Only the fact that they were Chinese works could possibly hold any importance, and even this is difficult to discern. Unless, of course, the fact that they are Chinese makes their antiquity all the more ancient or remote, or attaches some exotic glamour to their age. What this note does disclose is that Moore read this kind of literature and did so two years before this poem's initial publication. To invoke China almost as a random novelty also demonstrates how easily foreign elements can be incorporated into Moore's world-view—Chinese art embodying the 'sadness' of a 'reflective mind'—and can in this instance be used to justify the value and appropriateness of both significant emotion and the 'reflective mind' which feels it. Chinese art lends age and authenticity to that portion of the quotation which appears in 'Novices'. As John Hollander astutely remarks, 'Marianne Moore is quite capable of complex quotation of the sort that depends on a residue of the original text excluded by the fragment quoted.'[65] But a great many of her notes which have no Far Eastern references add little more than detail. Other quotations have no citation or note, and unquoted allusions or language which seems borrowed is similarly unexplained. There is no detectable scheme in Moore's citational activity, and yet it can be firmly linked to orientalist literature. When commenting on Oriental detail, Edward Said reminds us that 'each particle of the Orient told of its Orientalness'.[66]

In classical rhetoric, quotation functions as either illustration or ornament. As illustration (*auctoritas*), the quoted material is privileged over both the primary text and the author quoting. The quoting author is, in this case, meant to temporarily relinquish mastery over the primary text and thereby become subordinate to the quoted author[67] who, in Moore's words, has said a thing 'so well that it could not be said better'. But, in fact, very little of her quoted text displays language or a turn of phrase which

---

[65] Hollander, 'Observations on Moore's Syllabic Schemes', 89–90.

[66] Said, *Orientalism*, 231.

[67] Claudette Sartiliot, *Citation and Modernity: Derrida, Joyce, and Brecht* (Norman, Okla. and London: University of Oklahoma Press, 1993), 5.

could not be improved upon. The examples above attest to this, and even a cursory glance at the phrases she quotes throughout all of her poetry confirms it as well. So perhaps Moore has a hidden strategy in her processes of quotation and citation. Claudette Sartiliot offers an alternative reading of this kind of citational tribute, using Longinus as an example, whose essays often provided a framework for Moore's criticism:[68]

It is worth noting that the first meaning of *to cite* (*citer* in French) is to summon to appear in court. It is from this first meaning that the second meaning of citation as quotation is derived. If the quoted author is summoned to appear in court, the game of quotation, as discussed in Longinus, becomes more complicated: there is a confusion between the judge and the judged. If in the case of Longinus's discourse, the quoted discourse appears as that by which the discourse of the belated writer will be judged, in some modernist and postmodernist practices, and by an ironic game, even in Longinus, the quoting author exhibits the quoted fragment as evidence in the court of readers, all the while comfortably hidden behind it. In this sense, to quote, even under the pretense of extolling, of giving the example of excellence, could be an interesting game of exposing to ridicule. Indeed, citing as 'making appear,' 'offering as an example,' also means to present to scrutiny—the judgment does not have to be positive.[69]

If Moore is not demeaning or ridiculing her cited authors, which in some cases it is evident she is not, then her quotation functions as ornament and is meant to embellish the poems into which it has been inserted. Quotation as ornament 'imposes a grade', in Sartiliot's words, between the quoted text and the quoting text. 'In this respect, the quoted fragment appears as a mere appendage to the main discourse, something superfluous, but also paradoxically privileged, as it appears as a stylistic exemplum', Sartiliot explains; 'thus one sees the subtle ways in which the apparent respect displayed by the quoting author is compromised by a simultaneous and arrogant subornation of the authorities.'[70] In this respect, Moore's quotation and citation can be seen as another instance in which subversion underlies the idiosyncrasy of her poetry, that she is in a complex, and also genteel, way using her poetry to show that she knows the rules of citational

---

[68] See e.g. Moore's quotation of Longinus in her essay 'Feeling and Precision' (1944), and *CPR* 396–402.

[69] Sartiliot, *Citation and Modernity*, 22.   [70] Ibid. 5.

behaviour and yet flouts them in a seemingly capricious manner. There is a contest with, and for, authority in Moore's work which is played out in both her manner of quoting and, sometimes, her refusal to cite. Taffy Martin analyses the competing and simultaneous claims made by Moore for her borrowed words. 'These marked words are *less* important than others on this page because they have a more distant origin', and, at the same time, Martin notes, 'these words are *more* important than the others on the page and have been set off in order to make that difference evident and permanent.'[71]

Moore treats her quotations as dispensable fragments on which she sometimes wishes to amplify through citation, a process which levels all borrowed language and reduces it to a subsidiary status within her linguistic economy. Martin's remarks about quotation making words both 'less' and 'more' important call attention to the uncertain and, hence, unstable position of quoted material in Moore's poetry. In the end, this precariousness forces quotation to become intrinsic to language itself. By and large, Moore refrains from quoting authors whose words might be recognizable even if they weren't cited. She does not engage with her reader in a literary world. But Moore's poetry is almost instantly recognizable for its references, its idiosyncrasy, and its subject-matter. Through quotation and grafting, she has fabricated a style of prose writing and a method for constructing poetry which is always identifiable as her own.

The effect of Moore's personalization of co-opted language is to draw increased attention towards her homilies. The epigrammatic statements, or *luan*, extruding from the body of so many of her poetic texts, adopt the language and authority of an ancient wisdom. 'The power of the visible is the invisible', she writes in 'He "Digesteth Harde Yron"'. Early poems already exhibit a similar summoning of an originless, anonymous legacy from the past: 'But why dissect destiny with instruments | more highly specialized than components of destiny itself?' ('Those Various Scalpels'), 'The passion for setting people right is in itself an afflictive disease. | Distaste which takes no credit to itself is best' ('Snakes, Mongooses, Snake-Charmers, And The Like') and

---

[71] Taffy Martin, *Marianne Moore: Subversive Modernist* (Austin, Tex.: University of Texas Press, 1986), 106.

'we prove, we do not explain our birth' ('The Monkey Puzzle').
A scriptural tone inhabits these *luan* and yet, unlike other statements in her poetry, none of these aphorisms is quoted. Moore
gives no clues as to the source of this repository of knowledge,
and the reader is left to assume that it emanates from the poet
herself.

Moore makes her apophthegms her own, or assumes that
the debt she owes to some prior text is self-evident. Much like
the conventions of writing in ancient China that followed, as
Zhang Longxi notes, 'the settled practice of ancient writers
quoting earlier writings',[72] Moore is, both in these epigrams
and throughout her poems, creating an intertextual fabric of
reference in her work. 'While a deconstructive *intertexte* is a trace
without origin', Zhang Longxi reminds us, 'a Chinese intertext
is always a trace leading back to the origin, to the fountainhead
of tradition, the great thinkers of Taoism and Confucianism.'[73]
Thus Moore is either establishing her own poems as authoritative
texts or participating in an unacknowledged, or understood,
system of referral and attribution. Moore read Lao Tzu and
Confucius, and references to their writing and philosophy can
be found throughout her reading notebooks and among her prose
essays. 'The weak overcomes its | menace, the strong overcomes
itself', she writes in 'Nevertheless'. In Book One of the *Tao Te
Ching*, Lao Tzu writes, 'The submissive and weak will overcome
the hard and strong.'[74] Book Two again takes up the subject of
the power of weakness:

> Therefore a weapon that is strong will not vanquish;
> A tree that is strong will suffer the axe.
> The strong and big takes the lower position,
> The supple and weak takes the higher position.[75]

[72] Zhang Longxi, *The Tao and the Logos: Literary Hermeneutics, East and West*
(Durham, NC and London: Duke University Press, 1992), 33.
[73] Ibid.
[74] Lao Tzu, *Tao Te Ching*, Book One, 36: 79a, trans. D. C. Lau (New York:
Penguin, 1963), 95. The *Tao Te Ching* (as it is spelled in Pin Yin transliteration),
in two parts with eighty-one short sections, is one of two principal Taoist texts and
probably originates in the fourth or third century BC. Its authorship has traditionally
been attributed to Lao Tzu ('Old Master'). The *tao* literally means a 'way' or 'path'
and the *te* denotes the virtue or moral fortitude characteristic of an individual who
follows a correct course of conduct. Thus, *te* is the moral power one acquires by
being in accord with the *tao*.
[75] Ibid., Book Two, 76: 183; trans. Lau, p. 138.

And two chapters later Lao Tzu writes, 'That the weak overcomes the strong, I And the submissive overcomes the hard, I Everyone in the world knows yet no one can put this knowledge into practice.'[76] These lines naturally have much in common with the New Testament and with Confucian wisdom. Asked in 1965 what single book published in the previous decade she returned to most often, Moore cited Pound's translations of the *Analects* of Confucius.[77] Again, Moore echoes all of these texts in 'His Shield' when she writes, 'a formula safer than I an armorer's: The power of relinquishing I what one would keep; that is freedom'. 'The sage does not hoard', writes Lao Tzu, 'Having bestowed all he has on others, he has yet more; I Having given all he has to others, he is richer still.'[78] This stoical air is also evident in 'What Are Years?' (1940): 'He I sees deep and is glad, who I accedes to mortality'. And Lao Tzu offers effectively the same observation:

> The people treat death lightly:
> It is because the people set too much store by life
> That they treat death lightly.
> It is just because one has no use for life that one is
> wiser than the man who values life.[79]

Clearly, Taoist philosophy may well have informed Moore's work, as did Confucian thought, quoted in her prose writing and alluded to in several poems. The extreme terseness and compressed expression typical of these Chinese philosophical texts lends an aura of depth and urgency which transcends their semantic content. These sources are neither quoted nor cited, but it is clear that amidst these plentiful maxims lies a variety of spiritual and philosophical texts which never fully come to light. Even if they are not Far Eastern, Moore's poetry does in this light resemble a Chinese intertext in its continual return to recognizable traditions of thought.

Some hint of Moore's belief that 'kernels of wisdom' are a common inheritance can be found in a poem first published in 1950, 'Quoting an Also Private Thought'. 'Some speak of things

---

[76] Ibid., Book Two, 78: 187; trans. Lau, p. 140.
[77] Moore, *The American Scholar*, 36 (Summer 1965), 186, and *CPR* 671.
[78] Lao Tzu, *Tao Te Ching*, Book Two, 81: 195; trans. Lau, 143.
[79] Ibid., Book Two, 75: 181–181a; trans. Lau, 137.

we know, as new', she writes, 'And you, of things unknown as things forgot'. 'Disclosing the signature in an interior, | Mathematician's parenthesis— | Astute device quite different from the autograph', she later continues.[80] To quote private thoughts is to tell them accurately and also to demand a certain respect for their import-ance, or 'weight'. In this poem, too, the privacy of the thought is also a request for carefulness and delicacy on the part of the reader, an indication that a disclosure is being made, a personal truth told. The fact that all of these readings of the title obtain also makes each of them partial and unstable. The title renders quotation, and the poem as a whole, responsible for establishing veracity, and yet the primary text—'thought'—remains unverifiable and authority rests with the author. In fact, the 'private thought' becomes the poem itself, assembled from analyses of how 'some' people and 'you' treat recognition ('things we know') and memory ('things unknown as things forgot'), and the natural, literary, and mathematical instances in which both can be witnessed. Again, even in this poem, where there is a declared disclosure—a private thought—Moore does not actually quote but claims to quote, converting supposed intimacy into remove.

Moore maintained a network of habits throughout her writing career and many of them were strategic to satisfying her need to dominate her poetry while protecting her authorial sub-jectivity. Her orientalism, and her use of Chinese sources of all kinds, aided this central imperative of her poetry and expose the myriad ways that distance could be appropriated to define and bolster the identity of a nascent America. Moore's poetic collections of detail and quotation display her very personal method of coming to terms with the necessary exposure of writ-ing verse, at the same time that they shielded her from the audience she sought to address. In the early poem 'England', which situates America against the 'older' world of Europe and the East, she already perceived the attraction of China's ancient reserve: 'the East with its snails, its emotional | shorthand and jade cockroaches, its rock crystal and its imperturbability, | all of museum quality'. Moore's poetry continued to depend upon China to allow her to venture into resurrected poetic techniques,

---

[80] RL I:03:42 and first published in *University of Kansas City Review*, 16 (Spring 1950), 163. Not included in *CP*.

mythologies, philosophies, and artistic methods while it relied upon China's 'emotional shorthand' to defend her from any unwanted emotive dialogue with her reader. Her use of Chinese sources helped to guarantee that the reason and operation of her poetry would always remain undecipherable. As Moore wrote in the concluding lines to her unpublished poem 'An Ardent Platonist', 'one is under no | Fixed obligation then, to say what one thinks in order to be understood'.[81]

---

[81] RL I:01:08. The manuscript is not dated.

List of Chinese Terms

Ban Gu	班固
chuan-pien	传片
Chuci	楚辭
dian-ying	电影
fu	賦
fu-gu	復古
Guo Bu	郭璞
I Ching	易經
jiao	蛟
Jia Yi	賈誼
jing	景
ji xiang	吉祥
Lin-quan Gao-zhi ji	林泉高致集
Li Sao	離騷
Liu Xie	劉勰
long	龍
luan	矞
Lu Ji	陸機
Lun Yu	論語
Ming-shi	明詩
pien-wen	变文
qilin	麒麟
qing	情
qi xiang	騎象
Quan-fu	詮賦
Qu Yuan	屈原
shan-shui	山水
Shijing	詩經
Sima Qian	司馬遷
Ssu-ma Hsiang-ju	司馬相如
Sung Yu	宋玉
Tao Te Ching	道德經
t'u	圖
Tu Fu	杜甫

Wen Fu	文賦
Wen-xin tiao-long	文心雕龍
Xie Zhen	謝榛
Yang Xiong	楊雄
yin	陰
yu tao	油桃

List of Alternative Titles

'Abundance' : 'The Jerboa'
'Away With Appearances' : 'Style'
'Black Earth' : 'Melancthon'
'Blake' : 'Reprobate Silver'
'Brooklyn On the Mound' : 'Hometown Piece for Messers Alston and
     Reese' : Pitching in a Pinch
'Bulwark Against Fate' : 'Like a Bulwark'
'The Caduceus' : 'The Staff of Aesculapius'
'A Festival' : 'In the Public Garden'
'A Fool, A Foul Thing' : 'To Be Liked by You Would Be a Calamity'
'For Me Nothing Can Efface' : 'Style'
'A Glass-Ribbed Nest' : 'A Paper Nautilus'
'Glory' : 'Carnegie Hall: Rescued'
'A Graveyard' : 'A Grave' : 'A Graveyard in the Middle of the Sea'
'He Knew "Exactly How Many Yawns are Expressed by the Verb 'to
     Amuse One's Self' " ' : 'Ennui'
'It is Late, I Can Wait' : 'Nevertheless'
'It's Pencil Week' : 'Pencil Week'
'The Jewel' : 'To Victor Hugo of My Crow Plato'
'Kay Nielson in Cinderella' : 'Kay Nielson's Cinder-wench's Disembodied
     Glance'
'A Kind of Christmas Tree' : 'Rosemary'
'Letter Perfect is Not Perfect' : 'Tom Fool at Jamaica'
'A Macoronic? A Capric' : 'A Macaronic? No; Capric' : 'I've Been
     Thinking—I Mean Cogitating' : 'Occasionem Cognosce' : ' "Avec
     Ardeur" '
'The Mind is an Unobedient Thing' : 'The Mind, Intractable Thing'
'Nine Nectarines and Other Porcelain' : 'Nine Nectarines'
'The Past is the Present' : 'So far as the Future is Concerned, "Shall
     not one say, with the Russian Philosopher, 'How is one to know
     what one doesn't know?' " So far as the Present is Concerned' :
     'To George Moore'
'The Old Dominion' : 'Virginia Brittania'
'Perseus to Polydectes' : 'Progress' : 'I May, I Might, I Must'
'A Psalm to David' : 'That Harp You Play So Well'
'To a Cantankerous Poet Ignoring His Compeers—Thomas Hardy,
     Bernard Shaw, Joseph Conrad, Henry James' : 'Diogenes'

'To a Chameleon' : 'You Are Like the Realistic Product of an Idealistic Search for Gold at the Foot of the Rainbow'
'To Art Wishing For a Fortress Into Which She May Flee From Her Persecutors, Instead of Looking For a Jail In Which To Confine Them' : 'To Military Progress'
'To Civilization in Its Most Violent Form' : 'Pedantic Literalist'
'To Robert Browning in His Act of Vandalism' : 'Injudicious Gardening'
'Too Much' : 'The Jerboa'
'The Wizard in Words' : 'Reticence and Volubility'

Select Bibliography

PRINCIPAL WORKS BY MARIANNE MOORE

'The Accented Syllable', *The Egoist*, 3/10 (Oct. 1916).
Poems. London: Egoist Press, 1921.
'Is The Real The Actual?', *The Dial*, 73/6 (Dec. 1922), 620–2.
Marriage, Manikin, 3. New York: Monroe Wheeler, 1923.
Observations. New York: Dial Press, 1924.
'The Poem and the Print', *Poetry*, 43/2 (Nov. 1933), 92–5.
Selected Poems. New York: Macmillan; London: Faber & Faber, 1935.
The Pangolin and Other Verse. London: Brendin, 1936.
What Are Years. New York: Macmillan, 1941.
Nevertheless. New York: Macmillan, 1944.
Rock Crystal, trans. Marianne Moore and Elizabeth Mayer. New York: Pantheon, 1945.
Collected Poems. New York: Macmillan; London: Faber & Faber, 1951.
The Fables of La Fontaine, trans. Marianne Moore. New York: Viking, 1954.
Predilections. New York: Viking; London: Faber & Faber, 1955.
Selected Fables of La Fontaine. London: Faber & Faber, 1955.
Like A Bulwark. New York: Viking, 1956; London: Faber & Faber, 1957.
O To Be A Dragon. New York: Viking, 1959.
A Marianne Moore Reader. New York: Viking, 1961.
The Absentee [based on a novel by Maria Edgeworth]. New York: House of Books, 1962.
'Occasionem Cognosce' (poem) [first edition printed as a Lowell house Separatum]. Lunenburg, Vermont: The Stinehour Press, 1963.
Puss in Boots, The Sleeping Beauty & Cinderella [the tales of Charles Perrault translated and adapted by Marianne Moore]. New York: Macmillan, 1963.
The Arctic Ox. London: Faber & Faber, 1964.
Poetry and Criticism. Cambridge, Mass.: Adams House and Lowell House Printers, Apr. 1965.
Tell Me, Tell Me: Granite, Steel and Other Topics. New York: Viking, 1966.
The Complete Poems of Marianne Moore. New York: Macmillan, 1967; London: Faber & Faber, 1968.
Selected Poems. London: Faber & Faber, 1969.

Unfinished Poems by Marianne Moore. Philadelphia: Rosenbach Foundation, 1972.
'Answers to Some Questions Posed by Howard Nemerov', in Aquila Essays, no. 12. Isle of Skye, Scotland: Johnston Green & Co., 1982.
The Complete Prose of Marianne Moore, (ed.) Patricia C. Willis. London: Faber & Faber, 1987.
The Selected Letters of Marianne Moore. New York: Knopf, 1997.

SECONDARY SOURCES

ABBOTT, CRAIG S. *Marianne Moore: A Reference Guide.* London: Prior, 1978.
—— *Marianne Moore: A Descriptive Bibliography.* Pittsburgh: University of Pittsburgh Press, 1977.
ABRAMS, M. H. (ed.). *The Norton Anthology of English Literature,* 4th edn., vol. ii. New York and London: W. W. Norton, 1979.
ADAMS, JOHN. *Familiar Letters of John Adams and his wife Abigail Adams, During the Revolution,* (ed.) Charles Francis Adams. Cambridge, Mass.: Riverside Press, 1876.
AHMAD, AIJAZ. 'Orientalism and After: Ambivalence and Metropolitan Location in the Work of Edward Said', in *In Theory: Classes, Nations, Literatures.* London and New York: Verso, 1992, pp. 159–219.
ALDRIDGE, A. OWEN. Foreword to John J. Deeney (ed.), *Chinese–Western Comparative Literature Theory and Strategy.* Hong Kong: Chinese University Press, 1980.
Animal Sagacity: Exemplified by Facts. Dublin: W. Espy, 1824.
APPLETON, WILLIAM W. *A Cycle of Cathay: The Chinese Vogue in England During the Seventeenth and Eighteenth Centuries.* New York: Columbia University Press, 1951.
ARNHEIM, RUDOLPH. *Art and Visual Perception: A Psychology of the Creative Eye.* Berkeley and Los Angeles: University of California Press, 1974.
—— *Film.* London: Faber & Faber, 1933.
—— *The Power of the Center.* Berkeley: University of California Press, 1988.
BACHELARD, GASTON. *The Poetics of Space,* trans. Maria Jolas. Boston, Mass.: Beacon, 1969.
BATES, MARSTON. *Animal Worlds.* New York: Random House, 1963.
BAUDRILLARD, JEAN. 'The System of Collecting', trans. Roger Cardinal, in John Elsner and Roger Cardinal (eds.), *The Cultures of Collecting.* London: Reaktion, 1994, 7–24.
BAYLEY, JOHN. *The Romantic Survival.* London: Constable, 1957.

BEER, SIR GAVIN DE *Alps and Elephants.* London: Geoffrey Bles, 1955.

BENNETT, ARTHUR (ed.), *The Valley of Vision: A Collection of Puritan Prayers and Devotions.* Edinburgh: Banner of Truth Trust, 1975.

BEONGCHEON, YU. *The Great Circle: American Writers and the Orient.* Detroit: Wayne State University Press, 1983.

BERCOVITCH, SACVAN. *The Puritan Origins of the American Self.* New Haven and London: Yale University Press, 1975.

BERNARD, RICHARD. *Faithfull Shepheard . . . Wherein is . . . set forth the excellencie and necessitie of the Ministerie. . . .* London, 1607; Expanded version, London, 1621.

BINYON, LAURENCE. *The Flight of the Dragon.* London: John Murray, 1911.

—— *Little Poems from the Japanese.* Leeds: Swan Press, 1925.

—— *The Spirit of Man in Asian Art.* Charles Eliot Norton Lecture delivered at Harvard University, 1933–4. Cambridge, Mass.: Harvard University Press, 1935.

BIRCH, CYRIL (ed.). *Anthology of Chinese Literature.* Harmondsworth: Penguin, 1967.

BISHOP, ELIZABETH. 'Efforts of Affection: A Memoir of Marianne Moore', in *The Collected Prose,* (ed.) Robert Giroux. London: Chatto & Windus, 1984, 121–56.

—— *Complete Poems.* London: Chatto & Windus, 1983.

BORGES, JORGE LUIS. *The Book of Imaginary Beings.* New York: Dutton, 1969.

BOROFF, MARIE. *Language and the Poet: Verbal Artistry in Frost, Stevens and Moore.* Chicago and London: University of Chicago Press, 1979.

BROOKS, VAN WYCK. *Fenollosa and his Circle.* New York: E. P. Dutton, 1962.

BRYAN, WILLIAM JENNINGS. *Letters to a Chinese Official; Being a Western View of Eastern Civilization.* London and New York: Harper & Bros., 1906.

BURKHARDT, DIETRICH. *Signals in the Animal World.* New York: McGraw-Hill, 1967.

BUSH, SUSAN HILLES. *The Chinese Literati on Painting.* Cambridge, Mass.: Harvard–Yenching Institute Studies 27, 1971.

BUTLER, MARILYN. 'Orientalism', in David B. Pirie (ed.), *The Romantic Period.* London: Penguin, 1994, 395–447.

BYNNER, WITTER. *The Way of Life According to Lao Tzu.* New York, 1944.

CAHILL, JAMES. *Chinese Paintings: XI–XIV Centuries.* London: Elek, 1961.

CARDINAL, ROGER. 'Collecting and Collage-making: The Case of Kurt Schwitters', in John Elsner and Roger Cardinal (eds.), *The Cultures of Collecting.* London: Reaktion, 1994, 68–96.

CARPENTER, FREDERICK IVES. *Emerson and Asia.* Cambridge, Mass.: Harvard University Press, 1930.

CHENG, FRANÇOIS. 'Some Reflections on Chinese Poetic Language and its Relation to Chinese Cosmology', trans. Stephen Owen, in *The Vitality of the Lyric Voice*, (ed.) Shuen-fu Lin and Stephen Owen. Princeton, NJ: Princeton University Press, 1986.

CHISHOLM, LAWRENCE W. *Fenollosa: The Far East and American Culture.* New Haven and London: Yale University Press, 1963.

CHRISTY, ARTHUR E. *The Orient in American Transcendentalism.* New York: Octagon, 1932.

CLARK, SUZANNE. *Sentimental Modernism: Women Writers and the Revolution of the Word.* Bloomington and Indianapolis: Indiana University Press, 1991.

CLIFFORD, JAMES. 'On Collecting Art and Culture', in Russell Ferguson, Martha Gever, Trinh T. Minh-ha, and Cornel West (eds.), *Out There: Marginalization and Contemporary Cultures.* Cambridge Mass.: MIT Press, 1990, 141–69.

CONFUCIUS. *The Sayings of K'ung the Master*, trans. Allen Upward. London: The Orient Press, 1904.

COOPER, ARTHUR (trans.). *Li Po and Tu Fu.* Harmondsworth: Penguin, 1973.

COSTELLO, BONNIE. *Marianne Moore: Imaginary Possessions.* Cambridge, Mass. and London: Harvard University Press, 1981.

COTTRELL, ANNETTE B. *Dragons.* Boston, Mass.: Museum of Fine Arts, 1962.

CRARY, JONATHAN. *Techniques of the Observer: On Vision and Modernity in the Nineteenth Century.* Cambridge, Mass. and London: MIT Press, 1990.

DAVIS, BOB. 'Bob Davis Reveals: Facts about the Ear, Eye and Nose of Wild Animals', *The New York Times.* (dated by Moore 'November or December 21, 1931').

DAVIS, FRANK. 'The Chinese Dragon', *Illustrated London News* (23 Aug. 1930).

DAWSON, RAYMOND. *The Chinese Chameleon: An Analysis of European Conceptions of Chinese Civilization.* London: Oxford University Press, 1967.

DIEHL, JOANNE FEIT. *Elizabeth Bishop and Marianne Moore: The Psychodynamics of Creativity.* Princeton, NJ: Princeton University Press, 1993.

—— *Women Poets and the American Sublime.* Bloomington and Indianapolis: Indiana University Press, 1990.

DIJKSTRA, BRAM. *Hieroglyphics of a New Speech: Cubism, Stieglitz and the Early Poetry of William Carlos Williams.* Princeton, NJ: Princeton University Press, 1969.

DITMARS, RAYMOND L. *Strange Animals I have Known*. New York: Brewer, Warren & Putnam, 1931.

DONALDSON-EVANS, LANCE K. 'Demons, Portents, and Visions: Fantastic and Supernatural Elements in Ronsard's Poetry', in Maryanne Cline Horowitz, Anne J. Cruz, and Wendy A. Furman (eds.), *Renaissance Rereadings: Intertext & Context*. Urbana and Chicago: University of Illinois Press, 1988, 225–35.

DRISCOLL, LUCY, and TODA, KENJI. *Chinese Calligraphy*. Chicago, 1935.

EBERHARD, WOLFRAM. *Chinese Symbols: A Dictionary of Hidden Symbols in Chinese Life and Thought*, trans. G. L. Campbell. London and New York: Routledge & Kegan Paul, 1986.

EISENSTEIN, SERGEI. *Film Form*, trans. Jay Leyda. London: Dennis Dobson, 1951.

—— *The Film Sense*, trans. Jay Leyda. London: Faber & Faber, 1943.

—— *Nonindifferent Nature*, trans. Herbert Marshall. Cambridge: Cambridge University Press, 1987.

ELIOT, T. S. 'The Noh and the Image', *The Egoist*, 4/7 (Aug. 1917).

—— preface to *Anabase*. London: Faber & Faber, 1959.

ELLIOTT, EMORY. *Power and the Pulpit in Puritan New England*. Princeton, NJ: Princeton University Press, 1975.

ELSNER, JOHN, and CARDINAL, ROGER. Introduction to *The Cultures of Collecting*. London: Reaktion, 1994, 1–6.

EMERSON, RALPH WALDO. *The Journals and Miscellaneous Notebooks of Ralph Waldo Emerson*, vol. i–xv, (ed.) William H. Gilman, Alfred R. Ferguson, George P. Clark, and Merrell R. Davis. Cambridge, Mass.: Harvard University Press, 1960–82.

—— *The Journals of Ralph Waldo Emerson*, (ed.) Edward Waldo Emerson and Waldo Emerson Forbes. Boston, Mass., 1909–14.

—— 'Discipline' from *Nature* (1833–36) in *Selections from Ralph Waldo Emerson*, (ed.) Stephen E. Whicher. Boston, Mass.: Houghton Mifflin, 1957.

—— 'Self Reliance' in *Selections from Ralph Waldo Emerson*, (ed.) Stephen E. Whicher. Boston, Mass.: Houghton Mifflin, 1957.

ERICKSON, DARLENE WILLIAMS. *Illusion is More Precise than Precision: The Poetry of Marianne Moore*. Tuscaloosa, Ala. and London: University of Alabama Press, 1992.

FANG, ACHILLES. 'Rhymeprose on Literature', *Harvard Journal of Asiatic Studies*, 14/3 (Dec. 1951).

—— 'Rhymeprose on Literature', *New Mexico Quarterly* (Autumn 1952).

FENOLLOSA, ERNEST. 'The Chinese Written Character as a Medium for Poetry', (ed.) Ezra Pound, *Little Review*, 6/5–8 (Sept.–Dec. 1919); also published San Francisco: City Lights, 1936.

—— *Epochs of Chinese and Japanese Art*. London, 1912.

FENTON, JAMES. 'Becoming Marianne Moore', *New York Review of Books* (24 Apr. 1997), 40–5.

FITTER, RICHARD. *Vanishing Animals of the World*. New York, 1968.

FLETCHER, JOHN GOULD. *Life is My Song*. New York: Farrar & Rinehart, 1937.

FLINT, F. S. 'Imagisme', *Poetry*, 1/6 (Mar. 1913).

FONG, WEN. *Images of the Mind*. Princeton, NJ: The Art Museum, 1984.

FOUCAULT, MICHEL. *The Order of Things: An Archaeology of the Human Sciences*. London and New York: Routledge, 1970.

FOX, H. MUNRO. *The Personality of Animals*. London: Penguin, 1952.

FRANKEL, HANS. *The Flowering Plum and the Palace Lady: Interpretations of Chinese Poetry*. New Haven and London: Yale University Press, 1976.

GARRIGUE, JEAN. *Marianne Moore*, Pamphlets on American Writers 50, Minnesota: University of Minnesota Press, 1965.

GÉFIN, LASZLO K. *Ideogram: History of a Poetic Method*. Austin, Tex.: University of Texas Press, 1982.

GILBERT, SANDRA M. 'Marianne Moore as Female Female Impersonator', in Joseph Parisi (ed.), *Marianne Moore: The Art of a Modernist*. Ann Arbor, Mich. and London: UMI Research Press, 1990, 27–46.

The Golden Treasury of Puritan Quotations, compiled by I. D. E. Thomas. Edinburgh: Banner of Truth Trust, 1977.

GOLDSMITH, OLIVER. *The Citizen of the World; or, Letters from a Chinese Philosopher Residing in London to his Friends in the East*. London, 1762.

GOMBRICH, E. H. *Art and Illusion*. Princeton, NJ: Princeton University Press, 1960.

—— *The Image and the Eye*. Oxford: Phaidon, 1982.

GOODRIDGE, CELESTE. *Hints and Disguises: Marianne Moore and her Contemporaries*. Iowa City: University of Iowa Press, 1989.

GRAHAM, A. C. (trans.). *Poems of the Late T'ang*. Harmondsworth: Penguin, 1965.

GRAY, JAMES. *Animal Locomotion*. New York: W. W. Norton, 1968.

GRAY, RICHARD. *American Poetry of the Twentieth Century*. London and New York: Longman, 1990.

GROUSSET, RENÉ. *Chinese Art and Culture*, trans. Haakon Chevalier. London: Andre Deutsch, 1959.

GUILLORY, DANIEL L. 'Marianne Moore and Technology', in Patricia C. Willis (ed.), *Marianne Moore: Woman and Poet*. Orono, Maine: University of Maine Press, the National Poetry Foundation, 1990, 83–91.

HACKNEY, LOUISE WALLACE. *Guide-Posts to Chinese Painting*, (ed.) Paul Pelliot. New York: Houghton Mifflin, 1928.

HALL, DONALD. *Marianne Moore: The Cage and the Animal*. New York: Pegasus, 1970.

HAWKES, DAVID. 'The Quest of the Goddess', in Cyril Birch (ed.), *Studies in Chinese Literary Genres*. Berkeley, Los Angeles, and London: University of California Press, 1974.

—— *Ch'u Tz'u: The Songs of the South*. Oxford: Clarendon Press, 1959.

—— 'The Supernatural in Chinese Poetry', *University of Toronto Quarterly*, 30 (1960–1), 311–24.

H.D. [Hilda Doolittle]. *Hymen*. London: Egoist Press, 1921.

HEIMERT, ALAN, and DELBANCO, ANDREW (eds.). *The Puritans in America*. Cambridge, Mass. and London: Harvard University Press, 1985.

HERDER, JOHANN GOTTFRIED VON. *Ideen zur Philosophie der Geschichte der Menschheit*. Hanover, 1784–91.

HEUVING, JEANNE. *Omissions Are Not Accidents: Gender in the Art of Marianne Moore*. Detroit: Wayne State University Press, 1992.

HOLLANDER, JOHN. 'Observations on Moore's Syllabic Schemes', in Joseph Parisi (ed.), *Marianne Moore: The Art of a Modernist*. Ann Arbor, Mich. and London: UMI Research Press, 1990, 83–102.

HOLLEY, MARGARET. *The Poetry of Marianne Moore: A Study in Voice and Value*. Cambridge: Cambridge University Press, 1987.

HONOUR, HUGH. *Chinoiserie: The Vision of Cathay*. London: John Murray, 1961.

HOWARD, RICHARD, 'Marianne Moore and the Monkey Business of Modernism', in Joseph Parisi (ed.), *Marianne Moore: The Art of a Modernist*. Ann Arbor, Mich. and London: UMI Research Press, 1990.

HSI, KUO. *An Essay on Landscape Painting*, trans. Shio Sakanishi. London, 1935.

HUGHES, E. R. *The Art of Letters; Lu Chi's 'Wen Fu', A.D. 302*, Bollingen Series XXIX. New York: Pantheon, 1951.

HUGHES, TED. *Birthday Letters*. London: Faber & Faber, 1998.

I Ching, trans. Wilhelm and Baynes, Bollingen Series. New York: Pantheon, 1950.

INGERSOLL, ERNEST. *Dragons and Dragon Lore*. New York: Payson & Clarke, 1928.

ISANI, MUKHTAR A. 'The Oriental Tale in America through 1865: A Study in American Fiction'. Ph.D. diss., Princeton University, 1962.

JACKSON, CARL T. *The Oriental Religions and American Thought: Nineteenth-Century Explorations*. Westport, Conn.: Greenwood Press, 1981.

JAMES, WILLIAM. 'What Pragmatism Means', in *Pragmatism: A New Name for Some Old Ways of Thinking*. 1907; Cambridge Mass.: Harvard University Press, 1978, 27–44.

JARRELL, RANDALL. 'Two Essays on Marianne Moore: The Humble Animal; Her Shield', *Poetry and the Age*. New York: Vintage–Knopf, 1953, 162–6, 167–87.

JAY, MARTIN. 'Scopic Regimes of Modernity', in Hal Foster (ed.), *Vision and Visuality*. Seattle: Bay Press, 1988.

JOHNSON, SAMUEL. ' "Eubulus" On Chinese and English Manners', in *Yale Edition of the Works of Samuel Johnson*, (ed.) Donald J. Greene. New Haven and London: Yale University Press, 1977, 14–18.

KALSTONE, DAVID. *Becoming a Poet: Elizabeth Bishop with Marianne Moore and Robert Lowell*. London: Hogarth, 1989.

KAMMER, JEANNE. 'The Art of Silence and the Forms of Women's Poetry', in Sandra M. Gilbert and Susan Gubar (eds.), *Shakespeare's Sisters: Feminist Essays on Women Poets*. Bloomington, Ind. and London: Indiana University Press, 1979, 153–64.

KAPPEL, ANDREW J. 'Notes on the Presbyterian Poetry of Marianne Moore', in Patricia C. Willis (ed.), *Marianne Moore: Woman and Poet*. Orono, Maine: University of Maine Press, the National Poetry Foundation, 1990, 39–51.

KARLGREN, BERNARD. *Philology and Ancient China*. Oslo: Instituttet for Sammenlignende Kulturforskning, 1926.

—— *Sound and Symbol in Chinese*. Hong Kong: Hong Kong University Press, 1962.

—— *The Chinese Language: An Essay on its Nature and History*. New York: Ronald Press, 1949.

KEARNS, CLEO MCNELLY. *T. S. Eliot and Indic Traditions: A Study in Poetry and Belief*. Cambridge: Cambridge University Press, 1987.

KENG, JUNG. *The Bronzes of the Shang and Chou*, 2 vols., *Yenching Journal of Chinese Studies*, monograph series no. 17.

KENNER, HUGH. *The Poetry of Ezra Pound*. Lincoln, Nebr. and London: University of Nebraska Press, 1985.

—— *The Pound Era*. Berkeley and Los Angeles: University of California Press, 1971.

KNECHTGES, DAVID R. *The Han Rhapsody: A Study of the Fu of Yang Hsiung*. Cambridge: Cambridge University Press, 1976.

—— 'Two Studies on the Han Fu', *Parerga*, 1. Seattle: University of Washington Far Eastern and Russian Institute, 1968, 5–61.

KNOX, BRYANT. 'Allen Upward and Ezra Pound', *Paideuma*, 3/1 (1974), 71–83.

LACH, DONALD F., and FOSS, THEODORE NICHOLAS. 'Images of Asia and Asians in European Fiction, 1500–1800', in Robin W. Winks and James R. Rush (eds.), *Asia in Western Fiction*. Honolulu: University of Hawaii Press, 1990, 14–34.

—— and VAN KLEY, EDWIN J. *Asia in the Making of Europe*, vol. iii. Chicago and London: University of Chicago Press, 1993.

LANE, GARY (ed.). *A Concordance to the Poems of Marianne Moore*. New York: Haskell House, 1972.

LAO TZU. *Tao Te Ching*, trans. D. C. Lau. New York: Penguin, 1963.

LEASK, NIGEL. *British Romantic Writers and the East: Anxieties of Empire*. Cambridge: Cambridge University Press, 1992.

LEIBNIZ, GOTTFRIED WILHELM. *Novissima Sinica*. Hanover, 1697.

LIU, JAMES J. Y. *The Art of Chinese Poetry*. London: Routledge & Kegan Paul, 1962.

—— *Chinese Theories of Literature*. Chicago and London: University of Chicago Press, 1975.

—— *Essentials of Chinese Literary Art*. Belmont, Ca.: Wadsworth, 1979.

—— 'The Paradox of Poetics and the Poetics of Paradox', in Shuen-fu Lin and Stephen Owen (eds.), *The Vitality of the Lyric Voice*. Princeton, NJ: Princeton University Press, 1986.

—— 'Time, Space, and Self in Chinese Poetry', *Chinese Literature: Essays, Articles, Reviews*, 1/2 (July 1979), 137–56.

LIU, WU-CHI, and YUCHENG LO, IRVING (eds.). *Sunflower Splendor: Three Thousand Years of Chinese Poetry*. New York: Anchor Press/ Doubleday, 1988.

LONGINUS, CASSIUS. *On The Sublime*, Loeb Classical Library 199, trans. W. Hamilton Fyfe. Cambridge, Mass.: Harvard University Press; London: Heinemann, 1982.

LONGXI, ZHANG. 'The Myth of the Other: China in the Eyes of the West', *Critical Inquiry*, 15 (Autumn 1988).

—— *The Tao and the Logos: Literary Hermeneutics, East and West*. Durham, NC and London: Duke University Press, 1992.

LOURDEAUX, STANLEY. 'Marianne Moore and a Psychoanalytic Paradigm for the Dissociated Image', *Twentieth Century Literature*, 30/2–3 (Summer–Fall 1984).

MACKERRAS, COLIN. *Western Images of China*. Hong Kong, Oxford, and New York: Oxford University Press, 1991.

MAIR, VICTOR H. *Painting and Performance: Chinese Picture Recitation and its Indian Genesis*. Honolulu: University of Hawaii Press, 1988.

'Marianne Moore: The Art of a Modernist Master, A Symposium', in Joseph Parisi (ed.), *Marianne Moore: The Art of a Modernist*. Ann Arbor, Mich. and London: UMI Research Press, 1990, 105–23.

'Marianne Moore on Ezra Pound, 1909–1915', *Marianne Moore Newsletter*, 3/2 (Fall 1979), 5–8.

MARTIN, TAFFY. *Marianne Moore: Subversive Modernist*. Austin, Tex.: University of Texas Press, 1986.

MERRIN, JEREDITH. *An Enabling Humility: Marianne Moore, Elizabeth Bishop, and the Uses of Tradition*. New Brunswick, NJ and London: Rutgers University Press, 1990.

—— 'Marianne Moore and Elizabeth Bishop', in Jay Parini (ed.), *The Columbia History of American Poetry*. New York: Columbia University Press, 1993, 343–69.

MOLESWORTH, CHARLES. *Marianne Moore: A Literary Life*. New York: Athenaeum, 1990.

MONROE, HARRIET. 'A Symposium on Marianne Moore', *Poetry*, 19 (Jan. 1922), 208–16.

MONROE, MELISSA. 'Comparison and Synthesis: Marianne Moore's Natural and Unnatural Taxonomies', in Cynthia Goldin Bernstein (ed.), *The Text and Beyond: Essays in Literary Linguistics*. Tuscaloosa and London: University of Alabama Press, 1994), 56–83.

MORGAN, JOHN. *Godly Learning: Puritan Attitudes towards Reason, Learning, and Education, 1560–1640*. Cambridge: Cambridge University Press, 1986.

MUNDY, PETER. *The Travels of Peter Mundy in Europe and Asia, 1608–1667*. London, 1919.

MYERSON, JOEL (ed.). *American Transcendentalists*. Detroit: Gale, 1988.

—— *The New England Transcendentalists and the Dial: A History of the Magazine and its Contributors*. Rutherford NJ: Fairleigh Dickinson University Press, 1980.

NASH, ELIZABETH TODD. *One Hundred and One Legends of Flowers*. Boston, Mass.: Christopher Publishing House, 1927.

NIRANJANA, TEJASWINI. *Siting Translation: History, Post-Structuralism, and the Colonial Context*. Berkeley, Los Angeles, and Oxford: University of California Press, 1992.

OETTERMANN, STEPHEN. *The Panorama: History of a Mass Medium*. New York: Zone Books, 1997.

OSTRIKER, ALICIA. 'Marianne Moore, the Maternal Hero, and American Women's Poetry', in Joseph Parisi (ed.), *Marianne Moore: The Art of a Modernist*. Ann Arbor, Mich. and London: UMI Research Press, 1990, 49–66.

OWEN, STEPHEN. *Readings in Chinese Literary Thought*. Cambridge, Mass.: Harvard University Press, 1987.

—— *Remembrances: The Experience of the Past in Classical Chinese Literature*. Cambridge, Mass. and London: Harvard University Press, 1986.

PARISI, JOSEPH (ed.). *Marianne Moore: The Art of a Modernist*. Ann Arbor, Mich. and London: UMI Research Press, 1990.

PERKINS, DAVID (ed.). *English Romantic Writers*. New York, Chicago, San Francisco, and Atlanta: Harcourt, Brace, Jovanovich, 1967.

—— *A History of Modern Poetry: From the 1890s to the High Modernist Mode*. Cambridge, Mass. and London: Harvard University Press, 1976.

PERKINS, WILLIAM. *The Arte of Prophecying. Or a Treatise Concerning The Sacred And Onely True Manner And Methods Of Preaching.* Cambridge, 1609.

PERLOFF, MARJORIE. *The Dance of the Intellect: Studies in the Poetry of the Pound Tradition.* Cambridge: Cambridge University Press, 1985.

PETRUCCI, RAPHAEL. *Chinese Painters,* trans. Frances Seaver. New York, 1920.

PINSKY, ROBERT. 'American Poetry and American Life', in *Poetry and the World.* New York: Ecco Press, 1988, 122–39.

—— 'Marianne Moore: Idiom and Idiosyncrasy', in *Poetry and the World.* New York: Ecco Press, 1988, 47–60.

POINT, NICHOLAS. *Wilderness Kingdom.* New York: Holt, Rinehart & Winston, 1967.

POUND, EZRA. *The ABC of Reading.* London: Faber & Faber, 1951.

—— *Cathay.* London: Elkin Mathews, 1915.

—— *The Classic Anthology Defined by Confucius.* Cambridge, Mass.: Harvard University Press, 1954.

—— *Collected Shorter Poems.* London: Faber & Faber, 1952.

—— 'Dawn on the Mountains' and 'Wine', *Little Review,* 5/7 (Nov. 1918).

—— 'A Few Don'ts by an Imagiste', *Poetry,* 1/6 (Mar. 1913).

—— *Gaudier-Brzeska: A Memoir* (1916). New York: New Directions, 1979.

—— *Guide to Kulchur.* London: Faber & Faber, 1938.

—— *Literary Essays* (ed.) T. S. Eliot. London: Faber & Faber, 1954.

—— *Lustra of Ezra Pound.* London: Elkin Mathews, 1916.

—— *Pavannes and Divagations.* London: Peter Owen, 1958.

—— *The Selected Letters of Ezra Pound 1907–1941,* (ed.) D. D. Paige. New York: Harcourt, Brace, 1950.

—— *Selected Prose 1909–1965,* (ed.) William Cookson. New York: New Directions, 1975.

RAU, SANTHA RAMA. 'Built on a Fabled Past', *New York Times Book Review* (6 Oct. 1957), 5.

RECKERT, STEPHEN. *Beyond Chrysanthemums: Perspectives on Poetry East and West.* Oxford: Clarendon Press, 1993.

ROBINSON, G. W. (trans.). *Poems of Wang Wei.* Harmondsworth: Penguin, 1973.

RUDOLPH, RICHARD C. *China and the West: Culture and Commerce.* Los Angeles: UCLA, 1977.

SAID, EDWARD. *Orientalism.* New York: Vintage, 1979.

—— 'The Problem of Textuality: Two Exemplary Positions', *Critical Inquiry,* 4 (Summer 1978).

SAISSELIN, RÉMY G. *Bricabracomania: The Bourgeois and the Bibelot*. Rutgers: University of Rutgers Press, 1984; London: Thames & Hudson, 1985.

SARTILIOT, CLAUDETTE. *Citation and Modernity: Derrida, Joyce, and Brecht*. Norman, Okla. and London: University of Oklahoma Press, 1993.

SARTRE, JEAN-PAUL. *The Psychology of Imagination*. London: Methuen, 1978.

SCHAFER, EDWARD H. *The Divine Woman: Dragon Ladies and Rain Maidens in T'ang Literature*. Berkeley and Los Angeles: University of California Press, 1973.

—— *The Golden Peaches of Samarkand: A Study of T'ang Exotics*. Berkeley and Los Angeles: University of California Press, 1963.

—— *The Vermilion Bird: T'ang Images of the South*. Berkeley and Los Angeles: University of California Press, 1967.

SCHOR, NAOMI. *Reading in Detail: Aesthetics and the Feminine*. New York and London: Methuen, 1987.

SCHWAB, RAYMOND. *The Oriental Renaissance: Europe's Discovery of India and the East 1680–1880*. New York: Columbia University Press, 1984.

SHELTON, ANTHONY ALAN. 'Cabinets of Transgression: Renaissance Collections and the Incorporation of the New World', in John Elsner and Roger Cardinal (eds.), *The Cultures of Collecting*. London: Reaktion, 1994, 177–203.

SIEBURTH, RICHARD. *Instigations: Ezra Pound and Rémy de Gourmont*. Cambridge, Mass. and London: Harvard University Press, 1978.

SIRÉN, OSVALD. *The Chinese on the Art of Painting*. Peiping: Henri Vetch, 1936.

—— *Chinese Painting: Leading Masters and Principles*, vol. ii. London: Lund Humphries, 1956.

STEIN, GERTRUDE. *The Geographical History of America or the Relation of Human Nature to the Human Mind*. New York: Vintage, 1973.

—— 'The Gradual Making of the Making of Americans', in *Lectures in America*. London: Virago, 1988, 135–61.

—— *Useful Knowledge*. New York: Payson & Clarke, 1928.

STEINMAN, LISA M. *Made in America: Science, Technology, and American Modernist Poets*. New Haven and London: Yale University Press, 1987.

STEVENS, WALLACE. *The Collected Poems*. London: Faber & Faber, 1955.

—— *Letters*, (ed.) Holly Stevens. London: Faber & Faber, 1967.

—— *Opus Posthumous*, (ed.) Milton J. Bates. London: Faber & Faber, 1989.

STEWART, SUSAN. *On Longing: Narratives of the Miniature, the Gigantic, the Souvenir, the Collection*. Baltimore, Md. and London: Johns Hopkins University Press, 1984.

SULLIVAN, MICHAEL. *The Birth of Landscape Painting in China.* London: Routledge & Kegan Paul, 1962.

SZE, MAI-MAI. *The Tao of Painting.* Princeton, NJ: Princeton University Press, 1963.

TANNER, TONY. *Scenes of Nature, Signs of Men.* Cambridge: Cambridge University Press, 1987.

TEMPLE, SIR WILLIAM BART. 'An Essay on Popular Discontents', in *Miscellanea.* London: Jonathan Swift, 1701, 1–95.

TOCQUEVILLE, ALEXIS DE. *Democracy in America.* London: Patrick Campbell, 1994.

TODOROV, TZVETAN. *The Fantastic: A Structural Approach to a Literary Genre,* trans. Richard Howard. Ithaca, NY: Cornell University Press, 1975.

UPWARD, ALLEN. 'Scented Leaves—from a Chinese Jar', *Poetry,* 2/6 (Sept. 1913), 191–9.

URZIDIL, JOHANNES. *Das Elefantenblatt.* Munich: Erzählungen, 1964.

VAUGHAN-JACKSON, GENEVIEVE. *Animals and Men in Armor.* New York: Hastings House, 1958.

VERSLUIS, ARTHUR. *American Transcendentalism and Asian Religions.* New York and Oxford: Oxford University Press, 1993.

VOLTAIRE [FRANÇOIS MARIE AROUET]. *Essai sur les mœurs,* in *Mercure de France.* Paris, 1745–6 and 1750–1.

WALEY, ARTHUR (trans.). *The Analects of Confucius.* New York: Random; London: Allen & Unwin, 1938.

—— *The Temple and Other Poems.* London: George Allen & Unwin, 1923.

—— *Translations from the Chinese.* New York: Knopf, 1919.

—— *Zen Buddhism and its Relation to Art.* London, 1922.

WALPOLE, HORATIO. 'A Letter from Xo Ho, a Chinese Philosopher at London, To his Friend Lieu Chi, at Peking', in *The Works of Horatio Walpole, Earl of Oxford,* vol. i. London, 1798.

WAND, DAVID HSIN-FU. 'The Dragon and the Kylin: The Use of Chinese Symbols and Myths in Marianne Moore's Poetry', *Literature East and West,* 15/3 (1971), 470–84.

WATSON, BURTON. *Chinese Lyricism: Shih Poetry from the Second to the Twelfth Century, with Translations.* New York: Columbia University Press, 1971.

—— *Chinese Rhyme-Prose.* New York and London: Columbia University Press, 1971.

—— (trans. and (ed.)). *The Columbia Book of Chinese Poetry.* New York: Columbia University Press, 1984.

—— *Early Chinese Literature.* New York and London: Columbia University Press, 1962.

WATT, JAMES C. Y. (ed.). *The Translation of Art: Essays on Chinese Painting and Poetry*. Renditions, no. 6, special art issue. Seattle and London: University of Washington, 1976.

WILHELM, HELLMUT. 'The Scholar's Frustration: Notes on a Type of *Fu*', in John K. Fairbank (ed.), *Chinese Thought and Institutions*. Chicago: University of Chicago Press, 1957.

WILLIAMS, WILLIAM CARLOS. *The Collected Earlier Poems*. New York: New Directions, 1966.

—— *Imaginations*, (ed.) Webster Schott. New York: New Directions, 1970.

—— 'Marianne Moore (1925)', *The Dial*, 78/5 (May 1925), 393–401; repr. in *Imaginations*.

—— 'Marianne Moore (1948)', in *Selected Essays*. New York: New Directions, 1969.

—— *Selected Letters*, (ed.) John C. Thirlwall. New York: McDowell, 1957.

WILLIS, PATRICIA C. *Marianne Moore: Vision into Verse*. Philadelphia, Pa.: Rosenbach Museum and Library, 1987.

WINKS, ROBIN W., and RUSH, JAMES R. *Asia in Western Fiction*. Honolulu: University of Hawaii Press, 1990.

XIE, LIU. *The Literary Mind and the Carving of Dragons*, trans. Vincent Yu-chung Shih. Hong Kong: Chinese University Press, 1983.

XIN, YANG, LI, XIHUA, and XU, NAIXIANG. *The Art of the Dragon*. Boston, Mass.: Shambhala, 1988.

YEE, CHIANG. *Chinese Calligraphy*. London, 1938.

—— *The Chinese Eye*. London, 1935.

YIP, WAI-LIM (ed.) and trans.). *Chinese Poetry: Major Modes and Genres*. Berkeley, Los Angeles, and London: University of California Press, 1976.

—— *Diffusion of Distances: Dialogues between Chinese and Western Poetics*. Berkeley, Los Angeles, and Oxford: University of California Press, 1993.

YOUNG, ROBERT. 'Disorienting Orientalism', in *White Mythologies: Writing History and the West*. New York: Routledge, 1990, 119–40.

YU, PAULINE. *The Reading of Imagery in the Chinese Poetic Tradition*. Princeton, NJ: Princeton University Press, 1987.

YUTANG, LIN (trans.). *The Chinese Theory of Art*. London: William Heinemann, 1967.

Index